M000189686

NAVIGATING THE FICTION OF
ERNEST J. GAINES

NAVIGATING THE FICTION OF
ERNEST J. GAINES

A ROADMAP FOR READERS

KEITH CLARK

LOUISIANA STATE UNIVERSITY PRESS

BATON ROUGE

Published by Louisiana State University Press
Copyright © 2020 by Louisiana State University Press
All rights reserved
Manufactured in the United States of America
LSU Press Paperback Original
First printing

Designer: Mandy McDonald Scallan
Typeface: Sentinel
Printer and binder: LSI

The author's 2014 interview with Ernest Gaines is reproduced
with the permission of the Ernest Gaines family.

Library of Congress Cataloging-in-Publication Data

Names: Clark, Keith, 1963– author.
Title: Navigating the fiction of Ernest J. Gaines : a roadmap for readers /
  Keith Clark.
Description: Baton Rouge : Louisiana State University Press, [2020] |
  Includes bibliographical references and index.
Identifiers: LCCN 2019040507 (print) | LCCN 2019040508 (ebook) | ISBN
  978-0-8071-7104-2 (paperback ; alk. paper) | ISBN 978-0-8071-7338-1 (pdf) | ISBN
  978-0-8071-7339-8 (epub)
Subjects: LCSH: Gaines, Ernest J., 1933–2019—Criticism and interpretation.
  | Southern States—In literature. | African Americans in literature. |
  African Americans—Southern States—Social conditions.
Classification: LCC PS3557.A355 Z63 2020 (print) | LCC PS3557.A355
  (ebook) | DDC 813/.54—dc23
LC record available at https://lccn.loc.gov/2019040507
LC ebook record available at https://lccn.loc.gov/2019040508

The paper in this book meets the guidelines for permanence and durability of the Committee
on Production Guidelines for Book Longevity of the Council on Library Resources. ∞

For William Hall Jr.,

Kimberly Gregg Hall,

Joy Myree Mainor,

and the late

Dr. J. Lee Greene

and

Dr. James W. Coleman

In Memoriam

Ernest James Gaines

1933-2019

CONTENTS

ACKNOWLEDGMENTS

I am grateful for the support of colleagues at my home institution, George Mason University: Debra Lattanzi Shutika, English Department chair; Ann L. Ardis, dean of the College of Humanities and Social Sciences; Stefan Wheelock, exemplary intellectual, teacher, and friend; and Cynthia Fuchs, esteemed film/media studies scholar and a compassionate colleague who always manages to coax a smile.

I benefited from a residency at Virginia Humanities, which provided invaluable research time in Charlottesville at a particularly perilous moment in that city's—and our nation's—tumultuous racial history. I especially appreciated the generosity of Jeanne Nicholson Siler, director of the Fellowship Program, whose attentiveness covered everything from making sure payments arrived on time to recommending C'ville's best coffeehouses and eateries. Dear scholar/friend Maurice Wallace proved an indispensable presence during my Charlottesville sabbatical, providing scholarly support and, even more importantly, brotherly camaraderie in an unfamiliar environment.

I owe my unreserved gratitude to a community of persons whose identities overlap—friends, scholars, mentors: Trudier Harris (University of Alabama at Tuscaloosa) brought her formidable intellect and boundless generosity to an earlier draft of this work. Joy Myree Mainor (Morgan State University) and Hilary Holladay (biographer and journalist) also provided keen insights on portions of the manuscript.

I am indebted to former Gaines Center head Matthew Teutsch, who invited me to deliver the third annual Ernest J. Gaines Lecture in 2015, and to its current head, Cheylon Woods, who graciously facilitated and hosted my inaugural visit to the University of Louisiana at Lafayette.

Acknowledgments

Margaret Lovecraft, acquisitions editor at Louisiana State University Press, has been exceedingly supportive—unfailingly patient, professional, and gracious.

Longtime friends from my undergraduate days, Lola Singletary and Jacob Wilson, have remained steadfast in their love and support.

Finally, I'm inestimably indebted to William Hall Jr., Kimberly Gregg Hall, and Joy Myree Mainor: heaven-hearted friends, when the hot winds truly tested.

NAVIGATING THE FICTION OF
ERNEST J. GAINES

Introduction

When the young Alice Walker proclaimed in 1970 that Ernest Gaines was "perhaps the most gifted young black writer working today," one might have been inclined to view this avowal as the product of youthful insouciance and more than a tad bit premature (Walker, *In Search* 135). Since Gaines himself was still "emerging" in 1970 as a thirty-seven-year-old writer who had yet to compose the masterworks *The Autobiography of Miss Jane Pittman* (1971) and *A Lesson before Dying* (1993), one might have forgiven those who bristled at Walker's intrepid claim as an affront to more popular and widely published young voices: think of such firebrands as Amiri Baraka and Nikki Giovanni, not to mention a fortyish flame-throwing writer/activist named James Baldwin. But in light of Gaines's own blossoming over the subsequent five decades into the most acclaimed black southern male writer since Richard Wright, Walker's observation now seems keenly prophetic, her foresight a testament to an artist whose early, less well-known fiction probed the depths of human emotions with a subtlety, intensity, and sensitivity that may not have been appreciated at the time when more thundering expression was in vogue. Gaines maintained his prodigious output into his ninth decade, his fiction consisting of, in addition to the aforementioned works, the novels *Catherine Carmier* (1964), *Of Love and Dust* (1967), *In My Father's House* (1978), and *A Gathering of Old Men* (1983); *Bloodline* (1968), a

1

collection of the short stories; and most recently a novella, *The Tragedy of Brady Sims* (2017).

The African American southern male canon abounds with prominent and underread fiction writers who've chronicled the harrowing experiences of blacks below the Mason-Dixon Line, their works spanning over a hundred years: Charles W. Chesnutt, George Wylie Henderson, John Oliver Killens, Albert Murray, Raymond Andrews, Randall Kenan, and of course, the aforementioned patriarch, Wright. While we may debate whether Gaines, still writing into his eighties, supplanted the *Black Boy* and *Native Son* author whose influence he has disclaimed, Gaines's array of accomplishments is indisputable: the National Book Critics Circle Award for *Lesson*; Pulitzer nominations for *Jane Pittman* and *Lesson*; the Southern Book Award for Fiction; a MacArthur Foundation "genius" award; a Guggenheim Fellowship; a National Endowment for the Arts Award; the National Governors Association Award for Lifetime Achievement to the Arts; the National Medal of Arts, especially noteworthy because it was bestowed upon Gaines in 2012 by the nation's first African American president. To be sure, he has fulfilled his most ardent desire, expressed in a 1978 essay in which he ruminated on his tenure as an undergraduate in the mid-1950s: "When I told my adviser that I wanted to be a writer, he asked me what else I wanted to be. I told him nothing else. . . . I could not think of anything else I wanted to do" (*Mozart and Leadbelly* 12–13). Further reflecting on those early days at San Francisco State, Gaines would add: "There was something deep in me that I wanted to say—something that had been boiling in me ever since I left the South—and maybe before then" (13). His Bayonne, Louisiana, stands as the black fictive counterpart of Faulkner's mythic Yoknapatawpha, a hamlet where Gaines dramatizes the landscapes and personscapes of the rural southerners who kindled and cultivated his literary imagination.

As I was drafting this study, a colleague asked why Ernest Gaines was not as widely known as Ralph Ellison and Toni Morrison. Taken aback a bit—I've always "known" and esteemed Gaines's works, as evidenced by their recurrence on my syllabi—the question forced me to contemplate literary notoriety, celebrity, and audience. To be sure, Ellison's magnum opus, *Invisible Man* (1952), is *still* considered by many to be the greatest novel authored by an African American. And Toni Morrison has scaled heights that no black American writer before or since has: not *merely* earning the National Book Critics Circle Award and the Pulitzer, but the hallowed Nobel Prize for Literature in 1993, only twenty-three years after her debut novel, *The Bluest Eye.* One could legitimately claim that her masterpiece, *Beloved* (1987), single-handedly engendered the fields of literary memory and trauma studies and revitalized the area of neo-slave fiction as both a literary category and a scholarly field in and of itself. My colleague's query forced me to contemplate where to situate Gaines, a relatively well-known and even popular author whose works have been adapted into four well-received television films.

I concluded that what distinguishes Gaines from Ellison and Morrison relates to the politics of literary reception and valuation. Works such as *Invisible Man* and *Beloved* dazzle academic readers with their technical virtuosity, even showiness: they are dizzyingly intertextual, alluding to and conversing with a panoply of books and artists that critics/academics tend to esteem. For instance, consider the allusive breadth of *Invisible Man*—from *The Odyssey, Moby Dick, Huckleberry Finn,* and *The Souls of Black Folk* to Anton Dvorak and Louis Armstrong. As Ellison's literary heir, Morrison also awed "literary" readers in crafting a historically resonant neo–slave novel that is infused with elements of the gothic and ghost story, as well as the magic realism popularized by Gabriel García Márquez. Concomitantly, these works are modally rooted in (post)modern forms that critics privilege and laud: stream of consciousness, psychological realism, destabilized notions of time and space, past and present.

Let me be clear: I am not suggesting that Gaines's fictions lack technical deftness and complexity. What I am arguing is they are not stylistically ornate, as he foregrounds first and foremost the voices and stories of those routinely deemed unworthy of artistic representation. Specifically, he accentuates the voices and stories of what he classifies as "the peasantry"—the rural black Louisianans whose lives had been absent from southern fiction: "I could not write about anything except Louisiana, even though I spent most of my time in California. I could not write about anything except the land, the bayous, the rivers, the swamps. I had no interest in anything else. I could only write about the things that my people had experienced, my ancestors had experienced" (Brown, "Scribe" 207). This unwavering commitment has produced a fictive corpus that prioritizes individual and communal dramas rather than stylistic pyrotechnics, though Gaines's works reflect a technical finesse on the author's own terms. Without question, Gaines's work embodies Faulkner's assertion in his 1950 Nobel acceptance speech, that writers regardless of time and place must steadfastly probe "the human heart in conflict with itself."

"I Don't Hate It"
A Brief Bio-Sketch

The key to navigating Ernest Gaines's fiction is an understanding of Louisiana, the lifeblood of his art and life. This comes through when he recounts one friend's razor-sharp assessment: "You [Gaines] would not be able to write the things you have written had you not come up the way you did. You had to go into the fields, you had to work hard, you were around the old people a lot and you listened to them and you wrote letters for them and read papers for them—all kinds of things like that and this is the kind of thing you brought into the classroom" (Lowe, ed., *Conversations with Ernest Gaines* 246; hereafter cited as *Conversations*). His frequent remembrances of things past substantiate his friend's observations. One might, with good reason, ask "what's love got to do with it" vis-à-vis black southern writers who depict their homeland's history of racial hostility and terrorism. Southern literary trailblazer Wright's life and art epitomize the soul-crushing South which many African Americans understandably feared and therefore fled. And while Wright famously—and understandably—sought safe haven abroad, rarely to return, Gaines's relationship with the South differs markedly from Wright's and also from the protests-too-much Quentin Compson of Faulkner's *Absalom, Absalom!* who, despite his twice-uttered avowal "I don't hate it,"

4

does in fact despise his native land.

Even though he resided and composed almost all of his fiction in San Francisco, Gaines's was not an exile; his westward journey was a necessary and part-time hiatus from his known bucolic world: annually, he would make at least one pilgrimage back to his state of birth. He has constantly identified the peoples and places of Louisiana as his creative matrices, that state's people and places etched indelibly in his artistic imagination. Witness his indisputable love of Louisiana generally and his Pointe Coupee Parish whistle-stop specifically:

> Well, my folks have lived in the same place for over a hundred years in Pointe Coupee Parish in South Central Louisiana. I can't imagine writing about any other place, although everything I've written has been in San Francisco, in different apartments in San Francisco. I've tried to write about my army experiences; I've tried to write about San Francisco, about Bohemian life and that sort of thing. But everything comes back to Louisiana. People have asked me many times, why don't I write about other places? I tell them once I get my Louisiana stuff out of me, I will, but I hope I never do. I must write only about what my roots are, really, and my roots are there. (*Conversations* 298)

This underscores why Gaines uses rural Louisiana as the canvas for all of his literary portraitures. However, he doesn't mythologize or romanticize home. On the contrary, he unsentimentally conjectures that, had he not left as a teenager, he might have suffered the degradation that befell generations of southern black males—lives confined to soul- and body-sapping physical labor, penitentiaries, mental institutions—that culminated in premature death (279). His sojourns to and from Louisiana therefore provided the raw materials and connections that he would shape in the City by the Bay. From there he forged a mosaic of lives including—but not limited to—black people, some of whom suffer the grim fate that might have befallen him had he not left. This distance provided the vision and insight for Gaines to portray, with precision and poignancy, the various plights to which he

has alluded, most vividly in such characters as the valiant formerly enslaved Jane Pittman from the novel bearing her name, and death-row
inmate Jefferson in *Lesson.*

— — — — — — — —

Born January 15, 1933, in Oscar, a hamlet in Pointe Coupee Parish
that borders the larger town of New Roads, Louisiana, Gaines was the
oldest of the seven children that his mother, Adrienne, would bear by
her first husband, Manuel Gaines.[1] Like Wright, as a small boy Gaines
would experience being abandoned by his father. Adrienne Gaines
would later marry Ralph Norbert Colar Sr., with whom she would
have five more children. Dismal economic circumstances in the wake
of World War II would force Gaines's mother and stepfather to leave
River Lake Plantation to seek work in Vallejo, California. Gaines and
his siblings remained in Oscar to be raised by his paraplegic aunt, Augusteen Jefferson, whom he extols as having "the greatest impact on
my life, not only as a writer but as a man" (*Conversations* 121).

Similarly hellish compared to the lives of enslaved blacks in such
sentimentalized plantation epics as *Gone with the Wind,* Gaines's
young life sadly hearkened back to the deplorable living conditions
of the quarters' original occupants. Growing up on River Lake Plantation, he and his family resided in the former slave quarters, their
two-room cabin lacking running water, let alone an indoor toilet (278).
Physically and financially exploitative, plantation life in the thirties
was little more than a reincarnated form of serfdom. In addition to the
grueling demands faced by adult southern blacks working as sharecroppers and laborers, even small children were pressed into service
in this neo-bondage. Gaines himself remembers life on the plantation,
where he picked cotton and potatoes as an eight-year-old for fifty
cents a day (138). So onerous were these tasks that the length of African American children's school year was dictated by the agricultural
calendar, as interviewer Ruth Laney explains: "Five months out of the
year, when they could be spared from field work, the children of Cherie
Quarters went to school in the little white church at the head of the

lane. At the other end of the lane was the graveyard" (278). The church doubled as school because Pointe Coupee saw no need to provide a public school for its African American children. One can visualize the metaphoric if not literal narrow track to which poor southern black children were relegated, a path that one might legitimately compare to our twenty-first-century "classroom-to-prison-to-grave" pipeline—a situation produced by abysmal, ill-funded schools and the astronomical numbers of incarcerated and murdered African American young men. Still, the insufficient education young Gaines did receive, coupled with more nurturing experiences with his communal plantation family, provided the shoots that would germinate and blossom into a fecund literary life.

Because of his aunt's disability, her home became a communal gathering ground for what Gaines has deemed "the peasantry," those rural blacks whose lives were tethered to the land and the often-backbreaking work from which they wrung out a threadbare existence. As a precocious ten-year-old, Gaines listened attentively to these adult neighbors of the quarters, people for whom literacy was never an option given the viciousness and scope of the Jim Crow regime that controlled their lives. He recalls in a 2006 interview, "The people used to visit our house and they'd sit there and talk and talk and talk all the time. None of these people had ever gone to any school. No education at all" (Brown, "Scribe" 204). Thus, as a child who had himself received a slender education, he nevertheless became their default scribe, as he expounds in the same interview:

It was my aunt who told me that I should write their letters for them and read their letters for them when they received mail, which I did. They would come over there, and I'd sit on the floor by their chair. Sometimes, it was a man that I was writing a letter for, he'd sit on the floor or on the porch, or I'd be sitting on the steps, and I'd have my little yellow pencil and write on a tablet this wide, and I'd write their letters. They would know how to *begin* the letter, but they wouldn't know how to proceed. They'd say, for instance, "Hey, Sarah, how are you? I am well.

I'm hoping you are the same." And you'd sit there minutes after minutes, and they don't know what to talk about. And they'd say, "Say something about the garden," or "Say something about the field." So I'd just say, "OK." (204)

This passage elucidates the laying of the communal and verbal concrete that would form the foundation of Gaines's art and aesthetics. In marked contrast to young Richard Wright's family, who denigrated his writing abilities, Aunt Augusteen championed her young nephew's reading and writing prowess, encouraging him to use it practically in service to his community. By assigning him this responsibility, she also encouraged him to stand in the gap for his elders, to transform their lives into something legible and meaningful—to transcribe and embroider and transmit.

The stories of those black Oscar-ites, rural folks whom society would judge inarticulate and unworthy of artistic treatment, provided the raw materials from which Gaines would hew stories of unrivaled pain, power, and endurance. While he would go on to study creative writing at the august Stanford University in the late 1950s, his aunt Augusteen's humble dwelling became a literary incubator, an unofficial schoolroom that taught Gaines the intrinsic value of those whom society rendered voiceless and deemed dispensable. This unstinting commitment is reflected in his comments some five decades later: "What I'm always trying to do is show how this place and these people *are* important. They may think they're insignificant, but the great stories have been written about people who constantly question their significance" (*Conversations* 299).

Once he'd completed three years at St. Augustine Middle School for Catholic African American children in the neighboring town of New Roads, young Gaines's Louisiana education officially ended. Because of such truncated educational opportunities, his parents—now residents of "government-subsidized projects in Vallejo, California" (*Mozart and Leadbelly* 33)—sent for their now fifteen-year-old son, who left his small community in 1948. He poignantly recalls the departure day, a defining moment for the precocious man-child in whom the community invested so many of its hopes: "I went to each of the old people, shook their hands, and listened to their advice on how to live 'up North'" (6). Most bittersweet, however, was the last elder to whom he would bid goodbye. Gaines writes of the final time he would see her, an encounter true to the unsentimental, stiff-upper-lip tenor of their relationship:

> Then I went to my aunt. She sat on the floor—just inside the door. "I'm going, Aunty," I said. I did not lean over to kiss her—though I loved her more than I have loved anyone else in my life. I did not take her hand, as I had taken the other people's hands, because that would have been the most inappropriate thing in the world to do. I simply said, "I'm going Aunty." She looked up at me from the floor. I saw the tears in her eyes. She nodded her head and looked down again. When I came out into the road, I looked back at her. I waved and smiled; she waved back. (6)

And with this, young Ernest left on a segregated bus for the Big Easy, where he would board a train to the Golden State, a place that would prove instrumental in his evolution as griot for "Aunty" and the "black peasantry" whom other southern writers either ignored or reduced to "caricatures of human beings" (9).

When Horace Greeley exhorted young men to "Go West" in 1865, we can safely assume this wasn't directed at African Americans—regardless of gender—only a year after the Thirteenth Amendment's passage. And while literary critics have studied and almost exalted the global expatriatism of a cadre of African American writers—Wright, Chester Himes, and James Baldwin most famously—I would proffer that Gaines's relocation to the West Coast—"up North," in the words of his fellow Oscar natives—marks a cardinal moment. A far cry from a racial utopia, in much the same way that the actual North often failed its wayfaring sepia sons and daughters who had fled southern terrorism, California nevertheless became an alternative and intellectually affirming space. Gaines was especially struck by the exponential difference in the racial and ethnic composition of his new community.

He remembers post–World War II Vallejo as a melting pot, where he lived in Army housing alongside "poor whites, Japanese, Philipinos [*sic*], Latinos. . . . I went to school with them every day at an integrated high school" (*Conversations* 176). To be sure, this polyethnic, nonsegregated communal tapestry was a veritable Benetton ad compared to the South's impenetrable lines of caste and color. This might also explain the relatively measured tone of his fictions, which yet unsparingly depict a bevy of discriminations. In addition to addressing the omnipresent, virulent antiblack fervor on which southern whiteness is based, Gaines also depicts class and generational conflicts, as well intra-racial prejudices such as colorism. Whereas Wright's expatriate community was mostly white, Gaines's domestic repatriation included a dream coat of many colors, voices, and experiences. However, as integral as this multiethnic community was to the adolescent Gaines's racial and ethnic reeducation, perhaps even more vital in terms of his literary development was the presence of his stepfather.

Just as he spoke little of his mother, Gaines spoke very little of Ralph Norbert Colar Sr., who worked on a plantation near the one where Gaines and his mother lived prior to her relocation. While Adrienne Gaines found factory work in California, Colar became a merchant seaman; Gaines recalls him as a demanding but affirming presence (*Conversations* 59). Reminiscent of Gaines's meditation on what might have befallen him had he remained in spirit-killingly segregated Louisiana, Colar demanded that young Ernest "get off the block," where he "got caught up with some pretty rough guys." While this might seem inconsequential, as nothing more than a stepfather's performing that position's requisite duties, Colar's simple directive would have a seismic impact on his impressionable stepson: the library became the alternative, "safe" space—stoking a creative fire that would never have blazed had Gaines remained on that dehumanizing Louisiana plantation.

One of Gaines's friends, the late short-story writer and essayist James Alan McPherson, relates an anecdote that epitomizes the scope and lethality of Jim Crow and how it curtailed blacks' quest for literacy. Recalling an incident when he was "among the first to take advantage of the Atlanta Public Library after it was integrated in 1963," McPherson ruminates: "I remember being slapped by a white man on the street outside the library. For many years I believed that this enraged white man slapped me because I am black. Now I think it might have been because I was black *and* carrying a stack of books and several paintings away from the library" (McPherson, "A Region Not Home" 199). Given that white Americans so ferociously barred these bastions of knowledge from blacks, the premium placed on black literacy cannot be overstated. So, unsurprisingly, now-sixteen-year-old Ernest's visit to the public library in Vallejo was his maiden visit, a watershed moment in an America where literacy for African Americans had been previously proscribed by law. In a space which had historically been vigorously forbidden to African Americans, Gaines embarked on a reading regimen that would catalyze his desire to write.

If his letter writing in Pointe Coupee was the first phase of his writerly gestation, then his copious reading marked a crucial next juncture. Gaines devoured the contents of this newly discovered forbidden treasure: "So I went into the library and I saw all these books and I started reading, and I read, and I read, and read" (*Conversations* 173). Notably, it was here that he imbibed the writers who'd become indispensable influences: John Steinbeck, Willa Cather, and especially nineteenth-century Russian literary titans Dostoevsky and Turgenev. One can certainly detect the tangible connection between the fictions that Gaines would produce and the works of writers such as Steinbeck and Cather, regionalists and naturalists who depicted the woeful lives of impoverished "Okies" and European immigrants eking out lives in barren midwestern terrains—whites not unlike those Louisianans whose stories he had helped craft and disseminate through the letters he'd written on their behalf. These writers' works modeled for him how the lives of those dispossessed and devalued could in fact become the stuff of *literary* art. But even more important was what Gaines *didn't* see in the books he consumed: any trace of the rich, achingly compelling lives of his own people and their experiences, which were even more desolate than the downtrodden whites he encountered in *The Grapes of Wrath* or *My Ántonia.*

This glaring omission may have transformed Gaines from voracious reader into neophyte writer. He has commented extensively on how the robust, courageous women and men whose memories he transported with him to California were not on the radar of other southern writers (*Conversations* 8). Moreover, he lamented, those same writers "weren't up to portraying Black peasants as humans instead of clowns" (83). One might be inclined to question why works by such writers as Wright or Zora Neale Hurston, who featured in vivid detail black southerners in bucolic environs, didn't enter Gaines's constellation of writers. Because these writers are now stalwarts in American and African American literary canons, it is easy to forget that they didn't always occupy such a venerated place in the minds of publishers, readers, and library acquisitions staffs. While it would be unfathomable to imagine any library in the twenty-first century *not* having several works by Wright and Hurston, African American literature at mid-twentieth century had nowhere near the readership and currency as *serious* literature that it now maintains. In an interview exactly thirty years following his 1948 arrival to relatively progressive northern California (Vallejo is about thirty miles north of San Francisco), Gaines recollected, "There were no books by blacks or about blacks in any California libraries" (122). Still, if these bibliographical omissions had an upside, they impelled the blossoming young bibliophile to take pen to paper, with Gaines echoing the sentiments of fellow southern scribe Alice Walker: "I write all the things *I should have been able to read*" (*In Search* 13; author's emphasis).

Certainly, a writer's juvenilia may hold interest to only the most devoted readers and researchers. Yet those youthful if unpolished efforts often reveal something crucial about the topics and themes that would potentially crystallize in more mature writings. In addition to his aforementioned role as de facto scribe for the adults in his hamlet, preteen Ernest also wrote and staged plays for his local church (Lowe, "Chronology" xvii). So these early "scribblings" suggest that the seeds for a writing life were being planted in his native Louisiana soil, and that they began to germinate once he was transplanted to the West Coast. Given the absence of his native black Louisianans in the books he'd consumed, seventeen-year-old Gaines made a momentous decision: he decided to write a novel himself. Having written it in longhand, "in the summer of 1950," Gaines convinced his mother "to rent me a typewriter" (*Mozart and Leadbelly* 37). He "pecked and pecked" with his right index finger for twelve hours a day, producing a melancholic tale of doomed love between a dark-skinned man and a light-skinned Creole woman who cannot scale insurmountable barriers of skin color, prejudice, and familial loyalty in a rural Louisiana town. The manuscript was swiftly rejected and returned by a New York publisher. Yet this subsequently discarded work (actually, he set it ablaze) would nevertheless provide the sinews of his first fleshed-out novel, *Catherine Carmier*, published in 1964.

Unlike counterparts such as Wright and Baldwin, Gaines had extensive college experience, graduating first from Vallejo Junior College in 1953 before serving two years in the army. He then resumed his education, earning a degree from San Francisco State College in 1957, the year when he "started writing daily" (*Conversations* 54). His final years there marked a more official entrée into the world of fiction writing: Gaines published his first two short stories, "The Turtles" and "The Man in the Double-Breasted Suit," in *Transfer*, the university's student literary magazine. Perhaps the most pivotal portion of his training occurred during the next two years at Stanford, which had awarded him a Wallace Stegner Creative Writing Fellowship. Though he would return to Louisiana annually over the next several years, San Francisco would become his creative epicenter, the place where he would compose his first seven books of fiction. Though he resided exclusively in Louisiana after retiring from his teaching position at the University of Louisiana at Lafayette, the city held an inestimable place personally and professionally: "And I was fortunate enough at an early age to go to a place like San Francisco to be educated, a place so different and yet at the same time conducive to the imaginative mind" (119).

Upon leaving Stanford, and giving himself ten years to succeed as a writer, Gaines embarked earnestly upon the only career that appealed to him. His early years as a fledgling, wannabe writer in San Francisco are the stuff of literary cliché: "Gaines took odd jobs—washing dishes, working in the post office and delivering mail.... He lived in a small apartment [with a Murphy bed] and ate hot dogs or pork-and-beans" (295).[2] Though he walked a financial tightrope during these early years, Gaines began to reap some modest rewards, including grants and study awards that facilitated his writing.

Nineteen seventy-one was a red-letter year: he was appointed writer-in-residence at Denison University in Granville, Ohio, and he received his highest literary recognition to date with the publication of *The Autobiography of Miss Jane Pittman*. Not only did this retrospective account of the eponymous 110-year-old heroine's life from slavery to the civil rights movement place Gaines on the map of southern and African American writers of serious, "literary" fiction, but the book occasioned a breakthrough moment in television history: in 1974 CBS aired the film adaptation, which was seen by 43 million viewers and collected nine Emmy Awards, including two for Cicely Tyson in the starring role. As is too often the case for artists of any color whose works find their way onto the big or little screen, Gaines received scant financial remuneration.[3] Thus, despite the multiple accolades that the book and film brought, he was still on wobbly ground monetarily until he began in the early 1980s an enduring connection with the University of Southwest Louisiana (renamed the University of Louisiana at Lafayette in 1999). After he taught there for a semester during the 1982–83 academic year, not only was Gaines invited back the following year, but the university granted him tenure and gave him the key to his own home. The deal was mutually beneficial: the university could boast of a creative writing faculty that featured an artist who would go on to become arguably Louisiana's greatest contribution to American literature (though admirers of Kate Chopin and Walker Percy might take issue); and because he was required to teach only one semester, Gaines could return to San Francisco to focus on his own creative work.

That Gaines is so treasured for his undeterred commitment to portraying the lives of blacks who he felt merited more comprehensive and humane treatment than they had received makes his 1986 self-assessment a bit puzzling: "I don't think I'm taken seriously yet as a writer to a point where there can be long articles or comprehensive essays about me and my work" (*Conversations* 187). Nevertheless, over thirty years later, his "seriousness" is indisputable: his books and stories are staples on college and even high-school syllabi, his fiction the subject of doctoral dissertations and journal essays as well as monographs and edited volumes of critical essays. His native Louisiana has honored him handsomely: the Baton Rouge Area Foundation established the annual Ernest J. Gaines Award for Literary Excellence, which includes a cash prize of $10,000 awarded to the African American author who produces the best book of fiction in that year; and his longstanding home institution, the University of Louisiana at Lafayette, created the Ernest J. Gaines Center on its campus in 2008. This vibrant research site includes a trove of material, from original manuscripts to translated versions of his books to such personal effects as his typewriter. The present book is yet another indicator of his enduring importance, reflected in the manifold audiences who turn and return to his masterfully crafted tales of love, desire, disappointment, and endurance.

1

Sugarcane, Railroad Cars, Prisons, Peoples

Dominant Themes and Topics

> Surveying the writings of black men since Richard Wright shows us
> that other issues, other meanings, other forms of power are at stake.
> The southernness of the black male writer seems peripheral to the fic-
> tion many of them have written.
>
> —MICHAEL KREYLING, *Inventing Southern Literature*

Certainly, no one can dispute the *southernness* of Gaines's works: the
mythic pastoral past colliding with a modern, industrialized present;
a Jim Crow regime that provided legal ballast to separate and unequal;
white supremacist terrorism carried out by socially sanctioned hate
groups (the Knights of the White Camelia, the Ku Klux Klan, and so
forth); the omnipresent and intersecting color *lines*—not merely the
implacable, death-defying one separating black and white, but also
strictures separating "mulatto" from both "black" and "white" and
the wars waged in the name of a spurious racial "purity"; the way that
"progress" in the present moment is forever impeded by a southern
ethos of "go slow" gradualism. To be sure, these themes are preva-
lent in works by the colossus of southern literature, the writer who
casts an inescapable shadow over Gaines and every other southern writer regardless of race, gender, or period: William Faulkner.

Still, as the distinguished southern literature critic Michael Krey-ling observes, "Family and community, sense of place, the legacy of failure-poverty-defeat emit significantly different meanings in works by African-American southern men" (*Inventing Southern Literature* 77). With this distinction in mind, this chapter enumerates the fore-most concerns and themes that constitute the fabric of Gaines's fiction.

History, from the National to the Personal

Specific mention of Louisiana history might initially evoke such no-torious figures as Huey "Kingfish" Long, nefarious ones like David Duke, or natural catastrophes lacking surnames—Katrina, Rita, Camille. However, no less explosive in the history of American ra-cial jurisprudence was the infamous case that *Brown v. Board* abro-gated, *Plessy v. Ferguson,* the basis of which was an 1892 Louisiana statute that forbade a railroad passenger from entering "a coach or compartment to which by race he does not belong" (qtd. in Litwack, *Trouble in Mind* 243). Homer Plessy, a "quadroon" light enough to pass, was recruited by activists to challenge the law. After purchas-ing a first-class ticket on the East Louisiana Railway and sitting in the "whites-only" car, Plessy was arrested when he refused to exit. The case eventually reached the United States Supreme Court in 1896, and by an eight-to-one margin, the Louisiana law barring Plessy from the whites-only car was upheld. Sanctioning "separate but equal" accom-modations to legitimize racial segregation, the decision held that, "If one race be inferior to the other socially, the Constitution of the United States cannot put them upon the same plane" (242–43). Without question, this dreadful decision "mark[ed] the birth of Jim Crow and, in sad retrospect, the Supreme Court's and highest law of the land's endorsement of white supremacy and black subjugation as the na-tional legal norm" (Baker, "Incarceration" 18). Indeed, this case would become the bulwark for Jim Crow and mark the continuation of such oppressive judicial measures as the Slave Codes and the Black Codes.

I reference *Plessy v. Ferguson* to elucidate the scope of racism in Louisiana and the state's prominent role in our pestilential racial past. The specifics of *Plessy* also resonate in terms of Gaines's life and work: the law had a dismal effect on the lives of southern blacks, especially rural denizens like Gaines's family, in terms of economic opportunities, education, public accommodations, and voting. Legally barred from jobs that would pay what we in contemporary parlance call a "living wage," Gaines's family lived a sharecropping life which was little more than indentured servitude and peonage, a life that drove his mother and stepfather west and left his aunt and relatives to wrest what middling existence they could from the land. The tentacles of this case would reach down into an education system that severely stunted black children's academic development; at best, they might receive a middle-school education as young Gaines did. The quasi-slavery into which he was born and lived, coupled with the juridical racial strictures which fortified it, might explain Gaines's abiding interest in history: "So it's present [antebellum southern history]; it's always here. We still see the result of it among my own people. The effects and the legacy of slavery, it's always there" (*Conversations* 255). The most obvious artistic rendering of this belief is his 1971 novel *The Autobiography of Miss Jane Pittman*. Through his meticulous and sweeping creation of the heroine's life, he was "trying to go back, back, back into our experiences in this country, to find some kind of meaning to our present lives" (*Mozart and Leadbelly* 15).

Though Gaines never referenced *Plessy* specifically in interviews, he did cite another seismic episode in America's litany of them, James Meredith's integration of the University of Mississippi in 1962. Gaines stated that it "would change my life forever" (24). He abruptly cancelled a trip to Mexico and returned to Baton Rouge to reunite with friends, family, and community—all of whom heralded the Mississippian's bravery as evidence of the impact that one vigilant and courageous young man could have. It is these cumulative historical events, I would surmise, that informed Gaines's own unstinting interest not only in racially resonant historical inflection points and their impact on the community but, concomitantly, in how they can shape and motivate individuals on a much smaller, micro level. Throughout his canon, teachers and students, while not actors on the grand historical scale of ministers such as Martin Luther King and students such as Meredith, nevertheless perform noble acts on behalf of their families and communities.

Racial Tensions—In Black and White and Everything in Between

Though it might seem patently obvious that an African American southern writer would examine racial animus in his work, Gaines's treatment of this topic nevertheless warrants delineation. He himself has been unreservedly clear on its omnipresence in his fellow regional writers' fiction, regardless of their pigmentation: "I don't know if you can write at all, seriously, without invoking race, especially Southerners. . . . It's almost impossible for us to write seriously without bringing in race. From Twain's *Huckleberry Finn* to all of Faulkner's stuff, the best of that stuff, the best of, I would say, Southern literature would have involved race" (*Conversations* 254). Indeed, works such as *Jane Pittman,* which begins during the antebellum period and spans one hundred years, and *Of Love and Dust* (1967), set on a plantation in the late 1940s, by their very narrative situations are bound to depict racial disquietude. What distinguishes Gaines here from, say, black southern literary patriarch Wright, is that he complicates the standard black/white binary, populating his fictions with variations on these categories.

I would conjecture that there are two reasons for Gaines's more kaleidoscopic racial worlds. First, Louisiana, unlike other southern states, has more global origins: as a former French territory that stretched to Canada and was a major hub for enslaved Africans being transported both to America and the Caribbean, it is a *callaloo* of diverse ethnicities, nationalities, and cultures—black and white Creole, Haitian, and Acadian ("Cajun") to name a few. Add to this the profusion of New Orleans's brothels in the antebellum period (run by "mulâtresses"), as well as concubinage: "'kept women'—the famous New Orleans quadroon placées, mistresses of Louisiana's white elite, and their children" (Brasseaux, *French, Cajun, Creole, Houma* 107–8). With these various ethnic and sexual enmeshments come inevitable hierarchies within the black community based on skin color: the inexorable "color line," which includes a spectrum of hues, from blacks light enough to pass for white to the "blackest berries," to allude to the folk saying that inverts the usual elevating of the lightest-skinned black person. Secondly, recall the teenaged Gaines's relocation to Vallejo, where he lived among Japanese, Filipinos, Latinos, and poor whites. Hence, his impressionable teenage years were not marked by the searing physical and psychological racial violence Wright recalled in his autobiographical essay, "The Ethics of Living Jim Crow" (1938) and his nightmarish autobiography *Black Boy* (1945). Gaines's exceedingly more catholic experiences—and this is not to suggest that Gaines did not suffer the stings of race-specific enmity in the ostensibly more "liberal" Golden State—along with growing up in a more multicultural southern state, may have provided a unique insight and a different prism through which to reimagine and re-present southern life.

Another noteworthy dimension of Gaines's treatment of race relates specifically to the white southerners who populate his fictive universe. This topic has surfaced in some of the interviews he's granted, this response standing out: "A lot of whites have accused me of making my whites devils and my blacks angels. I don't agree with that at all. . . . I honestly think that I'm as fair with my white characters as most of, as probably all, of our white writers are with their black characters" (*Conversations* 176). Though one might grant a black southern writer of Gaines's generation a great deal of latitude if he or she were to paint white characters with the broad brush of viciousness and hatemongering, Gaines's portrayals belie such monochromatic characterizations. Indeed, just as he imagines the full scope of African American humanity—which includes such less-than-admirable features as greed, cowardice, and vengefulness—he also conceives whites in their comparable complexity and fullness. Though indeed some are unrepentant racists, he never reduces them to cardboard cutouts or racial straw men or women. One of the most tragic figures of any race in Gaines's canon is Tee Bob Samson, the "pure" white son (he has a mulatto half-brother) of the owner of the plantation on which Miss Jane Pittman works. He falls deeply in love with Mary Agnes LeFabre, a

Creole schoolteacher who, despite looking white, is an unacceptable mate in a South that forbids interracial love and intimacy. The narrative reveals the sobering but incontrovertible truth she has tried to impress upon Tee Bob, the one that compels his suicide: "She was a nigger, he was white, and they couldn't have nothing together. He couldn't understand that, he thought love was much stronger than that one drop of African blood" (*The Autobiography of Miss Jane Pittman* 242–43). Such sensitive depictions, in which whites too must pay an incalculable price for the toxic doctrine of white supremacy, substantiate Alice Walker's laudatory comment regarding the depth of Gaines's characters: "It is a credit to a writer like Ernest J. Gaines, a black writer who writes mainly about the people he grew up with in rural Louisiana, that he can write about whites and blacks exactly as he sees them and *knows* them, instead of writing of one group as a vast malignant lump and of the other as a conglomerate of perfect virtues" (Walker, *In Search* 19).

African American Men and the Rigors of Masculinity

The considerable number of studies devoted to Gaines's depictions of black male characters might reasonably lead one to think that this—more than what he's called "this Louisiana thing"—is the driving force behind his fiction.[1] To be sure, Gaines devotes much of his creative energy to the group one might arguably identify as the foremost scourge of the white South—the recipients of inapprehensible physical and psychological violence. Emmett Till, Martin Luther King Jr., Medgar Evers, James Byrd, Trayvon Martin: this too-brief catalog of mutilated, dragged, and shot male bodies is a jarring indictment of America generally and Gaines's native blood-soaked southern soil particularly. What seems to consume both author and characters is their often-elusive search for a socially sanctioned manhood, one rooted in self-sufficiency, independence, power, family control, integrity—all of which were forestalled once the first ships transporting human cargo landed on these shores in 1619. Gaines speaks to this historical quagmire:

You must understand that in this country the black man has been pushed into the position where he is not supposed to be a man. This is one of the things that the white man has tried to deny the black ever since he brought him here in chains. As Joe Pittman says in *Miss Jane Pittman,* a man must do something, no matter what it is, he must do something and he must do that something well. My heroes just try to be men; but because the white man has tried everything from the time of slavery to deny the black this chance, his attempts to be a man will lead toward danger. (*Conversations* 30)

From a twenty-first-century vantage point, Gaines's accounting of manhood might seem somewhat outdated, rooted in the idea that it has been the exclusive province of white men, whose unbridled domination and privilege have existed unabated. In Gaines's gender calculus, black men must wrest the prized masculinity from their white subjugators. But from the vantage point of an African American man growing up in Louisiana in the 1930s, this ostensibly parochial conceptualization of masculinity is understandable if not unproblematic.

Therefore, Gaines's canon is replete with black men who are battered and bereft, so devitalized by white supremacist southern culture that their prospects are few and unpalatable: violent death—either at the hands of other black men or white men who control figuratively if not literally every breath they take; life behind bars, with prisons functioning as contemporary reincarnations of the plantation; a resignation to their powerlessness and its attendant self-devaluation; and if not actual physical death, then psychological and spiritual death that eventuates their demise. One such character, schoolteacher Grant Wiggins in *A Lesson before Dying,* dissects the notion of "broken" black men, who might be deemed the South's unofficial human crop—the descendants of those shackled and degraded bodies that festered in the holds of slave ships: "We black men have failed to protect our women since the time of slavery. We stay here in the South and are broken, or we run away and leave them alone to look after the children and themselves. So each time a male child is born, they hope he will be the one to change this vicious circle—which he never does" (166–67). Such a situation produces what I delineate as an *anxiety of true black manhood,* where these men feel deprived of the rights and privileges they believe should accrue to them by their very biological status as men. As compensatory measures, many protagonists conform to white society's most debasing stereotypes of southern black malehood: "brutes" such as the incorrigibly violent Munford Bazille in "Three Men"; hyper-sexualized "bucks" like Marcus Payne in *Of Love and Dust;* docile figures such as Reverend Jameson in *A Gathering of Old Men,* so terrified of white men and the omnipresent threat of violence they wield that he preaches passivity and resignation to fellow blacks; and self-loathing men such as Professor Matthew Antoine, Grant's mulatto schoolteacher who harbors such rabid hatred of blackness that it engenders his premature death. Still, despite these men's severe deficiencies, they still serve an important function: they either model for other black men the consequences of the choices they've made, or they motivate their brethren to summon the fortitude to interrupt the "vicious circle," the predestined path of failure, futility, and death to which their native South relegates them.

African American Women
Beyond Mothers and Mammies

It is fitting that Alice Walker opens her landmark 1974 essay "In Search of Our Mothers' Gardens" with a quotation from and anecdote about Jean Toomer, one of the two African American writers Gaines embraced. Toomer was perhaps the only male writer before the 1950s to probe and portray the full complexity of black women's lives, not limiting them to domestics or, worse, stereotypical plantation mammies. That he titled several chapters for the women protagonists in his pioneering *Cane* speaks to his willingness to chart new ground by exploring black women's sexuality, spirituality, and relationship to a South at once vivifying and fear-inducing—his black women even endure racial violence, a fate almost exclusively limited to black male characters. While it would be misleading to suggest that Gaines devotes as much attention to women as he does to men in his fiction, he nevertheless echoes Toomer in offering more panoramic representations of black women's experiences vis-à-vis his southern male counterparts. But to get a fuller grasp of Gaines's interest in black women's experiences, I turn to Zora Neale Hurston, the writer he claimed influenced him most.

In her commitment to researching and spotlighting the lives of invisible southerners from the Florida swamps, Hurston is most obviously Gaines's literary godmother. Her now legendary depiction of both the physical and emotional struggles of a black woman, *Their Eyes Were Watching God* (1937), has drawn frequent comparisons to such contemporary classics as Walker's *The Color Purple* (1982). Like Hurston, Walker similarly mines her native southern milieu—for Walker, Eatonton, Georgia; Eatonville, Florida, for Alabama-transplant Hurston—to etch the harrowing experiences black rural women face, from familiar challenges of rearing and providing for children to more scalding and heretofore taboo scourges such as incest and domestic violence. However, just as one sees a similar arc in the personal and artistic lives of Gaines and Hurston, both writers' groundbreaking novels also contain some intriguing similarities.

Gaines follows Hurston in transforming oral and folkloric materials into literary art, through the privileging of authentic ways of speaking through the use of dialect, colloquialisms, and storytelling. As salient, however, is how both authors' heroines eschew convention and represent alternative modes of being/living for black women. For instance, many African American women characters, like their white counterparts, have been forced to conform to the protocols of the "cult of true womanhood," which privileges family, motherhood, wifehood, piety, and basic acceptance of patriarchal values that curtail women's personal growth and aspirations. Black women novelists who portray women bound by this ethos include Frances E. W. Harper (*Iola Leroy*) in the late nineteenth century and Jessie Faucet (*Plum Bun*) and Nella Larsen (*Quicksand*) from the Harlem Renaissance of the 1920s. But Janie Crawford of *Their Eyes* and the eponymous Jane

Pittman—perhaps Gaines was paying homage to his literary progenitor through his character's very name—defy prescribed, constricting gender roles, if not in the exact same fashion. Though both women marry, each manages to retain her independent spirit, neither censoring nor confining themselves to the home and the domestic duties therein. Moreover, both women are childless during eras when motherhood was considered de rigueur with respect to "true womanhood" (though Jane is unable to bear children, she does raise young Ned after his mother is murdered).

These characters' durability in the face of raced, gendered, and economic obstacles places them squarely in the orbit of Gaines's beloved aunt, Augusteen Jefferson. Though he denies that she served as a model for Jane Pittman specifically, "most of the women in my books are, somewhat, part of my aunt," whom he exalts as "the strongest person I've ever known in my life" (Brown, "Scribe" 217). But Gaines doesn't limit his women to possessing only the "strength" that is too often superimposed upon black women and thereby fails to account for their possible frailties, vulnerabilities, and imperfections—in effect, things that make them unfailingly human. Unlike the emotionally durable title character, another character from *Miss Jane Pittman,* "Black Harriet," embodies how a lifetime of hardship can leave one emotionally crippled. Black Harriet is reduced to a life of performing backbreaking field work under the oversight of unsympathetic overseers, resulting in a total mental implosion and her eventual institutionalization. Neither idealized nor romanticized, Gaines's black women are multidimensional and display the full gamut of human emotions and responses, even those who exhibit the most laudable qualities of his revered aunt. These variations help to explode a culturally enduring but reductive image of African American women that Georgia novelist Tina McElroy Ansa eloquently captures: "Perhaps it has been a heavier burden than readily realized, this assumption that black women, especially black Southern women, are stronger, more resilient, more reliable, more enduring—perdurable, in fact—than their Northern sisters, than their white counterparts, even their men" ("Women in the Movement" 190).

"Cabins and Gardens and Clotheslines"
Places and Spaces

In one of the most enlightening and comprehensive of the many interviews he has given, Gaines shares with Marcia Gaudet and Carl Wooton in a 1988 conversation that "My earlier teachers said I had that sense of place" (*Conversations* 224). In an interview in the *Southern Quarterly* almost twenty years later, Gaines with razor-sharp precision delineates the locale that birthed and nurtured him, the place and people from whom he vows never to "disconnect": "I'm not saying the South. I'm not saying all of Louisiana. I'm saying this general area here. This place" (Brown, "Scribe" 209). His picturesque recreations of his Oscar/Pointe Coupee landscapes stand out, perhaps akin to the aromatic smells of the peanuts and sweet potatoes that he says his people roasted during his boyhood. Enumerating a final thematic/topical concern that recurs in Gaines's oeuvre, I will discuss how different locations—outdoors, indoors, and in-between—are as pivotal to comprehending the works as are his profiles of peoples and the myriad circumstances in which they find themselves.[2]

Places

Land and Landscape are the *essence* of southern fiction: Twain's winding Mississippi River Valley, Mitchell's lush Georgia plantation pastoral, Wright's wretched Black Belt, O'Connor's bucolic but forebodingly tranquil country towns, the collective of creative writers and critics in the 1930s imbibing this sprit in branding themselves the "Southern Agrarians"—southern writers inherit "that sense of place" as their birthright, something embedded in their collective marrow. For Gaines, his art-inducing land- and water-scape is Pointe Coupee Parish on the False River. Note his deeply sentient, colloquial descriptions of what his Russian literary influences might have deemed "the old country," those places that were the incubator for his creative voice. In separate interviews he insists: "I must go back to the plantation where I was born and raised. I have to touch, I have to be, you melt into things and let them melt into you [. . .] the trees, the rivers, the bayous, the language, the sounds" (*Conversations* 69); "Much of this flat, rural part of the world is wrapped in a thick green carpet of sugarcane, notched at the edges here and there with tiny camps of cabins and gardens and clotheslines" (217); and "The old people would wash from the False River. That river was both a spiritual as well as physical part of us. We ate from the river—catching fish—and we washed our clothes there, and we washed our souls there, through baptism" (285). These descriptions reverberate with an almost Thoreauvian or Whitmanesque reverence for nature, the colloquial cadences of his southern speech bearing witness to his inseparable connection to soil and water. In his rendering, the False River and its surrounding terrain become hallowed, a sort of modern version of the sacred and cleansing Jordan River that provides physical sustenance and spiritual succor. While it might be an overstatement to designate Gaines an "environmental writer," the palpable, concrete dependence upon the earth is made plain in the above catalogue, which delineates nature's bounteous resources as the literal, metaphorical, and spiritual daily bread for Gaines's people.

If Gaines regards the False River region as life force and spiritual source, then he's also acutely aware of the desecration of the landscape, not only in the name of modernity and commercialization. As well, he grasps the unnatural disruption of one's and one's community's relationship to the soil. *A Gathering of Old Men* (1983) most eloquently renders Gaines's reverence for the land and his fellow bayou-dwellers' cultural and historical ties to it. While the novel's focal point is the titular collective's willingness to defend their community after decades of untrammeled white brutality, it also shines a light on the use of machinery to ravage the land and the simultaneous demolition of blacks' lifelong history on it. One white character decries the Cajuns "messing up the land with those tractors" (23), while one of the old men regrets how "The white people, they done bought up the river now, and you got nowhere to go but that one little spot" (27) where he and his buddy can now fish; and one of his compatriots claims that he murdered a member of a tractor-wielding Cajun clan because "that tractor is getting closer and closer to that graveyard [in which the black dead are buried], and I was scared if I didn't do it, one day that tractor was go'n come in there and plow up them graves, getting rid of all proof that we ever was" (92). The physical and psychological brutality inflicted upon black lives has often been part of an overarching objective: the categorical elimination of anything marking blacks' presence in or on a particular place, once upon a time.

Spaces

Gaines has frequently expressed his love of the land, embodied in characters such as Jane Pittman, who poetically extols the awesome power of rivers and unashamedly talks to trees. And if his works consistently demonstrate the interconnectedness between people and all of the earth's treasures, then he's even more attuned to the internal spaces his characters occupy. These various and disparate enclosures—bars/restaurants, prisons, dentists' offices, courtrooms, libraries, kitchens, and, in his most recent novella, barber shops—are the stages where the author dramatizes embroilments related to gender, race, age, power, and a bevy of other concerns. Just as the outdoor places of Gaines's youth, to which he has returned for revitalization throughout his writing life, underscore themes and characterizations, he imbues interior spaces with thematic and symbolic import. Such spaces are integral to his personal and artistic formation, most vitally the two regions where he's spent almost his whole life, Pointe Coupee and northern California. I have highlighted two especially notable ones: the two-room quarters' cabin where he lived as a child, which lacked indoor plumbing; and the public library in Vallejo (those in his home state barred blacks), where his stepfather demanded he go to avoid delinquency and the potential trouble that street life posed for an adolescent black male. A third space which he's identified as integral to his development and evolution as a writer is his San Francisco apartment.

Though he began dividing his time between California and Louisiana in 1983, when he became writer-in-residence at what is now the University of Louisiana at Lafayette, San Francisco was until that time the only locale in which he wrote. In this creative habitat, Gaines imagined and crafted almost all of the works that have now catapulted him to the pantheon of great writers of the American South, great African American writers—great *American* writers of any time or place or color. He resided in two apartments—both on Divisadero Street—where he composed the majority of his fiction (*Conversations* 194). Further, bearing a humility borne of his modest background, he describes the neighborhood thusly: "This is where I've done all my work," he says. "This is considered the ghetto, but most of the people here are just hard-working, middle-class folks. They'd be *embarrassed* if they ever saw a rat" (113). Time spent in these indoor environs—cabins, libraries, small apartments—perhaps has given Gaines a heightened sense of the tension and drama that can be built through placing characters in close quarters in sites that carry cultural, racial, class, and gendered implications alongside their denotative and connotative meanings.

The fiction teems with rooms that reinforce and magnify the works' central themes and meanings. Perhaps most noteworthy is the frequency with which Gaines deploys the prison as both setting and trope. Almost all of the action in his gripping 1968 short story "Three Men" occurs there, and it also provides the site for many of the critical scenes in his last novel, *A Lesson before Dying.* In both works, the prison clearly signifies a space that circumscribes black men's lives and is emblematic of a punishment industry that unfairly targets them. But in a more constructive vein, prisons are potentially redemptive spaces in which their inhabitants are stimulated to reevaluate their lives, undergo some form of reeducation, and reclaim the agency and sense of self-worth of which society has robbed them. Whereas one might think of Wright's use of the prison in *Native Son* (1940) as emblematic of Bigger Thomas's hopelessness and resignation to his impending physical death—in effect, a symbolic if not actual tomb—characters from the rebellious, violent Procter Lewis in "Three Men" to the formally educated, egotistical Grant Wiggins in *Lesson* undergo rigorous reeducation processes which are emotionally exacting but ultimately revitalizing. In more tragic situations, spaces exist in stark opposition to their socially intended function. The library in which the lovelorn Tee Bob Samson in *The Autobiography of Miss Jane Pittman* takes his life functions ironically, symbolizing not knowledge, enlightenment, and civilization, but their antitheses: ignorance, closed-mindedness, and tribalism. All of these highly charged spaces reflect the care and thought informing the author's choice of settings.

A Word about Porches and Plantations

Two regionally resonant realms specific to southern culture are the porch and the plantation. Recall Gaines's fond recollections of his Aunt Augusteen's porch, a communal gathering ground animating storytelling and the sharing of information. More germane to young Ernest's artistic genesis, this is where quarters' residents dictated the letters which he then augmented and embellished; in effect, it served as his imaginative cradle. However, the porch can take on more solemn and portentous meanings, as it does in his 1983 storytelling tour de force, *A Gathering of Old Men*. The nominative characters, who'd cravenly failed to defend themselves and their families in the face of white barbarity, gather on one of the quarters dwellers' porches; from here they begin the process of confessing their torturous histories of fear and retreat. Crucially, this event transpires in the presence of a brutal white sheriff, magnifying the men's newfound willingness to risk physical violence in collectively atoning for their transgressions. To be sure, this group storytelling becomes a ritual testifying, where the characters must relive and confess their painful pasts among those with whom they share physical and emotional space. This ritual exorcism signals the process of redemption and transformation. Thus, the porch is transformed into a potentially regenerative space, with the revelation of past transgressions and the possibility of healing.

However, plantations carry far graver implications than porches in terms of racial and economic history. Writing about the South's romanticizing of the plantation, Matthew Pratt Guterl illuminates its popular (mis)conceptualization: "This is an enduring myth, this idea of the plantation as an organic domestic space, with its various peoples arranged together in something like [Thomas] More's utopia" (26). Unlike the fantasy plantations memorialized in such grandiloquent epics as *Gone with the Wind,* well stocked with docile, "happy darkies" who not only labored but flourished under beneficent masters and doting mistresses, the plantations depicted in such works as *Of Love and Dust,* "Bloodline," and *The Autobiography of Miss Jane Pittman* are spheres of conflict, tension, and violence. Far from the picturesque monuments to a blissful, genteel antebellum South, Gaines's depictions of these edifices hearken back to the River Lake Plantation of his boyhood, which produced memories that were less than halcyon: "We were attached to the place"; consequently, "You couldn't move around and do whatever you wanted to do" (*Conversations* 217). Even in 1988, he observed the continuation of such inequitable conditions: "Plantations still control much of the agricultural land near False River. Black people still do much of the work" (217). Gaines's unsparing dramatizations of porches and plantations, then, complicate popular understandings of them as homespun, convivial meeting spots or Arcadian structures connoting a refined, bygone southern past.

2

Catherine Carmier

In 1949, when sixteen-year-old and recent West Coast transplant Ernest Gaines set out to write a novel, he probably had no idea that he was launching a literary career that would extend well into the twenty-first century. Though he would burn the manuscript he drafted in a single summer after its swift rejection by a New York publisher, he would nevertheless cultivate that manuscript's germ of an idea, a love story between a light-complexioned young woman and a dark-skinned man she's known since they were elementary-school playmates. *Catherine Carmier* required strenuous imaginative labor and time-consuming energy to complete, written and rewritten twenty times over five years (*Conversations* 42). While Gaines was awarded a Joseph Henry Jackson Literary Prize for an early draft, which enabled him to complete a polished version, he still had to take low-paying jobs (that is, washing dishes, working at the post office) to support himself during this time.

His commitment to finishing the book he began in 1957, the year he graduated from San Francisco State University, culminated in its publication seven years later. Though it didn't bring overnight literary stardom, Gaines's inaugural novel merits attention for its sensitive treatment of issues that might have easily lent themselves to the sensational: intra-racial skin-color stratification; internecine family battles pitting domineering parents and elders against adult children chafing under unbending expectations; and the potpourri of people—

blacks, whites, Cajuns—vying for land and resources in a South undergoing appreciable change if not necessarily progress.

More character-focused than plot driven, *Catherine Carmier* does in fact explore the complexities of the aforementioned relationship between rural blacks of different hues. The titular heroine is the daughter of a fiercely independent and prideful Creole farmer, Raoul Carmier, a man who loathes darker-skinned blacks with a hatred bordering on sociopathic. This feeling was no doubt instilled by his father, Robert, who had the gumption to ask white plantation owner Robert Grover if he and his family could work as sharecroppers on his plantation and occupy the abandoned house in which the former white overseer resided. In the novel's expositional chapters, the omniscient narrator reveals the following: "It was soon learned in the quarters that the Carmiers had little use for dark-skin people. They went by without speaking, and when you spoke to them they hardly nodded their heads" (12). Shortly after a physical confrontation with a neighboring Cajun farmer, Robert disappears, and his family relocates to another house on the plantation. The adult Raoul ascends to his dead father's position as family patriarch, continuing to work as a sharecropper and eventually marrying Della Johnson, another Creole woman who didn't harbor Raoul's unyielding anti-dark-skin prejudice and who "had a nice word to say to anyone else who went by the house" (14). However, she subsequently conforms to Raoul's warped light skin-centric mindset; in the words of one of the non-Creole women whom the formerly affable Della now ignores, "She couldn't stay that way for long, not around something like that" (15). This character's odd choice of pronoun, "that," speaks to the malevolent, borderline-inhumane shadow that Raoul casts, one that affects, and in the case of his wife and youngest child Lillian, *infects,* everyone under his roof.

The foreboding manner in which the family is spoken intimates their doomed fates in Gaines's tragic passion play, a novel that his British publishers marketed as a "black Romeo and Juliet" (*Conversations* 54). The firstborn Catherine, as a six-year old uninitiated into the strict color codes to which her father abides, informs her mother that she has a "boyfriend" (*Catherine Carmier* 15). Della's smile is eclipsed by panic when her daughter replies to her mother's query about the boy's color. Though Catherine describes him as darker than anyone in her family, Della doesn't terminate the budding friendship; instead, she only insists that, when Jackson visits to play, "he'll have to leave before Daddy gets home, you hear?" Meanwhile, Raoul lives a life consumed with work, as he manically fixates on farming and competing with Cajuns as a means of elevating himself to the vaunted level of white men—a status that will forever remain elusive given the impenetrable color hierarchies. It becomes apparent that Raoul's obsession with work is part of his grand design to attain a patriarchal status and the power and prerogative inherent therein. As Madame Bayonne, a longtime quarters' resident with deep communal knowledge, observes, "Della was for convenience sake. To look after the house, to bear his children, and other than that—nothing" (117). Della's de facto servitude in her own home drives her into the bed of "Bayou Walter," whose widely known indolence is only matched by his callousness: he abandons the pregnant Della. The birth of the darker-skinned Mark thereby seals her fate: in addition to her all-but-stated indentured servitude, Raoul further ostracizes her, now relying on eldest daughter Catherine as his sole source of emotional support and comfort.

Again, from Madame Bayonne: "And from the moment he found this out [Della's infidelity], Catherine has been the only person in the world to mean anything to him. There's no one else. There can't ever be anyone else" (117). Della and Raoul will conceive one more child together, though one of Raoul's class-conscious sisters in New Orleans seizes the infant Lillian so that she may "be brought up as a lady" (16). These youngest two children's lives will be especially fraught with calamity and inexorable emotional distress: Raoul brings about young Mark's death—his specific age is not given, but he's still referred to as a school-age boy—when a tree that Mark was helping his stepfather to saw crushes him, a death ruled "accidental" by the white authorities (16). The adult Lillian harbors seething resentment toward a mother and father she, with justification, blames for giving her away. As a result, Lillian inherits the Carmier family's revulsion of dark people, so much so that her rare visits to her family will cease once she permanently leaves the area to take up residence on the other side of the racial tracks: as a black woman who will pass for white.

Using juxtaposition as a key structural device, Gaines positions alongside the tormented Carmier family that of Miss or Aunt Charlotte Moses, a quarters matriarch who's often assisted by a young woman, Mary Louise, who now assumes Charlotte's place as a domestic for the Grover family. As Catherine awaits Lillian's arrival for what will be her final visit, Charlotte and Mary Louise simultaneously prepare for the return of Jackson Bradley, whom Charlotte raised until he left for California as a preteen. Having earned his college degree, he is returning to his native Louisiana for the first time in ten years, as Charlotte and Mary Louise anxiously prepare for a welcome-home supper in his honor. Arriving on the same bus, Lillian and Jackson are, in effect, the prodigal daughter and son: though separated by a chasm in terms of skin color and class background, both return reluctantly, wary of the demands placed on each by their respective families and communities. The novel's three sections unfold through the depiction of parallel family conflicts.

On the one side are the Carmiers' unabating hatred of dark-skinned people and Lillian's deep-seated hatred of her mother and father, the specter of little Mark's murder, and the pressure of being the only black family sharecropping in an environment where Cajuns are amassing more property and power. On the other is matriarch Charlotte, the nephew she's reared but hasn't seen, and the quarters community to which their fates are so intricately bound. Specifically, Charlotte (and to a lesser extent, the entire community) has assumed that Jackson has returned to assume the anointed position as "The One," specifically in the capacity of a schoolteacher devoted to uplifting the black community and ensuring its evolution and progress. Just as Raoul has encased Catherine in the role of nonsexual surrogate wife, Charlotte makes unabashedly clear her design for/on Jackson's life, a design that's seemingly foreordained by God himself: after kissing her just-arrived nephew "hard on the mouth," she exclaims, "I prayed. And, yes, He sent you back" (25). Though separated by a seemingly ineffaceable color line, the two families intersect at the nexus of desire: though a decade has elapsed, Catherine's attraction to the little boy she described to her mother as her "boyfriend" endures, as does Jackson's to the woman deemed off-limits by a tyrannical, color-obsessed father.

"He Hates One as Much as He Does the Other"
Hue and Cry

A light-skinned character in Zora Neale Hurston's *Their Eyes Were Watching God* exclaims "Ah can't stand black niggers"—that is, darker-skinned blacks—and then suggests "Us ougtha class off" (135) to the novel's mulatta heroine, Janie Crawford. This "solution" not only hints at the interracial color line separating black and white, but it exposes the *intra-racial* color hierarchy based on pigmentation. The term "Literature of the Color Line" is commonly applied to works by black writers that address issues of miscegenation and passing; among the most famous works in this category are Charles Chesnutt's *The House behind the Cedars* (1900), James Weldon Johnson's *The Autobiography of an Ex-Colored Man* (1912), and Nella Larsen's *Passing* (1929). But for an African American writer who hails from Louisiana, a place with a gumbo of races, ethnicities, and nationalities, skin-color variation *within* the black community takes center stage in fascinating ways. Instead of a singular black-white color line, the state's uniquely multicultural history has spawned color *lines* amongst blacks themselves. Consider the gamut of ethnic distinctions: Acadian, Creole, white Creole, black Creole, *gens de couleur libres* (free persons of color)—not to mention the dizzying class distinctions *within* these categorizations. Addressing the origins of these divisions, Louisiana history scholar Carl Brasseaux posits: "The enduring gulf between white and black Creoles did little to foster a sense of racial unity between Creoles of Color and blacks.... As postbellum black codes destroyed the traditional intermediate caste, the mulattoes began to segregate themselves more and more from their black neighbors by means of their own private schools and such inventions as the 'paper bag test' and the 'comb test'" (111). Gaines has commented on Louisiana's cosmopolitan mélange of colors and the seemingly ineradicable color yardstick which blacks use to measure and devalue each other: "I think we have a big problem among the darker skinned and the fairer skinned black people in this state, more than in any other state in the union. I see it all the time, and I live it" (*Conversations* 229). This heartfelt testimonial to oppressed people's propensity for internalizing and promulgating their tormentors' prejudices limns one of *Catherine Carmier*'s central conflicts: black-on-black hatred.

Raoul Carmier continues the legacy of his father's inviolable antiblack mindset, to the detriment of both his family as well as to himself. Madame Bayonne, Jackson's childhood teacher, tries to impart to her former pupil the depth of Raoul's racial *hatreds,* the byproduct of being racially liminal and therefore not fitting securely in any category. Della and Raoul are Creole, she observes, "But color is only skin deep, and below that Della is as much Negro as you or I. Raoul is not. No, he's not white either. He hates one as much as he does the other" (114). Indeed, while pigmentation is a key element in Raoul's racial loathing and dis-ease, the social dimension that allows blacks to form emotional and psychological bonds with their own kind is forever foreclosed for him because he's so imbibed society's *perception* of blackness as inferior, other, contaminated. What results is the condition to which many of those who occupy this racial limbo experience: a paradoxical desire for and hatred of whiteness—*Anglophilia* and *Anglophobia*; and an accompanying loathing of all things black—*Negrophobia,* which encompasses not only other black people, but most detrimentally, themselves. A few pages later, Madame Bayonne continues her master class on race: though Raoul's great-grandfather was phenotypically white, "he still had a drop of Negro blood, and because of that single drop of blood, it would be impossible to ever compete side by side with the white man. So he went to the land—away from the white man, away from the black man as well. The white man refused to let him compete with him, and he in turn refused to lower himself to the black man's level" (116). The malevolent racial tenets that have been passed from grandfather to father to son result not only in extreme isolation—Raoul finds community with no one in or out-side of his household—but they stanch his very humanity, the lifeblood of any individual regardless of her or his race.

As he psychically implodes upon learning of Catherine's potential tryst with Jackson at a dance he reluctantly allows her to attend, his mind wanders back to "the other boy." He then revisits his most egre-gious sin, orchestrating the "accidental" death of the nonbiological son he could never embrace: "(Contrary to what the others believed, he loved the boy. Ten thousand times he had wanted to pull the boy to him, to hold him against his chest, to cry, to whisper, 'I love you, I love you'; but something always kept him from doing so)" (228). His blighted moral infrastructure precludes even the most basic of hu-mane gestures: an adult accepting and expressing compassion for an innocent child in his care. Regrettably, the indelible stain of blackness *marks* Della's son Mark in Raoul's perverted racial ethos. And while "Marky" pays the steepest price for Raoul's hardwired prejudices, his biological daughters will pay emotionally as well. Raoul, along with his family in New Orleans, indoctrinates Lillian with venomous hatred of blacks, which she confesses to her sister in what will be her last visit to the family before she leaves permanently to pass as a white woman: "I'm not black, Cathy. I hate black. I hate black worse than the whites hate it" (48). But it is the beloved Catherine on whom Raoul will inflict the most emotional if not physical pain. Indeed, she suffers most as a result of Raoul's twin scourges: his chronic hatred of dark-skinned black people, and the cankered patriarchal masculinity that threatens to destroy all of the women within his household.

"Once These Rattlesnakes Get a Whiff of That Scent"
The Sins of Patriarchy, the Degradation of Women

Among its incalculable negative aspects, patriarchy sanctions and promulgates an ideology of male domination. This manifests itself in countless ways—from the seizure and exploitation of land for profit at the expense of the environment, to the reduction of people to laborers, servants, property, and even objects to sate one's emotional and sexual desires. Consider Madame Bayonne's characterization of Raoul: "He was taught to get everything from the land, which he did, and which he, through necessity, was taught to love and depend upon" (116). In Raoul's worldview, land is paradoxically idolized and objectified, something to be treasured but something to be exploited to fulfill emotional needs which should be met through relationships with other people. It is little wonder that, after he reduces his own wife to domestic servitude, he should transfer his emotional longings to his oldest daughter, who, like the land, will be the object of Raoul's "love" and on whom he will "depend upon" for emotional succor. These patently misplaced emotions don't result in as tragic an outcome as the death of the "lovechild" he was unable to love, but they do arrest Catherine's emotional, psychological, and sexual development and promulgate a situation that might be described as sexlessly incestuous.

From her adolescence into her young adulthood, Catherine is the recipient of her father's affection, affection that he withholds from both Della and Lillian and displaces onto his firstborn. The novel abounds with references to this aberrant situation: "'So he went to Catherine. She was to be victim now, cross-carrier now, as long as he was alive. If she goes for a visit, she must hurry back or he goes after her'" (118–19); "He had his Catherine; and that was enough" (205). These observations, semantically alluding to the criminal, pathological, and monomaniacal, mark Catherine as the child through which he will atone for the sin of infanticide and, even more troublingly, the daughter over which he claims ownership as some form of human property. Another crucial occurrence, which had the potential to become a distorted crime of passion comparable to Mark's murder, was Catherine's love for an unnamed Creole man whom Raoul had hired to do some work on his property. When the young man returns with the intent of taking the pregnant Catherine with him to New Orleans, "The only thing that kept Raoul from killing him was Della and Catherine getting in the way long enough for him to get out of that yard" (119). As is often the case in works by his southern literary "hero" Faulkner, these events collectively insinuate a more unseemly facet of this father-daughter relationship as well.[1] In addition to lavishing upon her expensive perfume and jewelry, he ruminates in the backseat as Catherine drives to his sister's house in Bayonne (where he will remain while another sister serves as the daughters' chaperone at the dance) that "He liked the way she combed her hair. . . . At the house he had wanted to tell her how lovely she looked, but he had not said anything" (204).

Moreover, it is not only Madame Bayonne who detects something unsettling about Raoul's fixation on his daughter. The only woman in his family to stand up to him, his sister Elvira, is unsparingly candid: "And no matter how much you love her, she can't take the place of a woman. . . . Let her go, Raoul" (212). Once Della learns that Catherine has been seeing Jackson secretly and warns her of the potentially destructive consequences it could bring were Raoul to find out, Catherine defensively chides her mother: "I'm not married to Daddy, Mama," to which Della incredulously responds, "Oh . . . You not?" (131). This exchange infers that both mother and daughter realize that the family's inner workings are atypical if not completely abnormal. Perhaps the most revelatory admission of this disquieting situation comes from Catherine herself, as she weighs her desire for Jackson against father's claims on her: "But she had waited up tonight [for her father to come in from the fields] for a special reason. Tonight she wanted to look at Raoul closely. She wanted to decide whether her entire life should be devoted to him, or whether she should be free to look at someone else" (135). Though Gaines himself admonished critics for exaggerating the extent of their relationship (*Conversations* 161), I concur with one of the novel's early commentators, Theodore Hudson, who describes Raoul's fascination with his daughter and Catherine's excessive display of commitment to him as "emotionally incestuous" ("Ernest J. Gaines" 513). Moreover, Raoul's adoration morphs into something more glaringly odious once he fully grasps what his wife already knows: their daughter's simmering longing for her darker-skinned childhood playmate.

With his own parcel of land to till and a household of women over which he wields financial and emotional control, Raoul has constructed his own version of a southern Eden, though not quite as grandiose as those mythic white plantations teeming with crops and human chattel to harvest them. Claiming dominion over people and property, he has clearly inculcated the values of the white men he claims to resent and loathe—a resentment, of course, which barely camouflages the esteem in which he holds those very same men. It is thematically apropos, then, that he'd respond thusly to Catherine's playful taunt about possibly having a boyfriend: "'You going to have lot more boyfriends than you barking for,' he said, 'once these rattlesnakes get a whiff of that scent [of her perfume]'" (*Catherine Carmier* 154). This rejoinder casts other black men as serpentine, potential sexual predators in the Eden over which he reigns supreme. The narrator subsequently conveys that the striped double-breasted suit-wearing, tilted gray felt hat–donning Raoul cuts "the perfect picture of the gangster made famous by Hollywood during the thirties and forties" (202-3)—a fitting description that implies outlaw behavior, male prerogative, and even the threat of violence if warranted. This behavior comes into full view after two black men, paid by the Cajuns whom Raoul detests and who would like to rid themselves of him as they did his father before, reveal to him that "Catherine fooling around up there" (224) at the dance with Jackson. This revelation engenders Raoul's emotional unspooling and exposes the havoc he's willing to wreak to keep his daughter tethered to him.

Now in the less comfortable position behind a steering wheel instead of his more familiar place atop a tractor, Raoul drives to the dance to thwart Catherine's pursuit of an intimate relationship outside the purview of his policing gaze. His mind careens, imagining his sole and most highly prized possession guilty of not only seeking out a Creole, who should be an acceptable companion, but also of violating his rigid anti-dark-skin tenet: "She will be dancing with someone her own color. . . . He will have his black arms around her waist. He will have his black mouth on her red lips[. . . .] I will raise the gun" (227-28). Domineering father has now recast himself as jilted lover in this quasi-incestuous love triangle. Though Jackson has convinced Catherine to go away with him, Raoul tracks them down at his own home before they can flee. Patriarchy and all of its malignant ingredients—

domination, ownership, misogyny, rage—come into sharp relief in the novel's violent climax. The psychically unravelling, enraged Raoul raises a gun as he offers both an admission and a warning: "Boy, I don't want any more blood on my hand" (236); "Get your hands off her" (237); "You're not taking her from here" (237). Further, a subsequent proclamation, "I'll die first," is accompanied by Raoul "knocking her [Catherine] to the side" (237). An apparent happenstance occurrence in this male duel for Catherine's affections, the physical harm which Catherine suffers here is not insignificant; on the contrary, it exposes the violent underpinnings of her father's actions which derive not from love but from some warped facet of his personality. There are numerous possible explanations for Raoul's obsessiveness and the psychic disintegration in which it culminates: he has fixated on his daughter to avoid confronting his own crime against her half-brother; he's forcing Catherine to atone for her sexual "sin" of bearing a child out of wedlock by cloistering her and preventing further sexual activity—in effect, punishing her as he's done her mother for the same transgression; he deems Catherine's coupling with a dark-skinned black man the worst breach in the minds of the southern white male patriarchs whom Raoul incongruously detests and idolizes.

Whatever the reasons, Gaines dramatizes the calamitous consequences of one man's unrelenting need to dominate place and people, especially women. One might even read *Catherine Carmier* as a quasi-black feminist text, given the degradation that the Carmier women suffer at the hands of a ruthless, uncontainable Raoul. Though he will create more intricately drawn women characters (most notably, the indomitable Miss Jane Pittman), Gaines's portrayal of the Carmier women nonetheless reveals his sensitivity to the devaluation of southern black women, perhaps heightened because he witnessed firsthand his aunt's struggles alongside those endured by other women in his community. Preceding Alice Walker's *The Third Life of Grange Copeland* by six years and *The Color Purple* by eighteen, *Catherine Carmier* treats issues that Walker will portray in even more harrowing hues: the numerous ways in which southern black women languish under conditions in which they have little if any control over

their economic and sexual lives, and how such dependence has ruinous consequences for them, as well as for their oppressors.

"Our Little Jackson"
The Yoke of Familial and Communal Expectations

Though Jackson superficially has little in common with the Carmiers,
his homecoming sparks divisions comparable to those that beset his
would-be lover's household. It is ironic that it would be Della who'd
use both the possessive pronoun "our" and the diminutive "little"
when Catherine informs her of Jackson's return, given that Della's
own household is suffused with dissension around issues of ownership versus independence and obligation versus self-fulfillment. Especially striking is that Jackson, like Catherine, is consistently seen
by those who reared him not as an adult capable of mapping his own
life's course; on the contrary, he, like his paramour, is frequently infan-
tilized regarding every facet of his life—from seemingly minor issues
such as his decision to occasionally gamble to more consequential
matters related to religion and, most ponderously, what, if anything,
he owes to a community that has invested so much of its hopes in him.
Though the pressure it imposes may not appear as insidious as Raoul's
psychological stranglehold on his older daughter, Jackson is cast as
the heroic native son through whom they hope to conquer longstanding social and racial inequities.

One the one hand, Aunt Charlotte is esteemed as the community
matriarch, a pillar who has earned respect for her long-suffering work
as a domestic for the plantation-owning white family, her churchgo-
ing and the moral values it instilled, and her overall steadfast commitment to her quarters' brethren and sistren. On the other hand, while
she is certainly no Raoul who shamelessly attempts to sequester and
monitor Catherine, Charlotte nevertheless does insinuate herself into
her nephew's life, attempting to shape his choices in ways that border
on the coercive. It is to Gaines's credit that he illuminates not only the
injurious effects of patriarchy, but he also demythologizes notions of
the black matriarch as infallible familial and communal presence, a

social and literary construct most evident in works such as Lorraine Hansberry's *A Raisin in the Sun*.[2] Like Della, it is Lillian who offers a telling comment about Jackson's maternal figure: when Catherine reveals that Aunt Charlotte "used to almost kill" Jackson when she learned that he'd visited the Carmier home as a child, Lillian replies, "I didn't know she was like that, too. . . . Then she's no better than daddy" (38). Though not quite as bad as "daddy," neither is Aunt Charlotte reluctant to display her authority, as the adult Jackson will soon relearn.

Unlike most of Gaines's fiction, *Catherine Carmier* is set in the time period in which it was published, the early 1960s. Hence, one can reasonably understand Aunt Charlotte's high hopes for Jackson's return to help advance the race through educational advancement; as one of the older people asks—or declares—at his homecoming supper, "And you ready to start your teaching, hanh?" (65). A formally educated black person in the South was a rarity, admired for his accomplishments but also one the community considers an investment and thereby expected to yield an appreciable return. Writing specifically about the racial dynamics of Louisiana's education system from 1936 to 1950, historian Michael Kurtz asserts that "Louisiana continued to rank near the bottom among the states . . . and one-quarter of Louisiana's adult black citizens could neither read nor write" ("Reform and Race" 346). Going back a bit further, historian Leon Litwack in his prodigious study *Trouble in Mind: Black Southerners in the Age of Jim Crow* quotes formerly enslaved African Americans in the postbellum South: "'Don't know much about education,' remarked a former slave who had served in the Civil War. 'All I got I got it out in the field. That was my fountain pen and pencil, the blade of the hoe, and my slate was the ground'" (127). This speaker might have been a contemporary of Aunt Charlotte; at the very least, her or his sobering, vernacular-rich reflection speaks to opportunities denied and their resignation to existences as human beasts of burden. Such summations pinpoint the inestimable role education plays in potentially improving their wretched circumstances.

Such sentiments underscore the earnestness of Charlotte's impassioned plea to Jackson, his return potentially buoying an under- and non-educated community of rural folk yoked to the field and the plow. After declaring "You everything, Jackson," she spells out why he's so highly valued and valuable:

> In ever' family they ought to be somebody to do something. We ain't had that somebody in this family yet. All the others, they been drunks, gamblers—and your pa, there, even 'fore you was born, he had packed up and left your mon [*sic*]. . . . I don't mean to be preaching. . . . But I just want you to know [. . .] you all they is left, Jackson. You all us can count on. If you fail, that's all for us. (*Catherine Carmier* 98)

Given the weight of his aunt's expectations, one can understand why he fears revealing his utmost belief, which informs his ultimate decision: because of the South's physical and psychological emasculating of black men—"No, the South was not home, it had not been home for a long time now" (94–95)—he concludes, "But there was no returning home" (93). Jackson has returned only for a brief sabbatical, which he can divulge to a kindred spirit such as the intellectual, less communally tied Madame Bayonne, but not to the aunt who has instilled in him the ability to discern "right from wrong." Because Charlotte might elicit more empathy because of the magnanimity of her expectations, readers may be inclined to reject Lillian's assertion that "she's no better than daddy." However, there are more troubling dimensions of the community matriarch's appeal, ones that make the comparisons to Raoul a bit less dubious.

Charlotte scolded Jackson for his occasional gambling, a sin for black southerners of Charlotte's generation if not so much in a twenty-first century where church busses ferry congregants to casinos. In battling the monstrousness of slavery and Jim Crow, southern African Americans especially maintained strong ties to morally (if not racially) conservative churches. Thus, a man of Jackson's age would have spent a great deal of time worshiping with his aunt and fellow churchgoers, Jesus being their primary armor in a war against the dangers, toils, and snares inflicted by southern whites. Choosing to gamble is heathenish enough; but Jackson subsequently commits an even more blasphemous act: he refuses to attend services with Aunt Charlotte and Mary Louise. After she accuses him of forgetting God as he has climbed the ladder of formal education, Jackson deals an emotional blow which elicits an actual physical one from his aunt:

> "I haven't forgotten God. But Christ, the church, I don't believe in that bourgeois farce—"
> Suddenly her hand came out and slapped him across the mouth. She had not intended to hit him. The hand had jerked forward to shut him up. (100)

This reenacts a decisive scene in Hansberry's legendary drama *A Raisin in the Sun,* when family matriarch Lena Younger delivers a blow to the face of twenty-year-old daughter Beneatha, who'd dared to exclaim "There simply is no blasted God" in her mother's living room (39). Both Beneatha and Jackson represent the emergence of more formally educated African Americans, a more incredulous younger generation who repudiate what they consider their elders' blind adherence to a Christianity they contend has and continues to oppress blacks. While Jackson is clearly guilty of insensitivity and even impudence, Charlotte's response is nevertheless troubling, as violence has often been deemed a reasonable response in the face of perceived opposition. It does lend credence to Lillian Carmier's comparison on some level, as Charlotte, like Raoul, brooks no dissent from the child who grew up under her roof, age and education level notwithstanding. However, unlike the Carmier patriarch, Charlotte is receptive to her pastor's attempts to curtail her expectations of Jackson, a message which Raoul would have dismissed categorically.

As these encounters with his aunt demonstrate, Jackson is considered the community's great black hope whose educational achievements may potentially "uplift the race," to evoke W. E. B. Du Bois's "Talented Tenth" concept. But that elevation is not without a downside and in fact comes with a price. To illuminate this final point regarding the paradox of community as it relates to "the One," I turn briefly to the elder to whom Jackson gravitates, Madame Bayonne. While comparing his aunt's emotionally asphyxiating homespace to a "prison" (*Catherine Carmier* 190), he frequently finds solace at Madame Bayonne's quarters dwelling; one might even consider Jackson her protégée, given that she, too, is a fellow intellectual who bucks conventional roles and ways of thinking. Childless, she lives alone in the quarters and does not adhere to the rigid Christian principles and practices that govern other older black southern women's lives. Though she attends Jackson's homecoming celebration, she "had very little to do with the people in the quarters now that she had retired from teaching" (71). She is respected for her keen insights as someone who understands people on a deeper psychological level, befitting her status as both elder and educator. In fact, in some ways she might even be said to be clairvoyant: for instance, even before Jackson expresses it, she intuits that he's only returned temporarily and insists that he inform his aunt sooner rather than later. Having already educated him about the psychology undergirding the Carmiers' warped family dynamics, she also elucidates for him his aunt's primary mode of being and thinking: "People like [her] never change.... The only important thing in her life was that you were coming back here one day" (70). However, Madame Bayonne's position in the community emblematizes the plight of the educated black southerner, whose achievements often have the unintended consequence of distancing them from the very people who respect them most. As the narrative reveals about the partygoers' reaction to her, "... though they respected her very much, [they] looked upon her as an eccentric old woman from whom they kept their distance" (71). That no one sits at the table she shares with Jackson denotes the chasm between those considered superior by way of their education and the very people who've placed them on a higher plane.

Like his former teacher, Jackson is made unequivocally aware of his difference from the very moment he returns. During the event ostensibly held in his honor, one of the women who remembers him as a child, Mrs. Viney, escorts him into his aunt's yard, where the "men folks" have gathered to socialize. Upon his entrance, "the conversation came to an abrupt end" (66–67). Jackson and the men maintain their silence, the latter because "They did not know how to meet and talk to educated people." Trying to ease the discomfort, Viney "tried to start a conversation by saying that Jackson had come back here to teach. The men looked at Jackson and said, 'Yes?' 'Un-hun.' 'That's good.'" Once she mercifully ushers Jackson back inside, "The men watched them go back up the steps, and their conversation was resumed only moments later." He had become a foreigner in his native land by way of his "educated-people" status, and the gulf separating Jackson from these men takes on a gendered dimension as well. In an environment where gender roles were fairly rigid if not wholly unalterable, teachers have tended to be women, performing what is indoor—if not domestic—work. Southern black men, conversely, have almost exclusively worked outdoors performing physical tasks. From the men in the yard's standpoint, Jackson's position has possibly "feminized" him in their eyes, widening the fissure which his education has already opened. Ostracized from the "men's talk" outdoors and the object of feigned interest inside, Jackson is other/othered in the place that he once called home but which is now even more alienating than the superficially integrated West Coast. A subsequent episode occurs on southern culture's premier stage, the porch, further dramatizing Jackson's liminality and isolation.

Fittingly enough, the only man with whom Jackson finds any sort of camaraderie is "Brother," a boyhood friend and staple in the community. Though Jackson admits to himself that "He could not make himself feel about Brother as he did before" (64), his childhood friend is one of few people around whom he feels relatively comfortable. As Brother speaks with other black men on the porch of a store, Jackson's arrival, again, brings all conversation to a halt. The primary difference between this scene and the previous example is manifold: this event takes place in a more public venue and includes both African American and Cajun men—both groups occupy the porch but don't interact. Moreover, the store is segregated, so if Brother and Jackson do purchase a beer (and Jackson admits that he "needed one badly"), they'd have to consume it in a separate area, which Jackson flatly refuses to do. They strike a compromise: Brother purchases two bottles of coke, which they consume on the porch. Though a bit lengthy, the following passages vividly display the level of scrutiny to which Jackson is subjected:

> He knew that the people on the porch were looking at him. But what did he care? It gave him a sense of importance to know they were concerned about him. He turned his head to the side. The Cajuns quickly looked away. He almost laughed. What fools. Just because he did not clown in front of them and drink in the sideroom with the other Negroes, they were suspicious of him. Already he had heard that they were asking whether or not he was a Freedom Rider. What a joke. He a Freedom Rider? And what would he try to integrate, this stupid grocery store? He felt like laughing in their stupid faces.
>
> He drank from the bottle. The Negroes were also looking at him. He could tell without turning around. No, they were no better than the Cajuns. Just as bad. Behind his back they called him "Mr. Stuck-up." He was not "Mr. Stuck-up"; he could not think of anything to talk with them about, and drinking in that sideroom was out of the question. He would never go in there. Let them call him what they wanted. (174–75)

The Cajun assessment of Jackson is predictable enough: any black who violates the "stay in your place" dictate that southern whites hold sacrosanct is suspiciously regarded as a malcontent and potential troublemaker. The allusion to the young activists who ventured South in the 1960s to register blacks to vote conjures up the "outside agitator" malediction southern white politicians foisted upon non-southerners who came to their cities to, from their vantage point, "stir up trouble" amongst *their* "contented Negroes."

But what's even more distressing is Jackson's own people's harsh scrutiny. The condemnatory gaze they fix upon any fellow black who refuses to conform to the South's poisonous racial practices speaks to the depth of internalized oppression; the Negro porch occupants have been so conditioned to demur to whites that those even *perceived* as offering token opposition are viewed with the utmost apprehension. Given the chilly reception he received from former quarters neighbors at this less than congenial homecoming, the public derision and ostracism to which he's subjected on the porch speak to the "crisis of the Negro intellectual." The close-knit black southern community, bound through its affirming cultural rituals and ability to endure, nevertheless can prove unnavigable, stifling, and unwelcoming for those who dare to push beyond the Jim Crow glass ceiling, which mandates black southerners remain less educated and resigned to their second-class status. If "Brother" is the sobriquet of Jackson's sole friend, the returnee's own outlier status renders him a type of "brother-outsider," one whose intellectual accomplishments and rejection of entrenched but demeaning racial protocols position him on the outskirts of both white and black worlds.

Jackson Bradley's betwixt-and-between status, Catherine's repression, a South moored to its past—these conflicts make Gaines's debut novel a compelling introduction to themes that he will revisit and complexify in subsequent novels and stories. For twenty-first-century readers, *Catherine Carmier*'s profundity evinces itself through the multiple forms and genres into which it can be situated. It might be read as Shakespearean tragedy (re: its British publishers marketing it as a "black *Romeo and Juliet*"), with Raoul ("fool"?) Carmier as a tyrannical, King Lear figure whose foolhardiness threatens to destroy Catherine's life. Or one might ponder its proximity to the fairy tale genre, given that the French translation of Raoul is "wolf counsel," apropos given his predatory nature and his obsessive attempt to guard his beautiful "princess" from Jackson, her potential ebony "prince" and savior.[3] Other fairy tale conventions include the presence of Jackson's "godmother" figure Madame Bayonne, a wise but foreboding presence (for example, "That old woman knew everything. Some of the children used to call her a witch" [198]). It is she who warns, "Don't go behind those trees, Jackson. It won't come to any good" (122), recalling the "hedge of thorns" that the prince must navigate on his way to resuscitating "Briar-Rose," also known as Sleeping Beauty. From an intra-racial perspective, issues related to beauty and desirability based on skin color, unfortunately, continue to ignite disagreements well into the twenty-first century among African Americans conditioned to think of dark skin as less than alluring. Actress/media mogul Oprah Winfrey took up this very question in her 2013 documentary *Dark Girls,* as did actor/director Bill Dukes in a follow-up film, *Light Girls* (2015). Gaines would not address this issue as overtly in subsequent fiction, though his heralded 1993 novel *A Lesson before Dying* does includes an affair between a light-skinned woman and a dark-complexioned man. His second novel, however, addresses more explicitly issues of miscegenation along with the plight of black people dependent upon the southern plantation for their livelihoods and their very lives.

3

Of Love and Dust

The late renowned playwright August Wilson has spoken to the un-quantifiable role communal spaces in Homewood, an African American community in his native Pittsburgh, played in his formative years. Bars, barbershops, bodegas—all became informal classrooms, indispensable venues where he learned as much if not more than he did in the schoolroom. It was in these exclusively black and often male-inhabited "joints" that he learned life lessons about race and sex, as well as the power of black expressive culture—the rhythms and wordplay of black vernacular speech, the power of storytelling and story-listening, and the ways seasoned black men could school up-and-coming young bloods.[1] Wilson acquired this informal educa-tion in the early 1960s in urban Pittsburgh; Ernest Gaines soaked up cultural lessons and practices in the 1950s, worlds away in the back-woods of his native Louisiana, experiences that would become core ingredients for *Of Love and Dust* (1967).

In essays and interviews, Gaines specified the concrete ways in which he mined two moments for first a short story and, subsequently, his second novel. The first occurred in 1956, when he was listening to a blues record by Lightnin' Hopkins: "As I was listening to his 'Mr. Tim Moore's Farm,' one of the verses of the song struck me. It went something like this: 'The worst thing this black man ever done, when I moved my wife and family to Mr. Tim Moore's farm. Mr. Tim Moore's man never stand and grin, say if you keep out the graveyard, nigger,

I'll keep you out the pen'" (*Conversations* 4). The other event that inspired *Of Love and Dust* occurred in 1958 during a visit to family in Baton Rouge, when he ventured to the White Eagle bar "out in the country"—a trip necessitated by Baton Rouge being "dry" on Sundays:

> My friend and I went to this bar, and in this bar I saw a fight between two young men. This bar is surrounded by fields—cane, corn, cotton—and most of the people who come here are from the country or from small towns not very far away. They come to drink; they come to dance; they come to gamble; they come to fight; they come to steal your woman; they come to steal your man; they come knowing they might end up in jail that night, but still they come. . . . So it was here that I saw the knife-fight between the two young men. Fortunately for both, the fight was stopped before either was fatally wounded. (4)

Gaines would draw upon both the music and the bar fight in fashioning two of his most engrossing works, the first a short story entitled "Three Men," which would be published a year after *Of Love and Dust*. In that story, a young black man is jailed for murdering another man in a dispute over a woman in a honky-tonk not unlike the White Eagle bar. Nineteen-year-old Procter Lewis faces two undesirable choices: he can allow a white plantation owner to bond him out of prison, a practice common throughout the South in the 1930s and 1940s in which black men awaiting trial consented to plantation owners paying their bond in exchange for their labor. The second unpalatable option would be for the imprisoned to forego bonding, meaning more jail time in addition to possibly being found guilty; consequently, such a verdict would bring a lengthy sentence in the body- and soul-crushing Angola State Penitentiary. Procter ultimately chooses the more self-affirming—albeit more potentially life-threatening—option and refuses to be bonded out by a white plantation lord. In conceiving *Of Love and Dust*, Gaines reimagines Procter as Marcus Payne, who vehemently rejects the penitentiary as a self-affirming alternative (*Conversations* 319).[2] Therefore, in this reworking and expanding of the short story, Marcus's spitfire temperament and masculine bravado will not allow him to place dignity before confinement.

The novel's exposition recalls that of *Catherine Carmier,* as an African American matriarch attempts to wield some measure of influence in the life of the young man she's reared. Marcus faces a potentially lengthy incarceration for knifing another young black man to death after trying to "claim" that man's woman as his own. At the behest of his godmother or "nan-nan," Miss Julie Rand, Marcus is bonded out of prison by plantation owner Marshall Hebert, for whom she'd worked as a cook for forty years. Though he has an ulterior motive, Hebert permits Marcus to work on his plantation until his trial, under the direction of its Cajun overseer, Sidney Bonbon (re: "Mr. Tim Moore's man"). The novel is narrated by thirty-one-year-old Frank James "Jim" Kelly, who has worked as the plantation's tractor driver for three years. When Jim takes Marcus back to his south Baton Rouge home to retrieve his belongings, Miss Julie explains that she raised Marcus because "His mama died and his daddy just ran off and left him" (*Of Love and Dust* 11). Forced to retire from Hebert's, she now recruits Jim to serve in her stead, imploring him to help make Marcus's life there as trouble free as possible under the circumstances. Well versed in Bonbon's racist attitudes and slave-overseer mentality, she beseeches Jim to intercede on her godson's behalf: "But first he [Bonbon] got to try you, he got to break you. I want you to talk to Marcus. I want you make him understand" (11). He reluctantly consents and comes to serve multiple roles for the newly arrived "convict": as the tractor driver, he works most closely with Marcus, who's assigned the task of pulling corn; he also provides Marcus lodging in his home in the quarters, where he also attends to his personal needs (for example, preparing meals, providing beer); and Jim attempts to school his obstinate young charge in the ways of plantation life and their subordinated place in its rigid racial hierarchy.

As predicted, Bonbon quickly proceeds to transform Marcus into a two-legged mule. Unable to keep pace with John and Freddie, a gay couple who also pull corn, a lagging Marcus must now face the full brunt of quasi-master Bonbon's brutal behavior: "And there was Bonbon leaning on the pommel of the saddle, looking down at Marcus. And there was that black stallion about six inches behind Marcus—and poor Marcus feeling the horse's hot breath on the back of his neck" (35). Reduced to tears by both the backbreaking work and the puncturing of his male ego, Marcus vows to run away, fervently rejecting Jim's advice that he adjust to his admittedly deplorable circumstances. In the interim, Marcus strives to preserve as much of his masculine persona as he can, dressing in flamboyant, "gangsta"-style clothing; Jim nicknames him "Playboy Marcus" prior to providing this description of his attire: "A short-sleeve green shirt and a pair of brown pants. No hat—not even a handkerchief round his neck. He had on a pair of brown and white shoes" (24). This "superfly" getup is totally unsuitable given the sweltering heat that compounds the laborers' misery.

Bent but not broken, Marcus commences to avenge Bonbon's castrating treatment by "taking that black woman," Pauline Guerin, Bonbon's black mistress and the plantation cook (54). Tired of doing field work, Pauline asked Bonbon to secure her an indoor position, which he orchestrated by persuading Hebert to relieve Miss Julie of the position. Bonbon's relationship with Pauline, like many proscribed couplings in the South, is an open secret, as are the mulatto twin boys she bears a year later and whose patrilineage no one dare utter in public. Though Jim warns him that "She's Bonbon's woman," Marcus in typical fashion scoffs at this fact: "Well, that sure don't cut no ice with me" (53). After Pauline steadfastly and sternly rebuffs his overtures, Marcus sets his sexual sights on Louise, Bonbon's waifish wife whose sole role in life is to care for their three-year-old daughter, Judy ("Tite"). After a lengthy period in which they silently ogle each other, Louise and Marcus begin a torrid affair which, like Bonbon's and Pauline's, is widely known if not discussed. The difference, of course, is that white southern patriarchal and sexual prerogatives mandate that Pauline "would have to lay with Bonbon if he wanted her to" (60), but this same sexual license is not extended to black men with white women. Without question, the gruesome lynching bee was founded upon black men's violation of this sexual code, in fact or perception.

Though admirable for his willingness to breach degrading plantation norms that have rendered blacks such as Jim and Aunt Margaret, the Bonbons' cook/nanny (that is, mammy), acquiescent and silent, Marcus is nevertheless shortsighted regarding the scope of white male domination. As Miss Julie and a few others know, Bonbon has killed on Hebert's behalf, a fact that has brought the Cajun—though white, an impoverished group relative to the plantation class Hebert represents—a degree of power that undercuts Hebert. Hoping to eliminate his potentially blackmailing overseer, Hebert promises the dupable Marcus that he will help him to escape with Louise by providing a car and money. In Hebert's grand scheme, he hopes that Marcus will kill Bonbon or, in a less desirable but still preferable possible outcome, Bonbon's ruthless Cajun brothers will kill him for failing to prevent Louise from abandoning him for/with a nigger. Marcus gullibly agrees, with predictably catastrophic results: a scythe-brandishing Bonbon kills him as Louise watches helplessly. Hebert engineers Bonbon's innocent verdict ("justifiable homicide" the result of a hearing, not a trial, which thereby ensures Bonbon's continued silence), and Bonbon immediately leaves the plantation with his daughter, joined by Pauline and their children shortly thereafter. While Marcus loses his life in this quest for freedom and forbidden love, Louise's mental state is a casualty of the climactic confrontation, as she is institutionalized in the mental hospital in Jackson. Unable to reconcile Marcus and Louise's merciless treatment, for which no one is held responsible, Jim abandons the plantation, having gleaned from the irremediably defiant young prisoner a greater understanding of how conscienceless men like Hebert and Bonbon will go to any lengths to maintain power and to whom black lives matter little, if at all.

As its steamy, slightly overwrought plot suggests, *Of Love and Dust* addresses hot-button racial tensions that beset the mid-twentieth-century South specifically and the nation as a whole more broadly. The action takes place in 1948, a tumultuous period in our racial history: that year saw the desegregation of the Armed Forces; one year earlier marked Jackie Robinson breaking baseball's color line; 1954 brought the landmark *Brown v. Topeka Board of Education* decision; one year after the desegregation of public schools,

Emmett Till was gruesomely murdered in Money, Mississippi; and in that same year, Rosa Parks made her historic sit that would spawn the Montgomery Bus Boycott. Within this maelstrom of racially reverberating events, the novel raises several germane issues: How has America's most grievous institution and sin, the enslavement of Africans and African Americans, continued to cast a pall over the lives of both its victims and its perpetrators? How has the antebellum plantation remained a hotbed of interracial and intra-racial turmoil, rooted in violence committed against people and land? How has an interminable legacy of male supremacy resulted in sexual violence, domination, and gender inequality? Given the seemingly insurmountable barriers separating black and white, can genuine love exist across racial lines? *Of Love and Dust,* with the durable southern plantation as its setting, is a pulsating examination of power, exploitation, and abuse, and the incalculable price paid by victimizers and victims alike.

"Baby Please Don't Go"
Blues and Survival

Critic Steven Tracy has written extensively on the crosscurrents between the blues and writers' use of this "major expressive African American form" ("The Blues Novel" 124). Thematically, the blues encompasses several emotions: "Loneliness, frustration, isolation, [and] sexual desire" (125). Further, the blues are inherently southern, given the region's pernicious history of inflicting pain and terror on its darker native sons and daughters; this accounts for the form's "down home" quality. Writers also replicate the blues' penchant for bawdy metaphor and double entendre found in such standards as Bessie Smith's "Nobody in Town Can Bake a Sweet Jelly Roll like Mine." *Of Love and Dust* insinuates such *bluesmatter* when Bonbon informs Marcus that Louise wants her yard "raked up," to which the self-styled stud responds, "I'll rake it. . . . Give it the best raking it ever had" (127–28). The blues mood is further evoked in the "House Fair" Jim vividly describes occurring at "Josie's" (think of "Harpo's Place," the juke joint opened to dull the pain of the owner losing his wife, Sofia, in Alice Walker's *The Color Purple*), which is steeped in the blues' decorum-flouting activities of drinking, gambling, whoring, and fighting. But it is through his portrayal of Jim that Gaines most dramatically accentuates the blues and its manifold meanings.

As narrator of a story chockfull of desire, frustration, and pain, Jim represents "an individual voice and style thoroughly rooted in the African American vernacular tradition, offering communal concerns through the voice of an individual member of the community" (Tracy, "The Blues Novel" 133). The long-suffering but resilient black community is comprised of a spate of bluespeople "laughing to keep from crying"—Miss Julie, Marcus, Pauline, Aunt Margaret, all scuffling to make a way out of no way. These characters' personal travails are, of course, exacerbated by systemically racist institutions such as the plantation and the convict-leasing program. But it is Jim's lived experiences that epitomize the form's power to paradoxically serve as an outlet for one's pain while also bespeaking the capacity for surviving it. Though Jim is a bystander to the novel's various sexual liaisons (specifically, the Louise-Bonbon-Pauline and the Bonbon-Marcus-Louise triangles), the novel frequently returns to his personal lamentations of abandonment and the unrelenting loneliness that accompanies them. Specifically, Jim can't rid himself of the memory of Billie Jean: "I had come to this plantation myself, when my woman left me for another man in New Orleans and when I was too shame-face to go back home" (*Of Love and Dust* 143). Jim's runaway wife resides in his memories like the ubiquitous dust that gets dislodged in the characters' emotionally charged comings and goings down the road connecting the quarters and the plantation.

Earlier, Jim recalls when he and Billie Jean lived together in Pointe Coupee (re: Gaines's home parish), a life of grueling labor by day tempered by rollickingly good times at night: "Remembering the nights coming in from the field and the big tub of hot water waiting for me, and Billie washing my back, and then us in that old Ford, heading for town. And dancing and dancing until late, and then hurrying back to that bed and loving, loving, loving until morning" (20). Jim's doleful remembrance exemplifies one of the form's most conventional situations: a life of physically taxing work made bearable by a doting spouse who knows how to satisfy her man in and out of bed. The transitory nature of love, usually represented by a capricious lover who seeks and finds another, is one of the genre's prominent themes. Appropriately enough, Billie Jean jilts Jim for a glitzier life in New Orleans, the home of Storyville—that city's legendary red-light district and the home of jazz and blues. His tale of marital bliss and abandonment is brought into full relief when he turns to the only solace he can find: the music itself.

Jim frequently strums his guitar on his "gallery" or porch, usually alone but occasionally accompanied by Jobbo, his "harp"-playing friend ("harp" = harmonica in southernese). After a few bars of bluesman Big Bill Broonzy's "Key to the Highway," which conjures painful reminders of Billie Jean's abandonment, a melancholic Jim finally asks Jobbo "to stop. I couldn't take it any more," after which Jim suggests that they strike up "something fast and hard" (48). This brief but affecting interlude demonstrates Gaines's adroit use of the blues as a vehicle through which black men can express torment, which often goes unarticulated and therefore unacknowledged. Though the blues might seem to deepen the depressive feelings, they function as an empowering coping mechanism. That is, Jim's very expression of them, importantly alongside a companion who fully grasps their depth, provides relief and respite. Gaines effectively infuses the novel with folk and cultural materials, spotlighting the enriching expressive traditions of rural southerners he believes have been minimized or overlooked altogether.

"That Wall"
The Ubiquity of Slavery

Speaking of another of his works set in the 1940s, Gaines articulates a concern that permeates *Of Love and Dust* as well: "So that when you say slavery ended one hundred thirty years ago, that wall is still there, that law is still there, although many things have broken down since the 1940s when 'The Sky Is Gray' took place, but there are many of those walls that are still there, invisible walls to most people, but they're still there" (*Conversations* 258). Gaines's observation lends credence to the fact that, "Nearly a century after their emancipation from slavery, tens of thousands of blacks in Louisiana still picked cotton and harvested sugar cane, living in conditions little different from those in which their ancestors had existed" (Kurtz, "Reform and Race" 361). The majority of the novel's black characters—from major ones such Jim, Marcus, Pauline, and Aunt Margaret, to minor ones such as Miss Julie, the gay field workers John and Freddie, and the house servant Bishop—are dependent on and beholden to the man at the apex of the plantation hierarchy, owner Marshall Hebert. Though he doesn't occupy as much fictive space as other white characters, Hebert is still the dominant white patriarchal authority, an omnipotent force whose decisions affect every facet of the lives of those blacks and whites he employs; little wonder that upon his first glimpse of him, Marcus deems Hebert "the big white man" (*Of Love and Dust* 114). The author's own abject plantation childhood gives him an unsentimental awareness of its harsh realities. Thus, Gaines's Hebert Plantation is a far cry from the sentimentalized ones peopled with beneficent white overlords and dutiful darkies, gargantuan white edifices hearkening to an idyllic southern past that conjure memories of Gerald O'Hara's "Tara" or James Madison's "Montpellier."

As an extension of the odiously exploitative plantation economy, the bonding system through which Hebert secures Marcus's release perpetuates the economic and physical violence that were slavery's stanchions. Gaines was well acquainted with this glaringly iniquitous arrangement; commenting specifically on the bonding of a black youth who had killed a peer, he explained: "The only catch here—when the prisoner, the convict, found himself bonded out of jail—was that he usually spent twice as much time on the plantation than he would have in the penitentiary" (*Conversations* 7). Unbeknownst to the newly "freed" Marcus, who naively asks, "How much they go'n pay me for working?" Jim offers a gut-punch of reality: "They don't pay 'bond people' anything, I said. They feed you, they clothe you. If you want anything else, you can charge it at the store out there. That adds to your time" (*Of Love and Dust* 30). In effect, the prison and the plantation become twin scourges, each cannibalistically feeding off the sweat of black men's bodies. The *bondage* of slavery is now reincarnated in *bonding* as practice, the lexical proximity of the terms bespeaking their mutually parasitic nature.

Hebert's financial bloodsucking of Marcus brings an attendant physical brutalizing, marked by bodily pain: the "crocker sack" [*sic*] Bonbon gives to Marcus—necessitated by Marcus's inability to keep pace with Jim and the other two corn-pullers—is now weighted down so heavily with corn that "the rope had started to eat through that green shirt at his shoulder" (36–37); "For the first couple hours in the field the next [second] day, Marcus could hardly straighten his back" (49); "He pulled it [the sack] on the left shoulder because the right shoulder was still sore." Bonbon's bestializing of Marcus—and the young man's John Henry–esque durability—is brought into full relief by Jim: "But working Marcus like a mule no more changed him than . . . Bonbon's riding that horse six inches behind his back" (168). In fact, when Jim informs a friend that Bonbon is "Trying to break" Marcus—"break" a popular practice during slavery referring to slave masters' and their overseers' efforts to destroy the enslaved person's will through unrelenting physical labor and, if necessary, violence— and the friend speculates that he'll succeed, Jim rejoins, "I wouldn't bet on it" (84). That a mule is biologically classified as the offspring of a donkey and a horse is apropos, given that slavery and its 1940s progeny, prisoner bonding, attempted to reduce African Americans to a different species—a sort of human-beast hybrid created to bear the white man's burden, the time period notwithstanding.

From Mule to Miscegenation
Sexual Taboos in Black and White

Crestfallen due to Bonbon's ability to bestialize and infantilize him—at one point he even reduces Marcus to performing chores delegated to the black children whose parents work on the plantation ("Them children we had unloading that corn there all took sick"; thus, "That's your job this evening"; "He [Marcus] cried so deep and fully, his whole body was shaking" 77)—the bonded "convict" resorts to a familiar compensatory strategy men often employ to recoup their tarnished manhood: competing for and sexually dominating women. Once Pauline refuses his attempt to seduce her away from Bonbon as a way to recoup his masculine/sexual pride—re: "I'm taking that black woman"—he redirects his attention to Bonbon's wife, Louise. Marcus adopts a hackneyed strategy that proceeds as follows: if he can't *be* a white man—with all of the prerogative and privilege and power inherent in that superior status—then he can at least seize what the southern white man treasures above all else: his white woman. I will address the sexist imperative underwriting Marcus warped sexual-racial calculus in the next section. However, in terms of the more frequent coupling depicted in canonical American literature, the white man–black woman pairing has been a longstanding if vexing taboo, one examined in works from the nineteenth century onward.

The white man–black woman linkage or coupling—terms I choose in lieu of the misnomer "relationship," since this coupling is historically rooted in unequal power dynamics—has been an enduring one in our history, popular culture, and literature. Indeed, a cursory consideration of this interracial pairing could yield an infinite catalog of fictional treatments, among them *Clotel; Narrative of the Life of Frederick Douglass; Incidents in the Life of a Slave Girl; The Autobiography of an Ex-Colored Man; Mulatto; Absalom, Absalom!; Their Eyes Were Watching God;* "Long Black Song"; and *Another Country*.[3] That historians and novelists alike continue to grapple well into the twenty-first century with one of our Founding Fathers' "relationship" with a teenager he owned speaks to the radioactive nature of this coupling, how it is embedded in America's historical and cultural DNA.[4] Perhaps at its core is this: could a white man and black woman genuinely, mutually love each other given the malignancy of slavery, where black women's status as chattel invited unfathomable sexual violence? Gaines offers a compelling portrayal in his 1967 novel. Coincidentally, *Of Love and Dust* appeared in the same year as the landmark *Loving v. Virginia* Supreme Court decision, which struck down anti-miscegenation laws throughout the land—a case as tectonic as *Brown v. Board* only thirteen years earlier.

A common if ignoble reality, sexual violence committed against black women on southern plantations—antebellum or postbellum, real or fictitious—was, sadly, so pervasive that it was neither startling nor remarkable. An unstated tenet of the Jim Crow South was that white men retained the sexual license they exercised during slavery, a point foregrounded in the novel during a brief recollection of the (unnamed) overseer who preceded Bonbon:

> It had started in the field, where he had all the right to call her [a black field worker] over into a patch of corn or cotton or cane or the ditch—the one he was closest to—and make her lay down and pull up her dress. Then after he had satisfied his lust, he would get back on the horse like nothing happened. And she would pull down her dress and go back to the work she was doing before he had called her to him. The other women wouldn't say anything to her, and she wouldn't say anything, either—like nothing in the world had happened. (59)

Where to begin, the situation abhorrent on so many levels. Bonbon, too, perpetuated this behavior when he assumed the overseer position: "At first he had laid with all and any of them" (59). One obvious point that nevertheless warrants highlighting is the racial-sexual inversion at play here: white men occupy the role historically and interminably projected onto so-considered "menacing" black men; white, not black, men are sexual predators, consumed by rapacious lusts. Indisputably, the gulf between the French translation of Bonbon's name and his actual self is vast; there is nothing singularly, let alone doubly *good* about a man who sexually terrorizes women triply doomed by their race, gender, and class. But Gaines raises a provocative question in light of the Loving case: can a white man extricate himself from this historical narrative of sexual predation and tap into a humanity that would permit genuine love for a woman belonging to the race white Americans have so despised and vilified?

The novel proffers an unforeseen response, given the South's history of reducing black women to the role of bed wench. In his inaugural trip to exercise his privilege, Bonbon approaches Pauline's home in the quarters (her home is connected to that of an elderly couple, the houses sharing a common porch), brandishing the power his whiteness and maleness endow: "It was summer just like it was now, and he had tied the horse at the gate and walked toward the house just like it was his own. He had not said anything to Aunt Ca'line or Pa Bully; he had said something softly to Pauline, who had been sitting in a chair by the door, and she followed him inside.... Anybody who had ever slept on a cornshuck mattress don't have to be told the noise one could make" (61). However, Bonbon's sexual domination evolves into something unexpected given the sexual and racial boundaries of the plantation: "He fell in love with one of the black women. He couldn't just take her like he was supposed to take her, like they had given him permission to take her—no, he had to fall in love. When the children came he loved them, though he wasn't allowed to tell them that. He probably never told it to Pauline, and maybe he never told it to himself. But he could feel it" (64). And because this relationship had its basis in sexual violation/prerogative, it is not surprising that "it took years for Pauline to fall in love with Bonbon" (62). Just as African Americans were forced to abide by inflexible strictures that prevented them from forming any type of relationship with whites beyond one of servitude, white men doing anything beyond exercising their region- and gender-sanctioned access to black women's bodies was similarly forbidden. Unsurprisingly, Louisiana, like all southern states, had anti-miscegenation laws on its books to provide legal ballast for its rigid cultural mores.[5]

Gaines demonstrates the limitations of Bonbon's ostensibly privileged white male status: he cannot openly express any emotions other than carnal ones, because loves like theirs dare not be made public below the Mason-Dixon Line. For example, Bonbon cannot openly take Pauline on a shopping trip to New Orleans. To avoid the very appearance of treating a black woman as anything more than a sexual pastime, Bonbon drafts an unsuspecting Jim to serve as a "beard," giving the public perception that *he*—and not Bonbon—is Pauline's paramour. Of course, none of this mitigates the unfettered sexual prerogative out of which the relationship germinated. As well, Bonbon's adultery merely compounds transgressions permitted in the name of white male supremacy. Still, Bonbon's love for Pauline and his inability to transcend southern whites' entrenched prohibitions disallowing its expression speak to Gaines's commitment to presenting balanced portraits of white characters (*Conversations* 176). His characters, regardless of race, ultimately belie reductive categories—white victimizer/black victim, black object/white subject—in possessing a full range of human attributes.

"It's Not Marcus, It's Them"
Whitemouths, Militants, and the Cult of True Black Manhood

Gaines has expressed his dismay over more stentorian contemporaries, writers who assailed him as insufficiently radical during the racially volcanic 1960s. However, *Of Love and Dust* is very much a novel of this whirlwind moment, despite its 1940s plantation setting. Its central plotline, Marcus's fierce disruption of a plantation apparatus that exploits its black workers physically, sexually, and economically, echoes black liberation struggles both domestic and global. The 1960s civil rights movement's raison d'être was to overturn the status quo; contemporaneously, colonized states in the "Motherland" were overthrowing their European colonizers, regimes which had seized and pillaged Africa's natural resources—this economic violence always expedited by the butchering of millions of African people. More specifically, Gaines modeled his rebellious young lion on one of the decade's most lionized figures: "In *Of Love and Dust,* Marcus had some of the characteristics of Muhammad Ali. He loved to talk, he said, I'm good and I can prove I'm good, like Muhammad Ali, Cassius Clay at the time" (*Conversations* 182). The irrepressible Clay/Ali—loud talking, self-promoting, principled draft dissenter—exemplified a vigorous, combative version of manhood that younger black activists glorified, one that informed Marcus's actions throughout the novel.

Gaines's representations of African American masculinity throughout the novel underscore one of his staunchest commitments: to inscribe characters doggedly, even valiantly attempting to forge identities as "strong black men" despite seemingly insurmountable conditions. However, in the twenty-first century, with the popular phrase "toxic masculinity" coined to describe the worst kinds of masculine excess—from powerful, often revered entertainers and politicians assaulting women without reprisal, to ordinary American men storing caches of weapons in the name of constitutional prerogative—the definition of manhood is neither uncomplicated nor uniform. Thus, it raises vexing concerns: Do the novel's black men covet the same form of manhood displayed by white men like Hebert and Bonbon, men who wield unimpeded and potentially destructive power? Do Gaines's black men achieve self-worth through physical domination and violence? Do they adopt the worst facets of white masculinity, which include unfettered access to women's bodies with the potential for sexual violence? In essence, do Gaines's men feel compelled to adhere to what I label the "Cult of True Black Manhood," which mandates a willingness to extol physical violence, to objectify women, and to deify white men as models of power, privilege, and authority?

Certainly, Marcus's heroic qualities are evident when he projects an audacious spirit associated with iconic historical figures: Frederick Douglass, Marcus (his namesake?) Garvey, the aforementioned Clay/Ali—also known as "The Greatest" and the "Louisville Lip." Upon their first meeting, even before he begins serving his bondage at the Hebert Plantation, Marcus unabashedly declares to Jim, "I'm running, 'way from there first chance I get" (6). Though Bonbon has attempted to "break" him without it having "done any good" according to Jim, Marcus intimates a physical indestructibility akin to the black folk hero John Henry. Hebert too hopes to further devalue Marcus by tricking him into killing Bonbon under the guise of supporting his escape, but Marcus fervently refuses: "I ain't no dog, Jim. . . . I ain't no hunting dog to go round killing people for nobody else" (192). This does not mean that Marcus eschews society's association of "real" manhood with aggressive behavior: his entire trouble stems from his knifing of another young black man ("Hotwater") in a dispute over a woman at a juke-joint. His spiteful contention, "I wasn't going to spend no five years in Angola for [killing] a chickenshit nigger like that," is deeply troubling, since this intra-racial and intra-gender violence conforms to poisonous stereotypes of black men as hyperviolent "thugs" who devalue each other's lives and thereby cheapen their own.[6]

Another aspect of Marcus's toxic masculinity is his admiration of the unbridled power that white men wield. Thus, in light of the slavish treatment he undergoes and Pauline's subsequent rejection of him, Marcus becomes fixated on his overseer-nemesis: "How could he hurt Bonbon? . . . And some kind of way he would get to his wife. So let them lynch him—let them. What did he care" (113). Marcus reveals a surfeit of flawed race, gender, and sexual valuations here. In his zeal to wound Bonbon for denting his masculine persona, he engages in misogyny and self-debasement, reducing himself to the walking phallus that white Americans have persistently equated with "menacing" black masculinity. Cumulatively, Marcus's violent behavior and brash repudiation of southern racial scripts render him as a variation of the "bad nigger," the legendary figure from African American folklore embodied by the likes of Stagolee. Literary/folklore scholar Jerry Bryant's definition of a "hard man" as one who "breaks the laws of mainstream society and turns his violence and surliness not only upon whites who get in his way, but also against the people in his own black community" is befitting of Marcus (*Born in a Mighty Bad Land* 3). Bishop's belief that a reckless Marcus "would do most anything" animates fear amongst his fellow blacks, who collectively keep silent to avoid the omnipresent threat of white vigilantism and vengeance (*Of Love and Dust* 210).

Still, despite these paradoxes and inconsistencies, the belligerent Marcus disturbs the plantation peace, such as it is, unlike the older quarters' dwellers and plantation workers—specifically Aunt Margaret and the house-servant Bishop, who, to varying degrees, "know their place" and contentedly accept that place at the bottom of the southern racial hierarchy in exchange for employment and spurious racial tranquility. Echoing their sentiments, Jim stresses maintaining the veneer of tranquility, warning Marcus not to "fuck with that woman [Pauline]," because "We don't want any trouble on this plantation" (118, 117). It is Bishop who paradoxically utters the quarters community's fear of Marcus's actions and the historical legacy of racism that perpetuates their virtual if not actual enslavement on the plantation. After Marcus forces his way past Bishop into Hebert's home by literally placing his foot inside the kitchen door, Bishop grouses: "The house his great-grandparents built. The house slavery built. He pushed his foot in that door" (209). Correlatively, Marcus is acutely aware that he is a cog in an institution that has and continues to press black bodies into servitude, rendering them chattel-like as an under-compensated labor force: "I'm a slave here now. And things can't get harder than slavery" (218). Upon Jim's entreaties that he accept his debilitating circumstance at Hebert, Marcus rejoins, "Be a contented old slave, huh?" (219). Refusing to accept the counterfeit "order" that his elders countenance, Marcus explicitly invokes the words of America's foremost freedom fighter, Frederick Douglass, who proclaimed in his 1845 *Narrative:* "I have found that, to make a contented slave, it is necessary to make a thoughtless one" (Douglass 135). Picking up Douglass's mantle, Marcus will invert his mentor-mentee relationship, imploring Jim to "stop being old-fashioned. . . . Where would people be if they didn't take a chance? You know where? Right here. Right here in this quarter the rest of they life" (*Of Love and Dust* 242). One hears in this unassailable call to get up, stand up, and shake off the chains of complacency the voices of younger 1960s activists—Angela Davis, Stokely Carmichael, Kathleen Cleaver, Huey Newton, and others.

However, Gaines does not idealize Marcus as an infallible hero. The character's minimizing of his murder of "Hotwater," despite legitimately defending himself, shows an ignorance regarding the dominant culture's longstanding devaluing of black people's lives. Moreover, he projects a cocksure and domineering attitude in the presence of women. In addition to using Louise as a means to wound Bonbon, he displays a callous disregard for Pauline that recalls the physical barbarity Louise's own father and brothers enacted and advocated. Knowing that Pauline is involved with Bonbon only fuels Marcus's rage, and when she rebuffs his advances, his behavior coarsens: "He hit her and knocked her down. She got up. . . . 'You white man bitch,' he said. He hit her again. She fell again. . . . 'You bitch,' Marcus said to her. 'You bloody whore'" (94). Marcus's physical assault stems from the assumption that he, not white men, possesses all rights and privileges when it comes to black women. But also worth noting here is his verbal barrage, where he invokes gender-specific epithets that society routinely thrusts onto women it deems inappropriately sexual. In this instance, a black woman *perceived* as preferring a white man to a black one is denounced as a type of racially traitorous Jezebel deserving any punishment the scorned black man deems appropriate. (It should also be noted that, when Pa Bully, the elderly black man who lives next to Pauline, attempts to intercede on her behalf, his wife, Aunt Ca'line, admonishes him; black sisterhood be damned.)

His misogynistic attitude and the concomitant violence severely undermine Marcus's otherwise enlightened understanding of his and his fellow blacks' demeaned place as peasants who help sustain "the house that slavery built." Despite grasping how men like Hebert and Bonbon dehumanize blacks as "dogs" for their own machinations, Marcus nevertheless falls into the trap of competing with them and craving the emblems of their privilege, thereby embracing perverted forms of white masculinity in order to, in effect, *become* white men in status if not hue. In the above scenario, Pauline becomes a scapegoat for his bruised male ego, the object of the violence he dare not direct toward Bonbon. He steadfastly believes, "I ain't nothing but a nigger. Bonbon is the man" (217), this declaration reflecting his adherence to a "Cult of True Black Manhood," whereby the vaunted status of manhood must be wrested from white men by any means necessary.

If the commendable—that is, non-chauvinistic—traits Marcus exhibits have affected anyone on the plantation, it is Jim Kelly, the woebegone bluesman-narrator. Recall that, in their initial meeting, Marcus branded Jim a "whitemouth"—a "self-hating black person" who "praises and idolizes" whites while demeaning fellow blacks ("whitemouth," *urbandictionary.com*). And while Jim would go on to perform a multitude of roles for his rebellious young housemate—

cook, clothier, co-worker, counselor, companion—it is Jim himself whose consciousness is raised, buoyed by Marcus's one-man assault on the mythologized southern plantation that "survives as this day as a touchstone for southern identity" (Guterl, "Plantation" 27). His many interactions with and exposure to Marcus stimulate a radical shift in Jim's complacent acceptance of degrading racial tenets and practices: "I had been thinking about this in the field all evening and I said to myself, 'Yes, yes: it's not Marcus, it's them. Marcus was just the tool'" (*Of Love and Dust* 263). In the novel's closing chapters, Jim arrives at a deeper understanding: the complex network of racial, gendered, class, and power dynamics that contributes to Marcus's fate also shapes his own and that of other blacks on and beyond the plantation.

This newfound sentiment comes into full view at workday's end, when Jim hurriedly returns the tractor to the plantation, hoping to express his gratitude to Marcus: "Why blame him? No, I didn't blame Marcus any more. I admired Marcus. I admired his great courage. . . . I wanted to tell him how brave I thought he was. He was the bravest man I knew, the bravest man I had ever met. Yes, yes, I wanted to tell him that" (264). Given his rather placid demeanor throughout the novel, Jim's excited repetition of laudatory words and phrases conjures images of a newfound religious convert—Jim's "religion" now a quasi-racial enlightenment regarding the inner workings of oppression. Jim's ideological transformation is solidified in the wake of Marcus's death, as he now realizes that its causes are far knottier than merely one white Cajun protecting the sanctity of his white wife by killing her nigger-lover.

The results of Jim's imbibing of Marcus's spirit of defiance are twofold. First, he vows to leave the plantation, not because Hebert advises him to do so lest Bonbon's fellow Cajuns kill him because of his association with Marcus, but because he can no longer tacitly abide the systemic oppression of himself and the other quarters denizens. Secondly, and more vitally, his final act concretizes his repudiation of the status quo: under the pretense of helping Jim to secure future farmwork, Hebert provides him a letter of recommendation, a paternalistic gesture to which Jim responds thusly: "After I had read the letter, I folded it neatly and put it back in the envelope. Then I laid the envelope on the desk" (274). Thus, his posthumous brotherhood with the young upstart is complete: Jim quietly but resolutely spurns the attempt to chart the future course of his life, whereas he had previously been content to allow treacherous whites like Hebert and Bonbon to intrude.

What readers glean when juxtaposing Gaines's maiden novel and his second one is a more socially and politically engaged writer addressing head-on the cancerous legacy of slavery, both within the novel's 1940s setting and the contemporary moment in which it appeared. It is the author's espousal in response to black students who ask, "why my young men must die?"—"young men who tried to change conditions have always died"—which reverberates upon concluding *Of Love and Dust* (*Mozart and Leadbelly* 50). Indeed, its decade of publication, the 1960s, abounds with black men who gave their lives in the name of elevating the plight of African American people—from Medgar to Malcolm to Martin. And while Marcus, like the Shakespearean heroes with whom Gaines was well acquainted, possesses grievously tragic flaws, the novel proposes that muted, smaller-scale acts of defiance, like comprehending how racial and class oppression infect every aspect of black life, can contribute to personal and collective liberation. The inevitable challenges African Americans experience in moving from endarkenment to enlightenment form the foundation of the short-story collection *Bloodline,* which commences from an innocent and expectant six-year-old boy's perspective and concludes with a dying black matriarch who's survived a lifetime of, in the words of the Negro spiritual, being "'buked and scorned."

4

Bloodline

Though his first two novels didn't capture as wide a readership as he might have hoped, it would be that genre in which Gaines would establish his reputation as one of our preeminent writers. However, many of his most faithful readers remain unaware that his first publications were short stories: "The Boy in the Double-Breasted Suit" and "The Turtles" appeared in *Transfer,* the literary journal at San Francisco State where Gaines studied in the mid-1950s. This oversight is indicative of a broader elision in African American literary studies, where scholars focus disproportionately on the novel. With notable exceptions such as Langston Hughes, Lorraine Hansberry, and August Wilson, poetry and drama remain comparably understudied. The same can be said of the short story, a genre to which black writers have richly contributed, from Charles Chesnutt and Ann Petry to James Alan McPherson, Toni Cade Bambara, and Edward P. Jones. Though not nearly as widely known or read as his novels, his 1968 collection *Bloodline* was Gaines's sole but lasting contribution to an underappreciated literary genre.

Although *Bloodline* chronologically followed his 1967 novel *Of Love and Dust,* three of the five stories appeared prior to its publication: "A Long Day in November" (1958), "Just Like a Tree" (1962), and "The Sky Is Gray" (1963). Gaines expressed confidence in his abilities as a short-story stylist in his 1998 essay "Mozart and Leadbelly." As a fledging writer in the mid-1960s, he was convinced that "the stories were good enough and long enough to make a book" (*Mozart and Leadbelly* 28). However, the sparse sales of *Catherine Carmier* hadn't earned him the kind of cachet that would compel Dial Press to publish a short-story collection on the basis of reputation alone. Though his editor agreed with Gaines, "he told me that I needed another novel out there before he would publish the stories. . . . 'Write a novel,' the publisher told me, 'and we will publish both the novel and the stories.' 'But those stories are good,' I said; 'they will make my name.' 'We know that,' they said, 'but no one knows your name now and we need a novel first'" (*Mozart and Leadbelly* 28). In addition to meeting his press's condition by completing *Of Love and Dust,* Gaines would write two additional stories for the forthcoming collection, "Three Men" and "Bloodline." While Gaines may have been overly optimistic in speculating that the stories would have a pronounced impact professionally, "A Long Day in November" and "The Sky Is Gray" have remained fixtures in literary anthologies from the 1970s into the twenty-first century.

The subject and scope of the five stories bring to mind the title of Romantic poet William Blake's collection *Songs of Innocence and of Experience.* The first four—"A Long Day in November," "The Sky Is Gray," "Three Men," and "Bloodline"—are presented from the first-person point of view that the author favors, the male narrators ranging from age six to young adulthood; the final story, "Just Like a Tree," focuses on the impending relocation and eventual death of an elderly woman and is told from multiple perspectives. Though Gaines has denied that the stories collectively form a unified novel, he identifies Faulkner's novel of interlocking tales, *Go Down, Moses,* and Toomer's multi–point of view, multi-genre novel *Cane* as primary influences (*Conversations* 222). "November" and "Sky" are companionate stories: told from the point of view of a six- and eight-year old, respectively, both reflect the author's deft ability to capture the rhythms and sensibilities of childhood. Cumulatively, the first four concentrate on these males' maturation in a menacing Jim Crow South. Though the experiences of the young protagonists are distinct and unique, Gaines explains that *"Bloodline* in the title means the common experience of all the male characters from the youngest to the oldest; they were all part of the same experience in the South at that time, between the 1940s and the 1960s" (*Mozart and Leadbelly* 28). While the final story appears to be an outlier in depicting multiple community members' responses to Aunt Fe's relocation, it is not out of place, given its concerns with both children's and adults' responses to a South for which change and progress prove unsettling though inevitable.

"We All Get Teached Something No Matter How Old We Get"
Education and Ritual in "A Long Day in November"

The collection's opening story depicts a day in the life of the young Howard family through the eyes of Sonny, the only child of Eddie and Amy. The setting is the canvas on which Gaines paints most of his stories: the white-owned plantation where blacks labor, and the plantation quarters in which they reside. The story offers a comic twist on the "other woman" plot: the homewrecker in this case is Eddie's automobile, which, according to Amy, is preventing from him from fulfilling his familial duties. As is often the case, young Sonny is thrust in the middle of his parents' tug-of-war, as the story opens with Amy informing him that they'll be moving the following day to her mother's house, because "I don't know what your daddy wants. . . . But for sure he don't want me" (6). Though one might expect the story to focus exclusively on Sonny's maturation, given his position as narrator, "November" is actually a dual initiation narrative, with both son and father learning crucial lessons related to masculinity and maturity—a point reinforced by both father and son's youthful-sounding nicknames. Eddie's immaturity if not outright childishness is evident in the first of the story's five vignettes. As he does throughout, he cries when frustrated or rebuffed, as when he attempts to engage a nonresponsive Amy in physical intimacy: "Then he starts crying" will become his default response whenever things ago amiss.

Once Eddie leaves for work the following morning, Amy follows through with her plan, packing their belongings and taking Sonny to her mother's nearby home. As has probably been her routine, Rachel begins admonishing her daughter for her dismal choice of a husband: "I warned you 'bout that nigger. . . . A yellow nigger with a gap like that 'tween his front teeth ain't no good. But you wouldn't listen" (18). While Gaines's flair for folk humor permeates the story, Rachel's actions aren't primarily humorous but intrusive: she invites Freddie Jackson into her home to woo her daughter, deciding that he's a much more suitable mate despite Amy's insistence that "I just feel it ain't right to leave one house and go to another house the same day" (31). As is the case at other times in the story, parent-child roles are reversed, with offspring expressing a more sensible attitude when a parent's judgment is wanting.

A great deal of the narrative consists of Eddie's attempts to restore domestic tranquility. To that end, he retrieves Sonny and the two trek through the quarters, Eddie enlisting the counsel of several community members to help him convince Amy to return. Father and son's alternately comic and serious odyssey will include encounters with the minister, the conjure woman, and several of Eddie's male friends—all of whom will attempt to bring about his fractured family's reunification. Following Reverend Simmons's unsuccessful intervention on his behalf, Eddie declares, "I hate to go to that old hoo-doo woman, but I reckon there ain't nothing else I can do" (44). It doesn't pose much of a clairvoyant challenge for Madame Toussaint to identify the purpose of his visit: "Your wife left you. . . . That's all you men come back here for" (46). Her advice, "Give it up," proves indecipherable to her rather obtuse client, who occasionally resorts to seeking out his young son's input. An increasingly exasperated Eddie finally turns to male friends who are working in the fields; Madame Toussaint's counsel has helped them to rekindle their own troubled marriages. But after concluding that her suggested cures are totally inapplicable to his circumstance, Eddie borrows three dollars and returns to Madame Toussaint, who clarifies her cryptic edict: to restore domestic bliss, he should not only "give up" the other woman—his cherished car—but she now commands him to "burn it." A reluctant Eddie returns to Amy, who concurs: "If you burn it up, yes, I'll come back" (65). What began as individual family strife climaxes with a burning ritual which includes both the family and the entire community. The return of familial order is conveyed in the story's denouement, when the still-innocent Sonny nevertheless infers that normality is restored when he hears "the spring on Mama and Daddy's bed" (79), their sexual intimacy indicating that the disruptive storm has passed.

Though Gaines privileges young Sonny in terms of point of view, "November" unfolds as a dual coming-of-age story. Sonny's day begins routinely with his reluctance to leave the literal and metaphorical warmth of home (Sonny frequently finds comfort near fireplaces or around outdoor fires) as his mother sends him off to school: "And I hate to leave Mama—and I hate to leave the fire. But I got to, because they want me to learn" (21), he surmises. The schoolhouse will play a key role in his maturation, but perhaps even more crucial are the life lessons he will learn after school when accompanying his father. Sonny's quest for knowledge, reflected in the disappointment he expresses in class while the other students are studying their lessons—"I wish I knowed [mine]" (23)—prefigures Eddie's own inability to grasp Madame Toussaint's advice: "I wish I knowed what she told them [other husbands she's advised]," Eddie exasperatedly mutters to his son. As he does throughout his fictive oeuvre, Gaines accentuates and complicates notions of masculinity, the enlightenment both father and son reach proving the validity of Rachel's aphorism, "We all get teached something no matter how old we get" (20).

Sonny's schoolhouse encounters impart various lessons—for instance, the humiliation he feels after urinating on himself in fear that his teacher will call on him illustrates the necessity of completing his homework. However, the communal advice Eddie receives will prove even more profitable. Eddie will directly absorb these lessons while Sonny's secondhand exposure to them has the potential to help him better navigate personal conflicts as he grows up. Their father-son journey first takes them to Reverend Simmons, who attempts to broker a solution when he accompanies them to Rachel's home and speaks with both mother and daughter. Although frustrated by the minister's inability to solve problems of this world, Eddie's decision to venture to Madame Toussaint speaks to his resourcefulness if not his desperation. Moreover, it conveys to Sonny the value of nontraditional sources of insight. Indeed, the "old hoo-doo woman" is the fount of insight on matters of domesticity and gender, as she lectures Eddie on why Amy prefers her own home to her mother's:

> Women like to be in their own house. That's their world. You men done messed up the outside world so bad that they feel lost and out of place in it. Her house is her world. Only there she can do what she want. She can't do that in anybody else house—mama or nobody else. But you men don't know any of this. Y'all never know how a woman feels, because you never ask how she feels. (61)

Madame Toussaint's quasi-feminist oration resonates on several levels, generally enumerating how the home has represented a sphere where women can feel some sense of control and comfort, and pointedly addressing the historical value of home to black women often forced to labor in white women's homes as domestics. Not only does Amy agree to return, provided that Eddie in fact incinerate his car, but there's further evidence that Sonny too has assimilated this lesson: he reinforces his mother's edict, "Come on, Daddy. . . . Let's go burn up the car" (67), as a prelude to the story's climactic event. The ensuing "car-burning party," in which a procession of quarters' residents (including Amy and Rachel) follow as Eddie's car is towed to a field to be set ablaze, is a restorative, affirming ritual, a stark contrast and antidote to the South's degenerate lynching and burning rituals. The gravity of this inclusive communal event is not lost on Sonny, who infers its sacredness: "Gran'mon the only person talking; everybody else is quiet. We stay there a long time and look at the fire" (72). Eddie's closing words to those present, "Thank y'all," become a benediction, thereby consecrating the restoration of the family that his car fetish helped to fracture.

"Neither Black nor White"
Races and Spaces in "The Sky Is Gray"

Though the 1962 story "Just Like a Tree" was published a year before "The Sky Is Gray," the latter story follows "A Long Day in November," its placement indicating the proximity of the stories in points of view. In "Sky" Gaines recasts six-year-old Sonny as eight-year-old James, a slightly older boy who ventures beyond the familiar confines of home and community and into the racially segregated town of Bayonne. Gaines drew upon his own childhood in depicting a brief but pivotal day in James's life, including his own boyhood experiences, such as riding on a segregated bus with his mother into town to have an aching tooth pulled (*Conversations* 182). Moreover, while "November" focused on both mother-son and father-son interactions, "Sky" concentrates exclusively on James's relationship with his mother, Octavia (her husband and James's father has been drafted into the army, his fate unknown). In addition to citing Faulkner's influence on the collection, Gaines acknowledged his indebtedness to another southern author for "Sky's" conception: ". . . but I don't know that I would have been able to write 'Sky' had I not read Eudora Welty's 'A Worn Path'" (245).[1]

Though set in the same decade as "November," the obstacles facing Octavia's family are far more formidable. The burden of head-of-household falls squarely on her shoulders as she, her sister Rosemary, and their children struggle to make ends meet as impoverished sharecroppers. While the story opens with James and Octavia awaiting the bus that will transport them to Bayonne, the first four sections concentrate primarily on past incidents at the family's home that have affected James's maturation. His early thoughts as they wait signal the vast difference between his still-evolving identity and his mother's stoic strength: "I love my mama and I want put my arm round her and tell her. But I'm not supposed to do that. She say that's weakness and that's crybaby stuff, and she don't want no crybaby round her" (*Bloodline* 84). This thought quickly triggers another in James's mind and reveals the purpose of their trip: "I can't ever be scared and I can't ever cry. And that's why I never said nothing 'bout my teeth." Thus, the story's opening vignette functions as a prologue, establishing many of the remaining twelve sections' core concerns: mother's and son's vastly different attitudes about intimacy and the expression of it, the comportment of oneself in public spaces, and the

ability to endure pain and hardship without complaint. The ensuing
mother-son journey (another slight but important variation on "November") and the various spaces they occupy while in Bayonne depict
not only Octavia's life lessons but, simultaneously, James forming his
own distinct way of observing and navigating the world that deviates
from his mother's.

Apropos of Gaines's unembellished way of integrating racial protest, James's understanding of the South's racial barriers is presented
subtly, without fanfare.[2] Once they board the bus, he knows that
whites and blacks are physically separated, even if he doesn't fully
grasp the perniciousness of Jim Crow's separate-and-unequal tenet:
upon passing "the little sign that say 'White' and 'Colored,'" he continues, "They got seats in the front, but I know I can't sit there, 'cause
I have to sit back of the sign" (91). As he and his mother walk to the
dentist's office, James notes the flag adorning the courthouse, which
differs from the one at his all-black school: "This one here ain't got but
a handful of stars" (93). Though James might not possess the vocabulary to describe these signposts, the reader clearly recognizes how
such emblems are byproducts of the same heinous racial codes that
render his family impoverished and disenfranchised.

The segregated dentist's office serves as his first informal classroom, as James primarily observes the interactions among the black
adults waiting to be served by the never-seen white dentist; the only
visible white person is his nurse, who doubles as receptionist. The
most *striking* encounter—literally and figuratively—involves a debate on race and religion between a "big and fat" minister bedecked
in "a black suit" and "a gold chain" and a young man who "looks like a
teacher or somebody that goes to college. . . . and he's got a book that
he's been reading" (95). What has agitated the minister is the student's
contention that nothing is beyond the bounds of critical scrutiny, including the Almighty. In response to the preacher's admonitory "Wait
now," the young man continues without trepidation: "His existence
as well as everything else. Everything" (96). Further, he insists that
"cold logic" is required when defining words such as "Freedom, Liberty, God, White, [and] Colored," which the student clearly interprets

as vacuous abstractions in a country that disempowers blacks by any and all necessary means, legal (Jim Crow statutes) and extralegal (hate groups such the KKK and the White Citizens Council). Though the minister requires little tangible proof of God's existence beyond his earnest conviction that "My heart tells me," the student remains unpersuaded: "A white man told you to believe in God. And why? To keep you ignorant so he can keep his feet on your neck" (97). Given that the story appeared during the rising popularity of Malcolm X and 1960s Black Nationalism, the young man's beliefs clearly reiterate their denunciation of American Christianity as "a relic of bondage, using God to keep black people down and reinforce their submission and dependence" (Litwack, *Trouble in Mind* 400).

This battle of warring ideologies abruptly ends when the preacher, having heard enough of the impious and impudent young whipper-snapper, demands he "get up"; once the student closes his book and complies, the man of the cloth goes into Joe Louis mode: "Preacher just hauls back and hit him in the face. The boy falls back 'gainst the wall, but he straightens himself up and looks right back at the preacher" (*Bloodline* 98). In response to the student's derisive retort, "You forgot the other cheek," the minister again "hauls back and hit him again on the other side. But this time the boy braces himself and don't fall." Though the not-so-nonviolent preacher has drawn blood, the student remains unbowed: not only does the holy man hastily depart, but the student "keeps on reading his book" after declaring to his would-be conqueror, "That hasn't changed a thing."

I outline this scene in extensive detail because of its tremendous impact on James's budding understanding of not only race and religion, but also of the potential power of education. However, one of James's childhood memories preceding their trip to Bayonne warrants mention here. Octavia had commanded James to kill two redbirds he'd trapped—the family's dire poverty precluded James the luxury of keeping them as pets when they could provide a meal. After James's repeated refusals, she "started hitting me 'cross the back. I went down on the ground, crying"; the corporal discipline doesn't end here, as James goes on to reveal that she "hit me and hit me and hit me" (90)—this despite Rosemary's entreaties that her sister "Explain to him. Just don't beat him. Explain to him" (90). Though James retrospectively declares that his aunt and her companion, Monsieur Bayonne, eventually "talked to me and made me see," he experienced firsthand how violence can be marshalled both to punish and to force a person to do something against his will. Therefore, the preacher's beating of the young man reinforces this: though the circumstances differ, like Octavia, he too resorts to violence when his authority is challenged. However, whereas James had no viable option but to acquiesce, the student enacts a potential defense: the intellect.

While James's intuitive understanding of this is evidenced when he points out some books to his mother and asks, "Want read one of them?" Octavia's response is equally revealing: "Mama looks at the books, but she don't answer me" (99). Though this silence is certainly in keeping with her nonverbal demeanor—she clearly prioritizes action over words—one wonders if she also ascertains that "book learning" might represent a potential defense James might one day deploy in response to the violence she relies on to punish and/or teach. This certainly doesn't negate the vital lessons his mother will model on race, pride, and agency in oppressive situations, yet the student also imparts an invaluable lesson: that brain has the potential to subdue brawn, a point reemphasized when James ruminates, "When I grow up I want be just like him. I want clothes like that and I want keep a book with me, too" (100). In this brief episode, the student nevertheless serves a potentially consequential role as surrogate father figure in the absence of James's biological one.

Having been informed that the dentist will not be seeing any more patients until after lunch, James and Octavia leave with the intention of returning. In the meantime, they venture to two distinctly racialized spaces: the "colored café" and an elderly white couple's hybrid home/store. Though Octavia sought refuge in the former only to allow James a few minutes to warm himself at the stove on this especially brisk day (re: the importance of fireplaces and fire in "November"), she then tells him they "Got to pay them something for they heat" (108) after James has lied that he's not hungry—further evidence that he is assimilating his mother's lesson regarding dispassionate endurance of discomfort. Not lost here is her attempt to instill a sense of responsibility to other black people. However, what should be a racially warm and warming space turns out to be anything but: a man with whom Octavia has agreed to dance mutters something sexually suggestive (at least her response implies this), to which she brandishes a knife and hastily retreats with son in tow. This contrasts sharply and ironically with their final refuge.

Trudging back to the dentist's, they encounter "a little old white lady up in front of us. . . . She's all in black and she's got a long black rag over her head" (112). Given that he'd moments earlier recalled an Edgar Allan Poe poem—the brutally cold day has reminded him how much school he's missed on account of inclement weather—the woman's ominous appearance might certainly bode ill (if not necessarily horror) for a black mother and son in a white part of town. But any potential fears are immediately dispelled when Helena volunteers to call the dentist on their behalf, her voice presumably carrying more weight than Octavia's. After Octavia responds "Yes ma'am" when Helena asks if they've eaten, the precocious narrator is perplexed: "The old lady looks at Mama a long time, like she's thinking Mama might be just saying that. Mama looks right back at her. The old lady looks at me to see what I have to say. I don't say nothing. I sure ain't going 'gainst my mama" (113). Again displaying the pluck and self-possession she displayed in an earlier encounter with the nurse (Octavia pleaded with her to allow James access to the dentist before lunchtime, given the immensity of his pain), Octavia demonstrates that blacks needn't obsequiously lower their gaze in the presence of a white person. As Octavia pivots to leave when offered what to her looks like a "handout" of a free meal, Helena quickly counters that, on the contrary, "I'm not handing out anything": James will have to move her garbage cans, to which Octavia consents. Like Octavia's willingness to engage the white nurse, this episode gainsays the often-accurate reality that, "For some black youths, an abrupt, often traumatic awakening to the impotence of their parents in a white world [becomes] in itself a racial baptism" (Litwack, *Trouble in Mind* 24). As well, these two strong-willed women are clearly working out the terms on which a cross-racial sisterhood can be consummated, one based on the recognition of mutual humanity and strength. Finally, Octavia is instructing James on the importance of not conforming to many whites' perception that blacks are interminably needy and therefore ever-dependent upon their largesse.

This parable-like scene concludes with Octavia offering heartfelt gratitude in the form of a blessing: "Your kindness will never be forgotten" (*Bloodline* 117). The darkness of the "colored café" is eclipsed by the sustenance and succor from the elderly white shopkeeper, who refuses to hide her light under the darkness of Jim Crow. As the author averred regarding the story's treatment of race, "the world is neither black nor white but there's a grayness there" (*Conversations* 241). Indeed, the story's subtle portrayal of encounters within and across races, where preconceptions and expectations are turned upside-down, marked a 1940s America in flux. The decade's monumental racial flex points—the obliteration of major league baseball's color line and the integration of the armed services—were a prelude to the 1954 *Brown* decision, which further grayed our heretofore separate and unequal racial skies.

"They Us"
Reimagining Race, Masculinity, and Family in "Three Men"

Whereas the first two *Bloodline* stories centered young boys' perceptions of family and society, the narrative perspective now shifts to that of a young adult. Nineteen-year-old Procter Lewis is a far cry from the innocent and impressionable Sonny and James: he has been arrested and jailed for murdering another young man in a barroom fight over a woman. While these stories are linked by the common theme of maturation and growth, the premise of "Three Men" had its genesis in another Gaines work, *Of Love and Dust*. Recall that the novel's protagonist, Marcus Payne, faced a lengthy jail sentence for killing another young black male but, in lieu of incarceration, he allowed himself to be bonded out of prison. Though Gaines has reconceived Marcus in the person of Procter, "Three Men" takes a vastly different turn from the novel: the story explores the circumstances leading to Procter's incarceration and the arduous emotional journey that leads him to choose the penitentiary over the plantation.

The story opens with Procter turning himself in at the local jail. After being taken to the "niggers' cell block on the second floor" (*Bloodline* 125), he reflects on the circumstances which occasioned his imprisonment. Passing the time at a local juke joint with his buddy Grinning Boy, Procter was drawn to Clara Johnson, who was dressed in "red, and she had two big dimples in her jaws" (128). But it isn't her jaws that ultimately enticed him: as is his wont, he perceives women solely as sexual playthings, admitting that "I was looking down at them two big pretty brown things poking that dress way out" (129). Convincing himself that he "had to touch her," despite Grinning Boy's warnings and Clara's own admission that her boyfriend has accompanied her, Procter engages her in a conversation in another part of the club. But this brief dalliance is rudely interrupted when Bayou bursts in, primed for a fight. Procter describes him in especially racially derogatory terms—"that ugly nigger" and "that big sweaty nigger." After inadvertently piercing the knife-wielding Bayou in the stomach with a broken bottle, Procter and Grinning Boy flee by car, pursued by a gang of his murdered adversary's friends. Once he and Grinning Boy have eluded them, Procter then decides to surrender, instructing his buddy to inform Procter's uncle about the murder. Procter does this, assuming that his uncle will persuade Roger Medlow, who owns the plantation where Procter lives, to bond him out of prison.

Though these violent and melodramatic events are crucial to the narrative's development, the story's pivotal action consists of Procter's interaction with his two older cellmates, Munford Bazille and Hattie Brown. Under their influence, he begins an internal journey in which he questions his assumptions about manhood, race, and responsibility. Through their influence and a night of wrenching soul-searching, he ultimately reaches a heightened sense of self and decides to forego the less onerous option of being bonded out. Though he faces a potentially dangerous stint in the penitentiary, he does so knowing that this choice breaks the cycle of southern black men indebted to white male benefactors, who view their criminality as indicative of their innate bestiality and inferiority.

Aside from the protagonists' ages, another notable difference between "Three Men" and the preceding stories is the absence of biological parents. In stark contrast to Sonny and James, Procter bemoans his parents' absence: "My daddy is somewhere up North—but where?" (145), while his mother suffered an apparently premature death— "Maybe I ain't never loved nobody since my mama died" (149). Both absences have orphaned Procter, leaving gaping emotional and spiritual deficits. Thus, the remaining two of the eponymous "three men," Munford and Hattie, will eventually serve as de facto parents, the three forming an all-male family unit. Procter is first engaged by Munford, a serial criminal habitually arrested and bonded out. The newly arrived prisoner describes his more seasoned counterpart thusly: "He must've been sixty; he had reddish-brown eyes, and a stubby gray beard. 'Cross his right jaw, from his cheekbone to his mouth, was a big shiny scar where somebody had gotten him with a razor" (133). Munford further expounds upon his criminal history to Procter: "Been going in and out of these jails here, I don't know how long... Forty, fifty years. Started out just like you—kilt a boy just like you did last night" (137). Such incorrigible behavior would seemingly disqualify Munford as a potential mentor. But given his surprising level of self-awareness and astute understanding of the South's debased and self-debasing racial customs, Munford is an appropriate surrogate father who can perhaps dissuade Procter from following in his lawbreaking footsteps.

The blues tune "Mr. Tim Moore's Farm" inspired Gaines's characterization of Marcus Payne. While Gaines conceptualized Procter as Marcus's fictive clone, it is Munford who best embodies the hard-won wisdom gleaned from a "blues life," his history of fisticuffs and brushes with the law testaments to such a badass existence. In his assumed role as the father figure Procter so woefully lacks, Munford parcels out penetrating insights on both race and manhood. About the former, he vividly recalls his late-arriving epiphany regarding why white men repeatedly have bonded him out of prison, a fate from which he's attempting to save his surrogate son: "Didn't wake up till

I got to be nearly old as I'm is now. Then I realized they kept getting me off because they needed a Munford Bazille. They need me to prove they human—just like they need that thing over there [Hattie]. They need us. Because without us, they don't know what they is—they don't know what they is out there. With us around, they can see us and they know what they ain't. They ain't us. Do you see? Do you see how they think?" (137–38).

That Munford concludes his remarks by posing direct questions to Procter iterates that this is in fact a teachable moment, one in which he expects his young charge to process and respond. Munford's revelation of when he "got woke" explicates for Procter how blackness is essential to whites' conceptualization of their own identities: whites can only conceive of themselves as human by equating blackness with the subhuman—as vicious thugs, as sexually lascivious, as lacking the capacity for moral behavior. Munford then proclaims the underlying truth behind whites' degrading racial sleight-of-hand: "But I got news for them. They us. I never tell them that, but inside I know it" (138). Munford emerges as an incisive race theorist, unpacking how whites project their own predilection for violence and degeneracy onto African Americans, whom they regard as not-themselves and thereby Other. Though a puzzled Procter thinks to himself, "I didn't know what he was talking about," he will eventually comprehend the truth his blemished but keenly insightful quasi-teacher/father is trying to illuminate.

Though his interactions with Procter are far less solemn, the cell's third occupant nevertheless exhibits behavior that Procter will subsequently emulate. As his name implies, Hattie is drawn in rather stereotypical strokes as an effeminate gay man, derided by the ostensibly heterosexual Munford as "a woman" and "bitch." Hattie's speech further solidifies his feminine persona: "What are you in for, honey?" (128), he asks Procter upon the young man's arrival. Munford gleefully blabs that Hattie was caught "playing with this man dick. . . . At this old flea-bitten show back of town there. Up front—front row—there he is playing with this man dick. Bitch" (127). Not surprisingly, the woman-chasing Procter will parrot Munford's derogatory language, frequently referring to Hattie as "the freak" and "a sad woman," language at once misogynistic and homophobic. Further, Hattie's oft-stated description of Munford as "just an animal out the black jungle" invokes the worst kinds of stereotypes ascribed to African Americans. Such a demeaning characterization intimates that Hattie is a type of race traitor who sees fellow blacks through the distorting, dehumanizing prism of whiteness.

Yet Hattie will disrupt and affect Procter's parochial understanding of masculinity in subtle, more muted ways that both counter and complement Munford's perspectives. Though Munford fervently denounced Christianity as yet another means by which society subdues and defangs black men, Procter takes notice when Hattie "started singing. He was singing a spiritual and he was singing it in a high-pitched voice like a woman" (143). While his not wanting "to have nothing to do with that freak" prevents him from asking Hattie to stop, Procter will display behavior in the story's climactic scene which suggests that his exposure to Hattie's singing has had an ameliorating, even moralizing effect. After Munford has been discharged, "a little boy—fourteen or fifteen" accused of stealing food is thrown into the cell. Gaines shines a light on the perverted southern justice system, which makes no distinction between black children's minor misdeeds and adults' far more serious transgressions. Moved by the child's tears, Hattie extends what stereotypically appears to be "motherly" comfort, at least from Procter's perch: "Hattie was holding the boy in his arms and whispering to him. I hated what Hattie was doing as much as I hated what the law had done" (150). Holding fast to hidebound but entrenched notions of masculinity where males must stifle pain and suppress the emotions that accompany it, Procter deems Hattie complicit with a white judicial system that similarly castrates and thereby feminizes black men. With Hattie now "rocking the boy in his arms the way a woman rocks a child" (151), Procter's simmering contempt for Hattie's "femininity" finally reaches its boiling point: "I grabbed two handsful of his shirt and jerked him up and slammed him 'cross the cell. He hit against that bunk and started crying—just laying there, holding his side and crying like a woman" (152). This spasm of violence implies that Procter still maintains his belief in a socially mono-lithic definition of manhood, where "true men" are contemptuous of anything hinting of "gay" or "feminine." However, his subsequent actions in the scene suggest that his views on gender may have evolved.

Once Procter has retrieved the unnamed younger teen (remember that he himself is only nineteen) from the unmanly Hattie's clutches, he immediately joins the child on his bunk, first forcing him to smoke a cigarette. Clearly, Procter has now inserted himself as conductor of the teen's jailhouse rite of passage, smoking being one marker of the transition from boyhood to manhood. Moreover, his next act, as-serting to the child that, "If Medlow come to get me, I'm not going" (153), reveals that he's accepted the challenge that Munford issued. Before leaving on bond himself, Munford exhorted Procter to refuse to be bonded out and instead accept incarceration at the perilous An-gola: "You go, saying, 'Go fuck yourself, Roger Medlow, I want to be a man, and by God I will be a man. For once in my life I will be a man'" (141). Realizing the potential harm that now awaits, Procter beseeches the boy to do something rather unexpected. Whereas Munford ve-hemently repudiated Christianity, and even though Procter himself doesn't "believe in God," he nevertheless implores the boy to "pray" for him once the guards extract him from the cell: "And I don't want you praying like a woman, I want you to pray like a man" (153). I believe this evinces the possible influence of Hattie's spirituals—that they may have, albeit subconsciously, elucidated for Procter the presence of a spiritual force greater than himself; in effect, the songs may have facilitated a partial conversion.

Procter's final gesture bespeaks a newly found nurturing spirit that, again, may be the direct result of the physical, nonsexual inti-macy Hattie modeled a few minutes earlier: "Let's wash your back.... Wash them bruises." After the child warns him "Don't mash too hard," Procter orders him to "Shut up.... and hold on" and commences: "I wet my handkerchief and dabbed at the bruises. Every time I touched his back, he flinched. But I didn't let that stop me. I washed his back good and clean" (154). In effect, Procter's act here reflects the adop-tion of both surrogate parents' teachings. In taking this young male under his wing, he has assumed Munford's role, now having metamorphosed from surrogate son to surrogate father. Reflecting Hattie's use of physical touch to sooth pain, Procter engages in the consecrated act of washing and comforting one's brother.[3] Comparable to the climactic encounter in "The Sky Is Gray," with its inferences of Christian charity, Procter's brief "ministering" to the newly imprisoned younger teen transforms the potentially suffocating prison into a spiritual womb, his own newly redeemed self aiding in the possible rebirth of another wayward young soul.

"I Didn't Write the Rules"
Interracial Blood Ties in "Bloodline"

The volume's titular tale, "Bloodline," bears out Gaines's commitment to crafting each story in a unique style (*Conversations* 106). While the story's presentation of an alienated and embittered young man dovetails with the collection's overall emphasis on young black southern males' experiences, it differs markedly. Whereas the first three stories privileged these characters with respect to point of view, "Bloodline" unfolds through the eyes of a septuagenarian, Felix. In fact, though most of the narrative revolves around the experiences of young adult Christian "Copper" Laurent, three much older characters figure as prominently in the unfolding drama. Moreover, while Gaines has identified *The Sound and the Fury* and *Go Down, Moses* as critical to *Bloodline*'s genesis, another Faulkner masterpiece, *Absalom, Absalom!* invites substantive comparisons. Gaines's story approximates that novel's dramatization of a domineering white southern patriarch's disavowal and dispossession of his half-black son in antebellum Mississippi. Though set over a century later on a Louisiana plantation, a similar event fuels the story's plotline. Whereas Thomas Sutpen learned of his former wife's Haitian heritage after the birth of their son, Walter Laurent was well aware of the race of the woman who worked on his family's plantation. While Copper will be dispossessed because of his "half-breed" status, he will mount a vigorous challenge to his father's brother Frank, "the last of the old Laurents" (*Bloodline*

164), from whom Copper will demand his "birthright." Thus, "Bloodline" deviates from the previous stories in structure and theme, with its portrayal of a southern landowning family's precipitous decline and how the "original sin" of miscegenation haunts the Laurents long after the act.

The story opens with a conversation between Felix, who has worked for decades in the Laurent Plantation's tool shop, and seventy-two-year-old Amalia ('Malia), the family's long-serving domestic. After lamenting that the plantation will become the property of Frank's niece upon his death due to Copper's tainted bloodlines, Amalia is especially perplexed by her and Frank's nephew's behavior: "Something disturbing Copper, Felix" (161). Though hosting him at her home in the quarters, Copper regards his aunt as a stranger: "This morning we was talking at the table, but he wasn't hearing me. He was just sitting there, looking out that door, looking far 'way." The opening vignette ends with Felix's revelations about Copper's father's background. Astride his aptly named horse "Black Terror," Walter Laurent delighted in barreling through the quarters to frighten its black denizens. Even more appalling was his history of sexual predation with respect to the women who worked and resided on his property: "That was one, that Walter. A black woman, no matter who she was, didn't have a chance if he wanted her. He didn't care if it was in the field, in the quarters, the store or that house; when he got his dick up, he hopped on any of them" (162). Though the story isn't clear on whether his sexual encounter with Amalia's unnamed niece was consensual, Felix's subsequent comments strongly imply that it was one of sexual violation. If this enactment of sexual prerogative sounds familiar, then it should: recall the vicious overseer Sidney Bonbon in *Of Love and Dust,* who also ruled with an iron penis. In his usual canny fashion, Gaines reverses one of the South's most corrosive if enduring myths: that of black men as sexually rapacious. In Felix's telling of what was one of slavery's most odious practices, *white* male sexual barbarity rendered women like Amalia's niece powerless prey. Walter's reign of carnal terror only ended with his accidental dragging death by his beloved equine.

As the narrative unfurls, Copper assumes control of the story and divulges further crucial information about his past. As a child, he accidentally witnessed his father raping his mother; after hearing her son vow to exact vengeance by killing Walter, Copper's mother relocates to the North and eventually marries a black man. After her death shortly thereafter, his stepfather immediately discards him as a white man's spawn, leaving him an orphan at the tender age of fourteen. During these years, Copper has traveled widely and encountered other wayfaring young mulatto men who have been similarly disclaimed and banished. His return to the Laurent Plantation years later is fueled not only by a desire to claim his rightful inheritance as a male Laurent, but also to warn of an inevitable war to be waged by these mixed-race sons against the white families who've rejected them. In this capacity, he assumes the moniker "General Christian Laurent" and dons an Army uniform.[4] While Frank will confess to Felix and Amalia that he regrets his brother's sexual profligacy, and though he plans to leave Copper "a few dollars" in his will as a gesture of atonement, Copper must comply with his uncle's nonnegotiable demand: "He must come through that back door" (187), a code mandated by the antebellum and postbellum ethos of black inferiority and subservience.

Perhaps more than any story in the volume, "Bloodline" portrays slavery's poisonous, perineal legacy. Frank embodies stasis: even in his decaying physical and emotional state (for example, "A tall, slim man with thin, gray hair. A very weak man; a very sick man" 190), he doggedly holds firm to the gospel of white supremacy. His stubborn refusal to recognize that the inevitable winds of racial change are blowing even on a deteriorating plantation he himself can no longer maintain (he rents much of it to Cajun sharecroppers) reflects slavery's mental vice grip on white southerners whose sense of self derives solely from the sanctity of their skin pigment. Though he maintains the utmost respect for Amalia as "a lady," Frank ordains that her contaminated black blood forever dooms her (like their nephew and Felix) to the bottom of the South's racial caste: "But she happens to be black, Felix, and because she's black she'll never enter this house through that door. Not while I'm alive. Because, you see, Felix, I didn't write the rules. I came and found them, and I shall die and leave them. They will be changed, of course; they will be changed, and soon, I hope. But I will not be the one to change them" (199). "The rules" to which Frank pledges eternal allegiance are the metaphorical ideological bloodlines connecting eras of white domination and black disenfranchisement—from slavery to Reconstruction to Jim Crow to the 1960s, in which the story is set. Ironically, the elder Felix announces that those winds of change have reached the rural South. Whereas older black "retainers" or long-term servants such as Amalia and he may have accepted if not embraced their lesser status, Copper is drum major for a rebellious younger generation: "Because it's not like it used to be, Mr. Frank. They not scared of you like they was scared of Mr. Walter" (200–201). Copper's refusal to abide by the white-written "rules" to which Frank clings is evidenced when the young "general" repeatedly refuses to come despite Frank's intransigent belief that "Any nigger on this place moves when I say move" (165).

Indeed, despite his repeated demands that Copper do so, Frank is reduced to meeting his noncompliant nephew at his aunt's home. Ultimately, Frank is forced to acknowledge what Felix (and other black characters) have dared to utter to him throughout the story—that Copper bears the indelible Laurent genes: "He looked more like Walter Laurent than Walter ever looked like himself" (167); "Copper is a Laurent. No Laurent's walking through any back door—'specially one he half figures belong to him, anyway" (187). During their charged encounter, Copper dismantles the myth of white humanity and black barbarism, his version of history correcting his uncle's supremacist, whitewashed one: he pronounces southern white men like his father and uncle "Rapists. . . . Murderers, plunderers—and they hide behind the law. The law they themselves created" (213). With Frank continuing to preach the sanctity of white superiority and Copper still refusing to submit to his uncle's demand, catastrophe is averted when "General Laurent" agrees to leave. Before doing so, however, he issues a chilling warning on behalf of his rejected mulatto brethren: "We'll be back, Uncle. And I'll take my share. I won't beg for it, I won't ask for it; I'll take it. I'll take it or I'll bathe this whole plantation in blood"

(217). Within the broader social-historical context in which "Blood-line" appeared, Copper's threat of a potential racial Armageddon is all the more jarring given when it was published: 1968, the year of Martin Luther King Jr.'s assassination and the radioactive response it sparked among younger blacks no longer becalmed by spirituals like "We Shall Overcome." Quite contrarily, one hears in Copper's pledge echoes of Nat Turner's blood-soaked 1831 rebellion and strains of Malcolm X's uncompromising declaration of full black humanity and self-determination, "by any means necessary."

"The Sky Is Black"
Changing Racial Weather in "Just Like a Tree"

Gaines has on more than one occasion identified the volume's thematic bloodline not as a literal biological kinship linking his child and young-adult male protagonists. Instead, the collection's title speaks to their common experiences in a segregated South which imperils their very existence (*Conversations* 246). However, I turn to another literary luminary, Toni Morrison, to frame my discussion of the collection's closing story, "Just Like a Tree." In her 1984 essay "Rootedness: The Ancestor as Foundation," Morrison identifies the indispensable presence of such wise elder figures in African American literature. For her, exemplary is Invisible Man's dying grandfather and the vital deathbed advice he dispenses in the first chapter of Ellison's 1952 magnum opus.[5] Further, she explains, "And these ancestors are not just parents, they are sort of timeless people whose relationships to the characters are benevolent, instructive, and protective, and they provide a certain kind of wisdom" (1070). A childless, elderly woman embodies such a presence in "Just Like a Tree." Though we only hear snippets of her actual voice in the latter portion of the story, the story revolves around Aunt Fe's imminent, involuntary move from the modest rural home she's occupied for the past thirty of her ninety-plus years. Several members of her family and community have gathered there on the eve of her departure, as her niece, Louise, and Louise's husband, James, have arrived to transport her to their home in an unnamed northern city. The reason for this unwanted upheaval is sobering: Louise has decided that recent "bombings" catalyzed by local civil rights demonstrations have made "auntie's" beloved southern abode unsafe.

Indeed, *Bloodline*'s final story is a departure in structure and focus if not theme. Whereas the first four stories were narrated solely from male perspectives, "Tree" marks Gaines's use of a storytelling mode that he'll perfect and showcase in a later work. The writer he claims as most influential, Faulkner, pioneered this technique nearly forty years earlier in *As I Lay Dying* (1930), where the transportation of a matriarch's body to her hometown for burial animates a chorus of multiple voices and perspectives. Prefiguring his 1983 novel, *A Gathering of Old Men,* "Tree" employs a *polyphonic* narrative approach, the story narrated by multiple characters who vary in age, gender, education level, and even geographic region. The story's opening recalls "A Long Day in November" as a verbally unsophisticated young boy, "Chuckkie," sets the narrative in motion. Older voices follow which shed more light on the story's central concern, Aunt Fe's ensuing move, as well as on their own lives, perspectives, and biases: some of these include Leola, Chuckkie's mother, who's served as Aunt Fe's occasional caretaker; James, a northern "city slicker" type who belittles Aunt Fe's visitors as "real country" hillbillies; Anne-Marie Duvall, a young white woman whom Fe cared for during the woman's childhood; and Aunt Lou, Chuckkie's grandmother and Fe's oldest friend. Despite its stylistic departure, "Just Like a Tree" retains the other stories' concerns with the challenges faced by rural blacks and their resilience; how various types of family—nuclear, extended, non-biological—support an individual in a time of crisis; intra-racial friction; and the changing racial landscape in a South still plagued by its hellish history.

As the only white narrator, Anne-Marie presents a narration that is one of the most portentous and self-revelatory of the story's ten voices. On the surface, her determination to see Aunt Fe prior to her departure appears racially magnanimous and genuine. Despite her husband's attempts to dissuade her on account of a torrential storm, she declares that "I must [go]. Father definitely would have gone if he were alive. Grandfather definitely would have gone, also. And, there-fore, I must" (*Bloodline* 240). Gaines deftly utilizes environment and weather metaphorically in this section. Her declaration that "The sky is black" prior to departing serves as a prelude to her ensuing pil-grimage: bearing a rather chintzy gift ("a seventy-nine-cents scarf"), she embarks on what becomes a tumultuous journey through rain, lightning, and downed trees. Having gotten out of her car to inspect a "water hole" that will prove impassable, Anne-Marie ruminates upon the ominous conditions: "The wind shoots through my body like needles. Lightning comes from towards the swamps and lights up the place. For a split second the night is as bright as day. The next sec-ond it is blacker than it has ever been" (241). The wildly vacillating shift between darkness and light, accompanied by sharp lightning and piercing winds that buffet her physically, signals something rather un-settling about the character herself. Moreover, her moribund descrip-tion dovetails with the hazardous racial climate which serves as the story's social backdrop.

Indeed, Anne-Marie's ostensibly benevolent motivation is belied throughout the course of her journey. Her turn down "that old muddy road" marks her trek toward a black milieu, a separate and unequal landscape of which she possesses grossly limited understanding. Turning her complaint that Aunt Fe "lives far back into the fields" into an existential query, Anne-Marie fashions a response in which she relinquishes any personal responsibility: "It was ordained before I—before father—was born—that she should live back there. So why should I try to understand it now?" (240). In this apathetic assessment, she shrinks from engaging deeper questions about why blacks are rel-egated to wooded areas separate from and invisible to whites. I would go so far as to posit that a common bloodline connects the stories' *white* characters as much as it does its black males: like Frank Laurent (and possibly the unseen niece who is his immediate heir) in "Blood-line," Anne-Marie accepts a segregated status quo as preordained, a situation sanctioned by male forebears who like her refused to ques-tion or lift a finger to effect social progress. This possibly benign or un-witting bigotry gives way to full-fledged antiblack sentiments once she arrives at Aunt Fe's celebration: "Sometimes I think niggers can laugh and joke even if they see somebody beaten to death"; "I go into the old crowded and smelly room"; "The other niggers gather around with all kinds of smiles on their faces.... Just think of it—a white lady coming through all of this for one old darky"; "I don't know how long I kneel there [at Aunt Fe's feet] crying, and when I stop, I get out of there as fast as I can" (242–43). This geyser of rancid observations and the racial panic it induces demonstrate how "Blacks do have a rather miraculous power over Southern whites, not to control them, but to upset them and drive them to frenzy" (Williamson, *A Rage for Order* 274).

In contrast to Anne-Marie's foreboding, "the-sky-is-black" perspective, a more optimistic if uncertain racial forecast is signaled by Emmanuel, who arrives after her departure. A precursor of the young race men portrayed in *The Autobiography of Miss Jane Pittman,* Emmanuel is at the vanguard of the struggle for equality, though some skepticism exists regarding his tactics. Despite some celebrants blaming him for inciting the recent bombing that has prompted Aunt Fe's niece to relocate her, Emmanuel remains resolute in confronting inequality by more forceful means. His prominent role as a burgeoning civil rights leader is captured metaphorically by Etienne, one of the narrators present at the gathering: "A big wind is rising, and when a big wind rise, the sea stirs, and the drop o' water you see laying on top the sea this day won't be there tomorrow.... [A]nd what this boy's doing is called the wind" (*Bloodline* 245). In light of this social vortex, Aunt Fe's removal might represent the passing of the "old guard" of African Americans resigned to the unequal status quo. However, Emmanuel casts her as an inspiring ancestral presence whose wisdom animated his own commitment to racial liberation. Fondly recalling childhood experiences when Aunt Fe was a constant presence in his life as a surrogate grandmother, Emmanuel reminds her of a story she'd shared about his great-grandfather, a lynching victim: "Just the two of us were sitting here beside the fire when you told me that. I was so angry I felt like killing. But it was you who told me get killing out of my mind. It was you who told me I would only bring harm to myself and sadness to the others if I killed" (246).

As he does with the elderly black characters in the title story, Gaines positions Aunt Fe as part of a continuum, a conduit between generations who are committed to equality even if their means differ. In Emmanuel's remembrance, Aunt Fe functions as griot, a storyteller who passes down invaluable historical information—a model ancestral presence according to Morrison's definition. She also serves as a moral beacon, echoing more moderate voices such as Rosa Parks and Martin Luther King Jr., who preached nonviolence as a morally grounded and therefore more effective strategy. Aunt Fe's indomitable spirit—projected in the words of the Negro spiritual from which the story derives its title, "Just like a tree that's/planted 'side the water./ Oh, I shall not be moved"—is also a precursor for Gaines's next book, a historical novel depicting a formerly enslaved 110-year old woman that would place him prominently on the roadmap of contemporary American writers.

5

The Autobiography of Miss Jane Pittman

Because he anchors his work in the folk cultures and vernacular traditions of his native black and rural Louisianans, Gaines's articulation of his own literary technique is apropos: "I do something very different from the experimental novel; my characters still say 'Yes' and 'No' and they say it in separate sentences, and I use commas and periods a lot. I don't use way-out adjectives and adverbs and long, 'subconscious,' sentences and all. All these dashes and parenthesis and little drawings and symbols—I don't do things like that. If anyone can, let him do it" (*Conversations* 155). Taken at face value, Gaines's description of his own stylistic approach appears to eschew modernist literature's distinguishing features—fragmentation, allusiveness, stream of consciousness. Paradoxically, he has repeatedly claimed such exemplars of American "high modernism" as Faulkner and Hemingway as artistic models. Thus, when he explains how he arrived at the title of what would become his first major literary achievement, one might not necessarily be surprised that he pinpoints yet another renowned modernist: "When I was working on *The Autobiography* [*of Miss Jane Pittman*], I kept Gertrude Stein's *The Autobiography of Alice B. Toklas* in mind because I liked the rhythm of the title. . . . *The Autobiography of Alice B. Toklas* is about everybody but Alice B. Toklas, so I felt I could do the same with Miss Jane" (249). Though Gaines doesn't engage in the same authorial sleight-of-hand, whereby Toklas functions as a proxy for Stein's own musing on her personal life and storied artistic milieu, the work he deems a "folk autobiography" concentrates not only on the personal travails faced by its 110-year-old formerly enslaved narrator. Simultaneously, it is a historical biography of the people, stories, and events often omitted from the annals of "official" American history. Gaines's Pulitzer-nominated third novel marked a pioneering achievement in its dramatization of slavery, its aftermath, and the indomitable survivalist spirit of African Americans not unlike those invisible and unlettered rural blacks who first stirred his creative impulses.

Given how story and voice provide the foundation for all of Gaines's fiction, it is paramount to consider them in outlining the novel's origins and underpinnings. Expounding upon both, Gaines again emphasizes his rural 1930s and 1940s upbringing—an era that not only predated the Internet and social media, but even those devices we might now consider in our technologically advanced twenty-first century antiquated forms of entertainment: given the absence of then-novel electronic devices such as radio and television, Gaines relied heavily on the conversations he'd heard throughout the plantation during his childhood for the novel's inspiration (*Conversations* 116–17). As fellow Louisiana writer Tom Dent observes, the novel "is built over a long established (possibly African) mode of Afro-American storytelling—elders passing down necessary historical knowledge to younger folk" (qtd. in Ward, "Foreword" 9). Speaking and hearing, storytelling and *story-listening,* provide the blueprint for *Jane Pittman,* whose genealogy the author traces to his boyhood.

Reminiscent of the "Prologue" that opens Ellison's *Invisible Man,* the novel begins with a prefatory "Introduction." Though its ostensible function is to introduce Miss Jane as the narrator/speaker— she had no formal education and could therefore not write her recollections—the section presents the vehicle through which her story will be transmitted: a history teacher is determined to capture the 110-year-old formerly enslaved woman's story by means of a tape recorder. The result of his project is the "autobiography" proper which he has transposed, Gaines deftly replicating the very methodology of the WPA interviewers who presumed to capture and inscribe the lives of ex-slaves "in their own words."[1] Following the "Introduction," the formal autobiography/novel is divided into four "books": "The War Years," "Reconstruction," "The Plantation," and "The Quarters." The novel is constructed primarily as a series of episodes, character profiles, and vignettes—this in lieu of a linear, overarching plot with sequential action. The various micro-stories and micro-biographies, which entail but are by no means limited to Miss Jane's, thereby form a coherent, composite novel rooted in personal recollections of people, places, events.

The novel proper begins shortly before the Civil War's conclusion, with ten-year-old "Ticey" fetching water for secessionist Confederate soldiers—"The Secesh Army" in her lexicon—who take respite at the plantation. Shortly thereafter, Union ("Yankee") troops arrive, and Ticey's mistress again orders her to retrieve water. One soldier, Corporal Brown, takes particular interest in the child, inquiring about her treatment. Knowledgeable enough to be wary of whites quizzing enslaved persons about other whites, Ticey offers no complaint. Colonel Brown attempts to dissuade her from calling him "Master," and this pivotal encounter climaxes with Brown declaring, "Ticey is a slave name, and I don't like slavery. I'm go'n call you Jane" (9); he takes the liberty of also bestowing his surname upon her as well. The newly christened "Jane Brown" beams upon her renaming, remarking, "It was the prettiest name I had ever heard." In the chapter entitled "Freedom," the master informs his chattel, "Y'all free. Proclamation papers just come to me and they say y'all free as I am" (11). A debate ensues between the older and younger enslaved, with a member of the latter group offering a spine-chilling view of the house that's never been their true home: "They got blood on this place, and I done stepped in all of it. I done waded in it to my waist" (16). This ghastly description is enough to convince Jane to join the younger cluster. They then strike out toward the northern promised land, led by a Harriet Tubman–like figure, "Big Laura." Their journey is short-lived, however: a ragtag vigilante group of former slave patrollers, "Secesh" soldiers, and KKK members ambush the group, slaughtering everyone—women, men, children—except Jane and Ned, Big Laura's son who's only a few years younger than Jane; the two hid during the onslaught. With their paltry provisions, Jane takes charge of Ned and the two continue their odyssey toward what they assume will be less a less hazardous existence above the Mason-Dixon Line.

The remainder of Book One focuses on their perilous journey; she and Ned in her words "ain't been doing nothing but walking and walking and walking ever since we heard of our freedom" (73), undeterred in her desire to reach Ohio. They encounter various persons—former slaves and plantation owners, poor whites eking out a living in the ravaged postbellum South, northerners working with the Freedman's Bureau—most helpful, others hostile or indifferent. Some of the more noteworthy figures include "Old Job," a poor but noble white man who shelters the children for a night, though his wife insists that they sleep in the barn lest they "stink up" their home (68). He stealthily shepherds them to a former plantation, now run by "Mr. Bone," where many of the formerly enslaved earn wages by doing field work. Here Jane, now "'leven or twelve," again displays her fierce independence. She counters Bone's admonition that he can't use a child to do the physical labor performed by adults—"I might be little and spare, but I can do any work them others can do" (72)—because, she declares, "I'm a woman" (73). Even more daringly, she negotiates equal pay: "'If I keep up with the other women, I can get as much as they get?' I asked him. 'Sure,' he said" (74). Just as "Big Laura" evoked comparisons to Harriet Tubman, one hears in Jane's retort echoes of Sojourner Truth's famous "Ain't I a Woman" speech, delivered at the Women's Rights Convention in Akron in 1851.[2]

As Book Two opens, Jane ponders their relative stability, with her working steadily and Ned excelling in his studies. She also expresses something of which both she and Ned had been robbed: a motherly bond. When the schoolteacher has Ned exhibit his reading prowess for her approval, Jane ruminates: "I stood there listening and smiling. Before then I doubt if I had ever looked at Ned like he was my own. I had always looked at him like he was a little boy that needed me. But listening to him read I knowed if it wasn't for me Ned wouldn't be here now. And I felt I hadn't just kept Ned from getting killed, I felt like I had born him out of my own body" (80). This revelation points to an appalling reality of enslaved persons' lives: the rupturing of the nuclear family unit—Jane's mother was killed by an overseer; her father never lived on the same plantation—and the vicious severing of bonds between parents and offspring. Still, Jane's maternal claim exemplifies how familial ties transcend DNA, how disenfranchised persons formulate kinship bonds despite unfathomably callous attempts to prevent them from doing so. However, with the North's retreat from the postwar South, racial violence and de facto re-enslavement filled the breach. Bone and the Freedmen's Bureau now gone, the plantation's former owner, Colonel Eugene I. Dye, reclaims his property and quickly reasserts his race-based dominance: the field workers can either remain and work for the same wages, or they can "catch up with that coattail-flying scalawag and the rest of them hot-foot niggers who was here two days ago" (84). As a dejected Jane observes, "It was slavery again, all right."

Having been convinced by Bone that the North was far from the hospitable environment blacks had imagined it to be, Jane commits to remaining on Dye's Plantation despite many of her fellow African Americans embarking upon "the Great Migration." Now a teenager on the cusp of manhood, Ned has developed intellectually—"too serious" in Jane's estimation—and always "had some kind of book round the house" (90). But Jane's incisive mother-wit leads her to another more doleful observation. Though he offers the pat response of "Nothing" whenever Jane asks the introspective youngster what he's thinking, she instinctively recognizes what troubles him: "But I knowed he was thinking about his mama. He never said it, he never talked about her (he used to call me mama) but I knowed he was thinking about her all the time" (89). Again, Gaines starkly portrays another grim dimension of enslavement: the emotional and psychological devastation visited upon those who physically survive the malignant "peculiar institution."

Evolving politically in direct proportion to his intellectual flowering, Ned rechristens himself Ned *Douglass,* an homage to the revered slave-turned-abolitionist freedom fighter. Ned redirects his unexpressed pain into activism, joining "the committee," a group of black ex-soldiers who monitor African Americans' treatment throughout Louisiana. His actions draw the attention of whites monitoring such "subversive" endeavors, resulting in a group of "riders" accosting and beating Jane in her home when she refuses to disclose Ned's whereabouts. When Ned returns, she poses a stark choice: he must either cease his activism or flee; he adamantly rejects the former option. Though he entreats her to join him, Jane refuses. As she has done and will continue to do throughout her life, she maintains her independence, lovingly but firmly declaring, "We doing what we both think is best."

After a lengthy stint of living alone, Jane becomes romantically involved with Joe Pittman, a widow raising two daughters. Though Jane discloses little about her intimate life, her decision to embark upon a relationship with Joe is informed by the most intimate of concerns: her reproductive prospects. Having been declared "barren" by an older woman on the plantation, Jane had this diagnosis corroborated when she visited a doctor: "'You barren, all right.' He told me it had happened when I was nothing but a tot. Said I had got hit or whipped in a way that had hurt me inside" (95). As he does through Ned's silent mourning, Gaines highlights another delicate—taboo?—issue: the boundlessness of slavery's violent tentacles, how they go beyond and beneath external scars. While enslaved women's bodies are often targeted as sites for white male pleasure through legally sanctioned rape, or sites for reproduction and profit, Gaines exposes a different iteration of savageness: how enslaved women were denied the very right to bear, deprived of the right to determine the terms of their sexual and reproductive choices. Despite Jane's trepidation, Joe assures her that her infertility has no bearing on his feelings: "Ain't we all been hurt by slavery?" (96), he asks, poignantly capturing the manifold ways that American's most monstrous institution has decimated countless lives underneath its mental and physical lash. An expert breaker of horses, Joe begins searching for an opportunity that would be financially beneficial and allow him to practice his trade. He, Jane, and their two daughters eventually leave Colonel Dye's Plantation, resettling on another near the "Luzana-Texas borderline" owned by "Mr. Clyde" (100). Having lived such itinerant existences, Jane and "Chief Breaker" Joe exult after moving into their cabin, which fulfills their desire to "find a little place of our own" (112). After ten years of relative stability at Mr. Clyde's, Jane will experience yet another catastrophe in a life saturated with them: her premonition that Joe will be killed by an untamable horse comes to fruition.

Though Ned had moved to Leavenworth, Kansas, she is elated when he returns twenty years later, accompanied by his wife, Vivian, and their three children. Now a seasoned veteran of the Spanish-American War, Ned returns a man on a mission: to uplift the race through the role of teacher. Marrying his passions for activism and education, he works assiduously to build a school for children whose learning was limited to three months a year. Continuing the work he began before his forced exile, Ned is now an evangelist for the ideology of Frederick Douglass, preaching throughout the parish about the value of fighting for racial equality. Reenacting the surveillance that teenaged Ned's activism garnered, whites again "knowed everything he did," including Albert Cluveau, a Cajun and neighbor. Cluveau and Jane have formed a relatively cordial relationship, which includes fishing together and occasionally sharing a meal. Their quasi-friendship prompts him to tell Jane that, not only do the local whites not want Ned to build a school, but more ominously, "They want him go back. Back where he came from" (132). In response to Jane's query as to whether he would actually carry out their diabolical threat, he declares without hesitation that, "If they say do it I must do it, Jane." But the whites' ominous desire that Cluveau shares defies logic: Ned is first and foremost a native son, from the very same Louisiana terrain Cluveau's now claiming as his and whites' exclusive domain—not an "outside agitator," in the parlance of white southerners demonizing anyone advocating an end to supremacist domination. In chapter 21, "Sermon on the River," Ned gathers the community for a wide-ranging oration, exhorting them to embrace an America that equally belongs to "red, white, and black men" and to struggle for full American citizenship in lieu of accepting a demeaned status of "nigger" (135–38). This sermon amounts to Ned's signing of his own death certificate, as Cluveau assassinates him shortly afterwards.[3]

As Book Three opens, Jane, now companionless and childless, relocates yet again. She takes up residence at the Samson Plantation, convincing the owner that she's still capable of working the fields some fifty years after first undertaking such exacting labor. More so than concentrating on Jane's life, the chapters in this section contain her remembrances of scores of blacks and whites on or near Samson; these now assume greater prominence in the narrative than her own life, though she figures in many of her recollections. Their sorrowful lives entail a number of solemn concerns—from madness to miscegenation to intra-racial skin-color prejudice to interracial love to suicide. In her own personal evolution, this chapter marks Jane's official affiliation with the church, which she had refused to join until now.

The final book stylistically differs from the previous ones: in lieu of individually titled chapters, it consists of a single, untitled long chapter which alternates between the life of another Ned-like heroic young man and Jane's personal, racial, and social flowering. At its locus is Jimmy Aaron, a child whom Jane herself "helped [bring] into this world" (248). Like Gaines himself, Jimmy is raised by an aunt until he joins his mother in adolescence. More significantly, Jimmy—from his birth through adulthood—is chosen and anointed by the community as "The One," the heroic figure who, like Frederick Douglass and Booker T. Washington, will elevate his people. His preselection as the race's Moses transforms him into the community's spiritual if not biological son, reflected in the adults' monitoring of his every move. Like the now deceased Ned, Jimmy is also intellectually gifted vis-à-vis the quarters' denizens to whom literacy was denied, restricted, or forbidden. Though he will subsequently join his mother in New Orleans to enhance his educational opportunities, he is not relieved of his foreordained duty: as one character opines, to "be a credit to his race" (266). However, the community's roadmap for Jimmy's life takes a wayward turn: though he "got religion" before he moved to the Big Easy, as Jane reveals, he now "no longer cared for the church . . . he didn't have the right interest no more" (268).

Upon another visit to the community, the now young adult Jimmy visits the church and is compelled to give his testimony. However, while the community had fashioned him as their local incarnation of Martin Luther King Jr. (whom the budding young activist had met and even been jailed with), Jimmy subsequently rejects religion if not the cause of racial equality; in lieu of professing God's grace, he exclaims to the congregation, "I don't go to church no more . . . because I lost faith in God" (278). Instead, he hopes to harness their god-induced fervor to effect secular, social change: "We have just the strength of our people, our Christian people. That's why I'm here. I left the church, but that don't mean I left my people. I care much for you now as I ever did—and every last one of you in here know me" (277). Though the church is divided over whether it will accept Jimmy's charge to engage in a civil rights march in Bayonne, he successfully enlists Jane in the cause. In fact, her courage convinces many of the quarters' residents—most of them women—to participate in the demonstration at Bayonne's courthouse. Incarnating Gaines's adoption of Hemingway's "grace under pressure" dictum, Jane proclaims: "I wasn't scared I might get hurt—when you get to be a hundred and eight or a hundred and nine you forget what scared is: I felt something funny in the air, but I didn't know what it was" (296). Ever prescient, Jane's sense of foreboding is again realized when plantation owner Robert Samson informs the would-be protesters of Jimmy's murder on the morning of the march.

Though Samson assumes that this will squelch the quarters' residents' nascent activism, the killing galvanizes them, with Jane emerging as de facto leader, evidenced by the novel's closing line: "Me and Robert looked at each other there a long time, then I went by him" (301). Therefore, in addition to profiling Jimmy as a composite Malcolm X–Fannie Lou Hamer–styled leader, "The Quarters" section of the novel marks Jane's full, multilayered blossoming—as a mentor to Jimmy, as an astute commentator on the civil rights movement, and as a community leader at the vanguard of the fight for racial equality; her eyes stayed on the prize, and in no way was she constrained by age or lack of formal education.

"Thank You for the Food, Misses, but We Going"
Miss Jane and a Community of Black Women

In her landmark 1974 essay "In Search of Our Mothers' Gardens," Gaines's fellow southern author Alice Walker decried the one-dimensional and often degrading representations of African American women: "We have also been called 'Matriarchs,' 'Superwomen,' and 'Mean and Evil Bitches.' Not to mention 'Castraters' and 'Sapphire's Mama'" (Walker, *Mothers' Gardens* 237). A composite of these demeaning categories, the southern mammy has been an enduring, nearly indestructible image, most vividly embodied in Margaret Mitchell's "Mammy" (no actual name bestowed upon the character Hattie McDaniel immortalized in the 1939 film). These women's lives first and foremost revolved around the white families they served, with their own lives and families either invisible or inconsequential. Even worse, they staunchly defended the racially disempowering status quo; any fellow blacks daring to push beyond their designated "place" would feel the full brunt of their disciplinary wrath. So when young Jane talks back to her mistress after she calls her "Ticey," she represents (in comportment if not quite in age) a radical departure from the nostalgic mammy of southern plantation lore. Though he never cited *Their Eyes Were Watching God*'s feminist heroine Janie Crawford as the source of his titular character's name or her formidable persona, Gaines did champion her creator, Zora Neale Hurston, as a literary foremother (*Conversations* 85). Gaines's boundary-busting women bear witness to the creative umbilical cord linking the Floridian Hurston to her Louisianan male literary progeny.

One sees not only in Jane Pittman but the women with whom she shares physical and emotional space their complexity as human beings—often heroic, sometimes flawed—in stark contradistinction to one-note, white-worshiping southern black women characters who were as mentally enslaved as they were institutionally bound. Deliberately or not, the fiercely independent Janie represents a fore-sister of Jane, refusing society's dwarfing roles for black women as subservient and/or man-dependent. Hence, when young Jane and Ned happen upon an assemblage of formerly enslaved blacks *willingly* accompanying their mistress back to their old plantation, she expresses her gratitude for the food the erstwhile plantation mistress has shared but adamantly refuses her invitation to join her reverse, "overground" railroad: "Thank you for the food, Misses, but we going" (35)—"we going" an early declaration of what will become her lifelong personal code, emblematic of her commitment to following her own road map and resisting any attempts to dissuade, dominate, or re-enslave.

Gaines's female "quilt," the many African American women who populate the novel's storyworld, begins with the title character herself, specifically her willingness to assert her voice regardless of the potential harm she risks for doing so. This is an apparently hereditary trait, evident when she recounts her mother's death to the above-referenced "Misses": "'My mama been dead,' I told her. 'The overseer we had said he was go'n whip my mama because the driver said she wasn't hoeing right. My mama told the overseer, 'You might try and whip me, but nobody say you go'n succeed'" (33). Though she dies in defending herself against the overseer's subsequent physical attack, Jane's mother models self-worth and the role of sass as a black woman's racial and gendered form of empowerment.

However, to his credit, Gaines avoids the trap of replacing one stereotype, the mammy, with another: the "strong black woman" (re: Walker's categorizations, for example, "Superwomen"). Instead, he provides a multifaceted picture of Jane capturing her *otherness*—other dimensions of her self that encompass a multitude of concerns and personality traits. In the scene in which she glowed as the schoolteacher exhibited Ned's reading ability, a relatively incidental part of that moment is nevertheless noteworthy: Jane's own recollection of the teacher himself. His "good manners" made him appealing to everyone, "'specially the ladies." Jane goes on, "I liked him, too, and I went to school couple times just to be near him. But I told myself I had no business thinking about somebody like that, and after I had gone maybe three times I didn't go no more" (80). This tender moment also reveals something not often associated with southern black women as self-possessed and independent as Jane: her possession of an *inner* life which includes the desire for companionship, intimacy, and possibly sex—something far beyond the purview of standard mammies, who were rendered asexual or completely sexless. This scene dovetails with the episode in which Jane expressed doubts about Joe Pittman desiring her as a mate given that slavery has robbed her of the ability to bear children, Gaines attentive to the character's intimate life alongside his treatment of her herculean quest for freedom.

Sensitive to the often-unnoticed challenges that beset black women, Gaines observed, "For every Miss Jane Pittman who made it, nine other Black women either went insane or died long before they were physically dead and put in the ground" (*Conversations* 158). In light of this point, one such character among the many women Jane encounters merits brief exploration. Now working in the fields at Samson plantation, she relates the tragic fate of a sister-toiler: "The worse thing happened in the field while I was out there was that thing with Black Harriet" (162); given her dark ("blue-black") complexion indicative of her "Singalee" (Senegalese) heritage, the community has inverted her actual name. Though described as developmentally challenged—"She didn't have all her faculties"—she nevertheless earns the honorific "queen of the field" because of her unmatched ability to pick and chop. In a folk set piece reminiscent of those in Hurston's *Their Eyes Were Watching God,* Jane describes the arrival of Katie Nelson, "a tight-butt woman from Bayonne," who brazenly vows to usurp Harriet as the most industrious field hand. In their ensuing duel, Katie proves a formidable foe, so much so that a flummoxed Harriet begins slicing cotton instead of chopping the undesirable "wire grass," which incenses the white overseer. What started as a light-hearted if intense battle of one-upwomanship takes a disturbing turn when Tom Joe "started beating her 'cross the back. He didn't try to take the hoe from her, he just rode down there and started beating her with the bridle reins" (165).

However, his violent intervention has the opposite effect: "But the more he beat her, the more cotton she was digging up." Acutely aware of this now volatile and potentially fatal situation, Harriet's sister-workers spring to action:

Grace Turner was the first one to run down there. She pushed Harriet down and laid on top of her. Now Tom Joe started beating Grace because she was trying to protect Harriet. Bessie Hebert ran down there with the hoe and threatened to chop his head off, and now Grace jumped up off Harriet and grabbed Bessie. . . . Harriet was just laying there laughing and talking in that Singalee tongue. Looking at us with her eyes all big and white one second, then say something in that Singalee tongue the next second, then all of a sudden bust out laughing. (*Miss Jane Pittman* 165–66)

Her mind having clearly unraveled as a result of the chaos and wanton brutality, Harriet is sent to the state mental hospital in Jackson. While Tom Joe eludes any type of discipline, the women who came to Harriet's aid are severely punished—Katie "fired," Bessie told "she had to leave the place."

This brief but disheartening episode teems with potential meanings. Harriet's tireless commitment to physical labor elicits comparisons to the legendary black folk hero John Henry; one wonders if a lifetime of field work as a sort of *Jane* Henry subsumed any sense of self—if Harriet could only experience self-actualization by engaging in physically debilitating labor on behalf of the white plantation owners who for all intents and purposes owned their workers. But in a more positive vein, one might interpret her ensuing madness as her path to freedom from such drudgery. Like the iconic trickster figures of African American folklore ("Br'er Rabbit" probably the most famous), perhaps there's an underlying method to Harriet's "madness," as institutionalization might represent a desirable alternative to the quasi-slavery of Samson Plantation. Moreover, Harriet's coworkers' swift intervention represents an instance of black women's communal resistance to systemic oppression that often takes bloodthirsty forms. The episode's outcome, where women who speak and act on their own behalf are both attacked and expelled while the white men who batter them go unpunished, attests to slavery's enduring legacy. Still, this galvanizing moment displays black women's collaborative efforts in combating their ongoing oppression, a core theme that the novel's heroine-narrator exemplifies.

Three White Men: Menacing and Moderated Masculinities

In response to an interviewer's stunningly obtuse query/accusation—"All of your white characters seem to be racist, cruel and/or stupid. Why?"—Gaines offered a pique-free rebuttal: "I try to create the type of white character whom I can best understand. I might be prejudiced toward the character, but I try to do as well as I can with that character" (*Conversations* 147). As evidenced by the range of whites whom Jane encounters on her travels—some racially malevolent, others relatively enlightened, still some invaluably helpful—Gaines avoids such reductive characterizations, envisioning the full palate of whites' humanness. In a work that foregrounds the travails of a woman who experienced slavery's horrors firsthand, Gaines proffers nuanced portraits of white men that reflect the breadth of his artistic imagination.

At the menacing end of the spectrum is Albert Cluveau, Jane's Cajun fishing companion. But Cluveau is foremost a sadistic "fisher of men," an unrepentant version of the Apostle Paul, who was transformed from a life of persecuting and executing Christians into one of Christ's most ardent acolytes. Assigned to "patrol" Jane's community, Cluveau serves as a mercenary for local whites hell-bent on tamping down any hint of black advancement—educational, economical, political. So consumed with and buoyed by his violent exploits, Cluveau openly brags to Jane about his murderous crusades: "Sometime I got him off talking about killing. . . . But in the end killing always came back in Albert Cluveau's mind"; "Albert Cluveau had killed so many people he couldn't talk about nothing else but" (*Miss Jane Pittman* 129–30). True to his religion of racial cleansing, Cluveau shoots Ned in cold blood—this despite telling his fellow adherents that "Jane good nigger woman just like you see me [with] there" (132). Cluveau's actions expose a clear racial cognitive dissonance, which permits him to nurture a relatively cordial relationship with Jane as he demeans her with racial epithets and ultimately snuffs out the life of the man she reared as her own son. This contradictory inhumanity within the context of interracial community exposes the precarious position Cluveau inhabits, which might best be captured by the man for whom Ned has renamed himself. In Frederick Douglass's 1845 *Narrative,* he reflected upon Mrs. Auld, his white mistress, who initially took it upon herself to educate the precocious young Frederick, only to turn viciously against the child when her husband warns her of the imminent danger of teaching the enslaved regardless of their age: "If you give a nigger an inch, he will take an ell" (78). Now embracing her husband's precepts, she "finally became even more violent in her opposition than her husband himself," a devolution that Douglass laments in one of his most poignant reflections: "Slavery proved as injurious to her as it did to me. . . . Under its influence, the tender heart became stone, and the lamblike disposition gave way to one of tiger-like fierceness" (81–82).

So encumbered by the scourge and ideology of white supremacy, Cluveau similarly forfeits his humanity, rendering him both a victim and a victimizer. Though clearly an incorrigible assassin, Cluveau might also be a victim of the very white ideology that underwrites his vigilantism: as a Cajun, a category of poorer whites of French Canadian ancestry, he might feel pressured to prove his loyalty to the "pure" white southerners who incessantly preach racial division. His "diluted" white status might lead him to engage in excessive displays of racial hatred in order to compensate for his non-southern roots, lest his loyalties be doubted and he be accused of being a "nigger lover," an unpardonable sin in the minds of many southern whites. In this racial calculus, his whiteness is contingent upon his willingness to do the violent bidding of powerful whites such as the plantation-owning Samsons; he must pledge allegiance to them to shore up his own tenuous hold upon that esteemed racial identity. Gaines's complex rendering of Cluveau's tortured racial identity culminates in the character's tormenting guilt, which results in madness and death.

If Albert Cluveau's agonizing ending is of his own making, another white character, Robert Samson Jr., also known as Tee Bob, is a victim of calcified racial boundaries that he ultimately refuses to accept. Tee Bob is introduced in a chapter entitled "Two Brothers of the South."

As in the case of Sidney Bonbon in *Of Love and Dust,* Robert Samson Sr. fully exploits his gender and racial privilege, fathering a child with a black woman (Verda) who works on his plantation. The entire community—from Samson's wife, Amma Dean, to the black field workers residing in the quarters—knows of Timmy's origins, which Samson himself doesn't even attempt to conceal. Moreover, in his abrasive and arrogant demeanor, the biracial Timmy is the spirit and image of his father—much more so than the sensitive Tee Bob, who's described as being "small and delicate all his life" (*Miss Jane Pittman* 173). The boys' father totally flouts the norms that their mixed-race offspring not be recognized: against Verda's wishes, Samson demands she send their son to live on the plantation. Twelve-year-old Timmy becomes the inseparable companion to his white half-brother, despite the five-year age difference. But the boys' strong bond is permanently severed as a result of overseer Tom Joe's (re: the "Black Harriet" episode) attack on Timmy. Though ostensibly angered by what Tom Joe views as Timmy's neglect—he blames him for an injury Tee Bob suffers when the boys are riding horses—the roots of the overseer's rage go much deeper: Timmy fails to act in the deferential and obsequious manner that Jim Crow codes mandate.

Put more plainly, he acts more "Samson" than "nigger." This racial face-off reaches its breaking point when Timmy calls Tom Joe by his first name; infuriated by this egregious breach of southern racial protocol, he commands Timmy to "Call me Mister, nigger" (181). Timmy's rejoinder, "I wouldn't call white trash Mister if I was dying," provokes the overseer's white-hot rage: he beats Timmy "bloody and unconscious" with a pole. His son's blood *not* being thicker than Samson's staunch belief in white superiority, he punishes Timmy for daring to stand up to any white man, Tom Joe's low-rent, "poor white trash" status notwithstanding: "A few days later Robert called Timmy to the house to give him some money and send him away" (182), Timmy's fate hearkening back to that of the women who rushed to Black Harriet's defense. Young Tee Bob becomes a collateral victim of the entrenched racial codes all white men are expected to accept and enforce. Despite his family's and even Jane's attempts to explain these codes, he simply can't grasp why his best friend—and blood kin—is banished. As Jane surmises, "Robert thought he didn't have to tell Tee Bob about these things. They was part of life, like the sun and the rain was part of life" (183). But Tee Bob will fail to subscribe to the corrosive racial hierarchies his father assumes are natural, even sacrosanct—a failure that takes a more tragic turn when he enters adulthood.

As he did in *Of Love and Dust,* Gaines again examines the potentially tragic consequences of proscribed interracial desire. Burdened by her mixed-race heritage and her native Creoles' own exclusionary, antiblack ethos, Mary Agnes LaFabre does penance for what she considers their racial sins by becoming the new schoolteacher at Samson Plantation. Now attending Louisiana State University, a visiting Tee Bob is immediately smitten by the new schoolteacher and quizzes Jane about her racial makeup: in response to his query, "That girl almost white, ain't she?" Jane replies, "Almost, but not quite" (206), the *almost* becoming the pivotal word in the delicate balance that determines life and love on the South's hazardous color axis. During subsequent visits, Tee Bob becomes a constant presence at the school—doing chores for Mary Agnes, accompanying her on horseback on her walks home. What begins as a schoolboy crush blossoms, at least in his mind, into a full-fledged romance. Though Jane attempts to warn her about the potentially fatal outcome of such a relationship, Mary Agnes insists that Tee Bob comprehends that racial barriers preclude such a coupling; moreover, she insists, "Robert is more human being than he is white man . . . Robert is good . . . That's why I don't fear walking with him. The day he get out of line I'll tell him he's too decent for that" (212–13). Despite the lesson Jane is attempting to impart to the young teacher, Mary Agnes continues what she considers a platonic though deep friendship, her racial naivete preventing her from realizing the depth of Tee Bob's feelings for her, despite his impending marriage to the daughter of another respectable southern family. Tee Bob's yearning is an open secret, whites and blacks aware of why he's uninterested in Judy Major: "He found something on his daddy's place. One of them high yellow from New Orleans almost white there" (211).

Mary Agnes's contention that Tee Bob is both "more human than white" and "too decent for that" merits further comment. As her incisive observations insinuate if not make explicit, whiteness and maleness in the South are markers not simply of privilege but of license and domination—thus, Robert Samson Sr.'s sexual licentiousness with the *black* woman he employs and his unabashed flaunting of this indiscretion in front of his *white* wife. True to the moderate, measured maleness he exhibited as a child, Tee Bob has developed into a man who does not exercise the rights and privileges that are endowed by his very whiteness and maleness; in essence, the apple has fallen far from the paternal tree. His countenance and manner cast him as an alternative to the toxic masculinity brandished by men as lofty as his father and as lowly as Tom Joe. Nevertheless, Tee Bob is subjected to the very same rigid expectations that brought about Timmy's expulsion, a point made achingly clear in a discussion with his close college buddy Jimmy Caya. When he confesses that he "loved a nigger woman more than he loved his own life" (216), Caya offers a dose of racial castor oil that he hopes will cure his friend's lovesickness. He first hones in on the pollutive "mighty drop," the speck of black blood that contaminates Mary Agnes's entire personhood: "That woman is a nigger, Robert. A nigger. She just look white. But Africa is in her veins." Caya then underscores the racial and sexual privilege that their whiteness automatically confers in a lesson that many have already attempted to teach the racially aloof, "more human than white," Robert Jr.: "If you want her you go to that house and take her. If you want her at that school, you make them children go out in the yard and wait. Take her in that ditch if you can't wait to get her home. But she's there for that and nothing else" (217).

No subtlety in Jimmy's tutorial: as evidenced by Tee Bob's father and others in Gaines's fictive universe (Walter Laurent in "Bloodline," Sidney Bonbon in *Of Love and Dust*), white men have unbridled access to black women's bodies without the encumbrance of law or public sanction. Though Tee Bob attempts to convince Mary Agnes to leave with him, she seconds Jimmy's repellent but accurate unpacking of southern racial and sexual mores. Unable to reconcile either socially accorded white male privilege or socially mandated black subhumanity, Tee Bob returns to his home where, ironically, his parents are hosting an engagement party for him and Judy Major. Once there, he barricades himself in the family library and takes his own life with a letter opener in a sort of aristocratic form of self-lynching. Though not on par with the loss of her surrogate son Ned, Jane suffers yet another senseless death of a young man she helped rear and who valued her as a guiding and loving elder.

Jules Raynard, Tee Bob's *parrain* (godfather), is the final character in this triptych of white men. Though not without his own classist beliefs—he considers Jimmy Caya representative of "just rednecks who had come up" (234)—he nevertheless represents a moderating presence in light of the malignant form of white maleness that compelled Tee Bob's suicide. He first brings calm and fair-mindedness to a combustible situation, seizing Tee Bob's suicide letter after Samson has broken the library door with an ax. When Caya claims "That nigger wench did it" (235), thereby blaming Mary Agnes for his suicide, Raynard rejects this assumption categorically. Referencing the contents of Tee Bob's letter, Raynard then speaks the fateful truth that none of the other whites in his midst dare utter: "'And we know that letter is true, don't we, Robert?' Jules Raynard said. 'Because we know what everybody else know in this parish, and that's he loved her. And because she couldn't love him back, because she knowed better, he killed himself. We know that, don't we, Robert?'" (236). Once the hard-nose Sheriff Guidry arrives and is satisfied that Mary Agnes was neither raped nor played any role in Tee Bob's death, Raynard still apprehends the volatility of the situation and the potential peril she faces. Given that the white community—if not the white law in this instance—might hold her responsible on the fallacious grounds Jimmy Caya claims and snuff out an innocent woman's life, Raynard intercedes and presents Mary Agnes with her only option: "He told her he wanted her to leave for New Orleans tonight, and he wanted her to leave New Orleans as soon as she could. He told her not to tell nobody where she was going, not even him" (241). Though his command may seem harsh and dictatorial, it reflects Raynard's clear-sighted understanding of the South's history of and proclivity for vengeful violence—its mob-like demand for black blood in the face of white death, the innocence or guilt of its target seemingly inconsequential.

For twenty-first-century audiences, there is a relative abundance of stories exploring slavery and its aftermath: from lavishly praised Pulitzer Prize–winning novels such as Toni Morrison's *Beloved* (1987) and Colson Whitehead's *The Underground Railroad* (2017) to the 2013 Oscar-nominated *12 Years a Slave,* artists in multiple mediums continue to revisit and dramatize a period that still haunts the collective American psyche. But at the time he was composing *The Autobiography of Miss Jane Pittman,* Gaines faced a far different literary landscape. During the racial tinderbox of the late 1960s, when readers flocked to the works of Black Arts Movement flamethrowers like Eldridge Cleaver and Sonia Sanchez, Gaines resisted the calls for rage and destruction emanating from his peers' pens. Criticized for composing a "fictive biography" of a formerly enslaved 110-year-old woman, Gaines stuck to his creative principles in bucking the more militant trend. And while his first literary triumph brought a Pulitzer nomination and, later, $50,000 for the rights to the highly acclaimed television film version, Gaines would claim in his signature droll fashion that, in the wake of its success, "I can buy better whiskey now" (*Conversations* 85). His distillation of Miss Jane Pittman's panoramic life story—in her voice, in her own language—now stands as a momentous occasion in American literary history, its creator helping make the creative terrain fallow for future artists to retrieve and reexamine our still-to-be unraveled dark racial past.

6

In My Father's House

By 1978, Gaines was well on his way to establishing himself as a prominent if not preeminent black southern writer. Just four years after the televised version of his breakthrough novel, he was indeed fulfilling his artistic creed: to forge into literary art the experiences of his fellow "peasants": rural black Louisianans relegated to substandard living conditions as field workers and domestics, enduring racial, economic, and psychological degradation through their dogged strength and spiritual moorings. Gaines's 1982 remark succinctly identifies his blossoming fictive corpus and hints at literary terrain that lay ahead: "I feel that *Miss Jane, Catherine Carmier, Of Love and Dust,* and *Bloodline,* are all part of the big book because no one book ever captures everything. So you write another book" (*Conversations* 148). And given the critical and popular acclaim of the Pulitzer-nominated novel and the Emmy-winning television adaptation, Gaines might have been forgiven for writing "another book" in the same vein of *The Autobiography of Miss Jane Pittman.* He might have revisited the subject of slavery, which the wildly successful—and financially lucrative— ABC miniseries *Roots* had thrust onto the national stage in 1976; or he might have dramatized another invincible black heroine at a time when such characters were still a novelty. Readers might have been understandably perplexed, then, with Gaines's distinctly different fourth novel, which took him seven years to complete.

Gaines in fact ventured slightly beyond his Pointe Coupee postage stamp with *In My Father's House,* a work set in contemporary—early 1970s—Louisiana with much less emphasis on the land than on the material and spiritual lifeblood of the characters. Not that the novel completely abandons what has become the connective vein that courses through his fictive corpus. As he himself reiterates, though *Father's House* is "post Martin Luther King," "I'm still talking about the plantation life" (*Conversations* 189). But this work deviates a bit in setting, characterization, and form. He moves beyond the rigidly segregated St. Raphael and Bayonne, the settings for his previous fiction. The novel's many upper- and middle-class black characters reside not in the quarters but the more citified world of fictive St. Adrienne Parish, the novel's primary setting (though the quarters does figure in some characters' pasts). As well, he expands his geographic contours beyond Louisiana: though not the novel's primary setting, crucial events transpire in his second home of San Francisco. If critics regard *Father's House* as anomalous, Gaines's own bewildering, even exasperated descriptions of the novel's composition history bespeak its outlier status. He has spoken of the unique challenges posed by what might best be described as a laborious literary gestation and subsequent post-publication, postpartum dis-ease (162). The book maintains a vexing place in his creative memory in the several decades since its publication: "I was never absolutely satisfied at all with what I did with the book, whether I'm working with the omniscient point of view or with the plot of the story. I wasn't very satisfied" (Brown, "Scribe" 215).

The book's title spotlights what the author himself identifies as its animating force: the pervasive conflict bedeviling and separating fathers and sons (*Conversations* 63). Protagonist Phillip J. Martin is a well-respected minister-activist who evokes comparisons to Martin Luther King Jr. The novel is set in 1970, in the wake of the "king of love's" assassination. In its opening pages, a character heralds Phillip's vaunted communal status: "He's our civil rights leader round here. Everybody proud of him" (*Father's House* 10). Leveraging the power, authority, and wealth accrued as a venerated preacher and leader, Phillip now basks in the trappings of the American Dream: a ranch-style brick house, "the most expensive and elegant owned by a black family in St. Adrienne"; a "big Chrysler"; "two big rings on his fingers and the gold watch band round his wrist"; Alma, his doting wife; and three young children attending elite schools (35). But Phillip, like the historically amnesic America in which he resides, has attempted to simply expunge the decadent life he previously led. As a younger, unsaved man in the preceding decades, Phillip lived in relative economic comfort with his parents, exercising sexual, class, and male prerogatives. This resulted in his fathering three children by Johanna Rey, who resided in the nearby plantation quarters as she barely eked out a living by toiling in the fields with no financial assistance from Phillip. Shortly thereafter and now residing with another woman, he passively witnesses—and the novel isn't clear if he plays a role in this—his shadow family's relocation to California, as his best friend ferries them to the bus that will remove them from Phillip's immediate orbit if not his memory. Reverend Martin erroneously convinces himself that the chasm separating South and West will swallow his past in which he cavalierly disposed of his *illegitimate* family, one he will subsequently replace through his marriage and the three *legitimate* children it produces.

Still haunted by his morally bankrupt actions some twenty years later, Phillip is stunned when he gazes upon Etienne, the oldest child, some twenty years later, physically bedraggled and emotionally wrecked. The twenty-seven-year-old has renamed himself "Robert X" and just returned to St. Adrienne to, in his rather ominous words, attend a "black man's conference" (16). By happenstance, Elijah Green, a young schoolteacher who lives with Phillip and his family, plays good Samaritan by giving Robert X—dubbed "The Tenant" when it's learned that he is renting a room in the home of one of the community's best-known citizens, Virginia Colar—a ride and inviting him to a party to be given at the Martins' residence. But Robert X's unanticipated appearance in his father's house causes Reverend Martin's physical collapse, a literal fall that effectuates Phillip's journey to a past he'd considered just that, passed. Exacerbating Phillip's momentary loss of consciousness are the two powerful white men

in attendance, pharmacist Octave Bacheron and attorney Anthony
McVay, who take charge during the crisis: Despite his claims that's
he's regained his faculties, they "insisted on helping him to his feet,
and they made him lean on them as they followed Alma down the hall
to the bedroom" (42). Thus, Phillip's brief seizure now assumes racial
as well as paternal implications; rendered prostrate by the gaze of his
castaway firstborn, he risks further degradation in his physical depen-
dency on white men. (Revisiting this episode, he admits as much: ". . .
like some cowardly frightened little nigger, he lay there and let them
do all the talking for him" [55].) This instance of behind-the-scenes
white control foreshadows another action that will draw the ire of the
men who constitute the St. Adrienne civil rights committee and lead
to Phillip's removal as its leader: In exchange for his son's release from
prison, Phillip unilaterally agrees to the white sheriff's demand that
he call off a planned march outside a local business that refuses to hire
blacks.

The fainting spell induces Phillip's excruciating but necessary excursion through his past, which entails geographic, spiritual, and psychological movement. While Etienne catalyzes Phillip's reconnection
to a past life he'd just as soon have remain hidden, the fallen minister
must still seek out and rely upon a bevy of other characters—from denizens of the black Baton Rouge folk community from which he is now
estranged, to Chippo Simon, his closest friend from his pre-saved days
who learns the fate of Phillip's illicit family—to garner the sordid, violent history of the family he has forsaken. Once the history of sexual
and emotional trauma that befell that family is ultimately revealed,
the novel climaxes with the tragic death of the son whose initial presence so stunned Phillip. These devastating revelations puncture the
facade of respectable minister/civil rights leader that he so carefully
cultivated. As a result, his marriage is barely intact, and he is stripped
of his leadership post of the civil rights organization he'd helmed. The
novel's denouement is decidedly ambiguous if not altogether hope-
less: Though somewhat chastened, Phillip still lacks the moral clarity
and self-critique that might propel him to a greater understanding of
his moral failings and the calamitous repercussions they've had for

so many—Alma, Johanna and their tormented children, and the black community he purportedly leads in its enduring battle against an enduringly Jim Crow St. Adrienne. The personal and collective despair that permeate the entire novel might explain the conclusion reached by longtime Gaines critic Keith Byerman, who deems *Father's House* "one of the most pessimistic of Gaines's books" ("Ernest J. Gaines," 92). The novel acutely illustrates how personal transgressions must ultimately be confronted, and that to delay or avoid the inevitable accounting of that past may result in one's ruination.

To frame my exploration of the novel's most prominent themes, I turn to Gaines's summation of its genesis: "It was something I'd always wanted to do—to write a tragedy that has a lot to do with the Black male and his history in this country" (*Conversations* 167). The concerns certainly cohere with the author's oft-stated interest in a theme that has universal, national, racial, and personal implications: the fractured and seemingly irremediable father-son bond. Without question, Etienne's reverse pilgrimage from San Francisco to St. Adrienne to locate—and his words intimate, slay—the father who virtually exiled him when he was only six years old is the novel's spark plug. This homecoming, in turn, launches Phillip's own odyssey, in which he attempts to expiate for this biblical-sized transgression by reclaiming his firstborn. Consequently, he will embark upon a geographic and personal journey into his own discarded history to unravel what became of the family he rejected before his self-proclaimed redemption and reincarnation as "Reverend Phillip Martin." But to limit this manifold novel's scope to a male-centric "search for the father" would reduce it to a well-worn literary category. Aside from the dramatic tensions that evolve from it, the father-son conflict becomes a thematic prism through which Gaines elucidates a spectrum of equally cogent concerns: the modus operandi of the civil rights movement itself, with its "heroic" leadership model that elevates—deifies?—a singular, exalted male figure; the emotional toll those within such a dominant and domineering figure's orbit pay; and the inexorable impact of the past on the present and the woeful wrongheadedness of repressing, denying, or expunging that past.

Correlatively, the novel raises a more veiled but equally vexing issue that Gaines's overview paradoxically discloses *and* conceals—re: his desire to author a tragedy about the *Black male* and his *history* (emphasis added). I interpret the "history" to which Gaines refers as the thematic umbilical cord linking *In My Father's House* to *The Autobiography of Miss Jane Pittman*: America's primordial sin, slavery. But the author's stated emphasis renders invisible a key dimension of that monstrous history: the plight of African American women and *their* history, which is inextricably bound up with the privileged black male's. Phillip's moral lapses—his sexual exploitation of Johanna and subsequent repudiation of her and their offspring—are the manifestation of the nation's own enduring and chronic affliction: a failure to acknowledge, condemn, and reconcile an institution based on the brutalizing of black men *and* black women. Though not as explicitly as *Miss Jane,* the novel nevertheless condemns America's historical downplaying of slavery and the multitude of ills it sanctioned: physical violence, sexual violence, economic violence, and untrammeled lawlessness. *Father's House* dramatizes what slavery *spawned*—intra-racial hatred, illegitimacy, shame, silence, and self-degradation. Phillip's actions are individually tragic but also metaphorical, his disclaimed family emblematic of African Americans' historical exclusion from the larger American family which citizenship should automatically guarantee, as codified in the Fourteenth Amendment. Thus, like the neo-slave novel that preceded it, *In My Father's House* painstakingly registers the repercussions of forsaking history in any form—personal or political, racial or national.

"King Martin Himself"
The Pitfalls of Male Ministerial Heroism

The novel's title directly references the famous biblical injunction inscribed in the fourth gospel, John 14:2: "In my Father's house are many mansions: if it were not so, I would have told you. I go to prepare a place for you." As is the case when any author highlights a biblical passage, such a prominent allusion teems with denotative and connotative possibilities; in this instance such potential meanings range from the ecclesiastical to spatial to the familial and racial. The unknown biblical scribe may have been assuring Christ's disciples that they "would have a place with Him, that He would not abandon them" ("What Did Jesus Christ Mean?"). Or if "mansions" can be interpreted as "dwelling places," perhaps the assurance is that within the capacious "House" of God's afterlife kingdom would be rooms in which they could reside, anointed souls abiding in close proximity to their redeemer. Ascribing a more racio-historical gloss, one might consider the passage in the context of African Americans' centuries-long oppression on their native American soil, where they were perpetually relegated to the status of wayfaring foreigner. If their ebony hues insured their interminable displacement and homelessness, then their heavenly, color-blind Father would flip the racial script in the afterlife, not only elevating the black outcasts, but rewarding their steadfast faith by welcoming them into his celestial mansion. Within the novel's central narrative conflict, the word "mansion" insinuates patrilineal and economic realities, denoting Phillip's palatial homeplace and connoting the ironic situation that sparks the narrative action: though Robert X pitifully laments that "I had a home once" (26), his earthly father has failed to prepare a room for his banished, disinherited firstborn. The manifold forms of father the fictional Phillip assumes—theological, biological, civic—invite comparisons to the larger-than-life pastoral presence that towers over American culture and permeates the novel itself: Phillip's namesake, Martin Luther King.

One the one hand, Gaines categorically insists that he neither modeled his character after the civil rights colossus nor used the character's moral failings to cast aspersions on the slain leader: "Some people thought I attacked King because I named him Martin. Martin is a common name along False River where I come from. If I have six heroes, Martin Luther King is one of them" (*Conversations* 164). But on the other hand, the close temporal proximity between King's 1968 death and the novel's early 1970s setting, coupled with specific references to the civil rights icon throughout, makes such comparisons with Gaines's protagonist inevitable. Early in the novel, Elijah Green beamingly points out Reverend Martin's house to the newly arrived Robert X, adding: "'Our civil rights leader round here,' Elijah said. 'Our Martin Luther King, you might say'" (16). Thus, such characters' recognition of King's elevated status in the community echoes the author's own reverential sentiments. Elijah subsequently brings Robert X to the gathering at the Martin household, where another of Phillip's supporters, Shepherd Lewis, identifies long-lost father for recently returned son: "'Over there by the piano,' he said to the tenant. 'Big man in the dark suit, talking to the white folks. King Martin himself'" (30). Shepherd's tongue-in-cheek name-play—labeling Reverend Martin "King Martin"—furthers the link, which is underscored when Phillip spells out the philosophy that underpins his civil rights activism: "Love is the only thing. Understanding the only thing. Persistence, the only thing. . . . You got some out there screaming Black Power. I say, what is Black Power but what we already doing and what we been trying to do all these years?" (37). His impassioned belief in an ideology of love and equally fervent denunciation of what he considers a more militant ideology make him King's ideological twin; King's landmark 1963 "Letter from Birmingham Jail" expressed these sentiments almost verbatim.[1]

Still, I would contend that, while the novel does not critique King personally, it nevertheless raises thorny questions about a crucial if uncertain juncture in African America and the nation's history. First and foremost, the novel problematizes the civil rights movement's reliance on a heroic or "great leader" and the inherent risks of imbuing a single charismatic figure with so much power/prestige that his personal moral compass becomes severely compromised. To what degree does the attainment of such absolute power and privilege almost inevitably lead to personal crises that potentially derail the movement's very reason for existing? And given that the community has tied so many of its aspirations to the success of this singular figure, does the community risk an inevitable loss of purpose if not outright collapse with the hero's inevitable demise? Thus, while the novel might not depict its protagonist as a "smaller-than-life" version of King, the physically and morally attenuated Reverend Martin becomes a lens through which Gaines foregrounds the deleterious effects of lionizing *any* man. The hero's fall brings the unintended consequence of jeopardizing the struggle for equality, the community's ultimate prize.

As the community's secular and spiritual leader whose past and present misdeeds affect all within and beyond his orbit, Phillip is the whirlwind force that drives the narrative. His commanding presence as a preacher-activist is reinforced through his physical immensity. In addition to being pointed out to Robert X as the "Big man in the dark suit," he is further described as "sixty years old, just over six feet tall, and he weighed around two hundred pounds" (*Father's House* 34). That Gaines delays Phillip's actual appearance until the fourth chapter effectively heightens the magnitude of his fall, his somatic response to the son on whom he has trained his gaze despite the presence of more than three dozen people in the room. Attempting to acknowledge the son whom he had forsaken but who has now encroached upon his hallowed home-ground, Phillip "pushed his way out of the crowd and started across the room. He had taken only two or three steps when he suddenly staggered and fell heavily to the floor" (40). This episode becomes one of the novel's cardinal moments, shining a spotlight on his multitude of offenses—from the superficial, such as his material profligacy, to the more substantive, his discarding of his first family—for which he has failed to take ownership.

Indeed, the lofty perch from which Phillip tumbles and the disreputable past that must be excavated approximates the experiences of black clergymen, real and fictitious: Father Divine, the Honorable Elijah Muhammad, Reverend Ike, Eddie Long, James Baldwin's character Gabriel Grimes, Martin Luther King Jr. himself.[2] These holy men displayed varying levels of patriarchal power and, often, unbounded excess—material, sexual—that their communities often accepted, or at the least turned a blind eye to. This situation raises questions about the paradoxical nature of heroism in the African American community, a subject literary scholar Trudier Harris addresses in her study *Martin Luther King Jr., Heroism, and African American Literature:*

> The African America folk heroic tradition allows for the some-
> times ambiguous and questionable nature of African American
> heroic actions and African American heroic figures. Work for
> the common good outweighs individual fault within that work.
> Moral lapses, even (or especially) from ministers, are simply
> something to which African Americans are accustomed. If they
> do not embrace such actions, they simultaneously do not call
> the perpetrator evil and turn permanently away from him. (19)

Thus, Phillip's exalted status as God's sacred ambassador and secular leader exposes a tendency among many such figures to see their
rampant materialism as permissible—just desserts for their efforts on
behalf of their various constituencies. His opulent lifestyle, evidenced
by his bejeweled fingers and other extravagant gewgaws, is recognizable to readers familiar with actual pastors who, as Harris's assessment suggests, are extolled so much for their communal good works
that their intemperate spending is either ignored or, in some quarters,
even celebrated. Gaines dramatizes the material chasm separating father and son most vividly in the quality of the men's garments: while
Robert X dons "a wrinkled brown shirt and wrinkled brown slacks"
(*Father's House* 24), his father is resplendent in "a black pinstriped
suit, a light gray shirt, and a red polka-dot tie" (34). But Reverend Martin's lifestyle also raises nagging questions about the objectives of the
movement he spearheads: is its purpose to provide St. Adrienne residents access to economic and political opportunities and power to
elevate the collective, or is its objective to transform blacks into individually driven consumers who gorge themselves on cars and houses
and other accoutrements of a vacuous American Dream?

In addition to identifying the potential for rampant consumerism
as an implicit pitfall in African Americans' quest for equality, Gaines
further problematizes Phillip's outsized sense of self through the near
godlike power he asserts as his prerogative. While such power wielded
in the service of the community may, as Harris posits, spare the heroic
figure communal judgment, such unrestrained privilege may auger a
god complex, where one's personal breaches are minimized if not out-

right dismissed. Such a whitewashing of one's own foibles by claiming a greater proximity to the Divine can potentially be used to excuse heinous acts committed against others. Perhaps the most striking instance of Phillip's self-proclaimed godhead status occurs when he attempts to explain how he has atoned for his earlier life of libidinal indulgence, embodied in the disowned firstborn who now craves retribution. After being struck down by Robert X's gaze, Phillip retreats to his office and pleads with *his* Father in less than humble—if not outright accusatory—fashion: "Why? Why? Why? Is this punishment for my past. Is that why he's here, to remind me? But I asked forgiveness for my past. And You've forgiven me for my past" (69). His self-piety becomes more pronounced when he faces Robert X's wrath, in their only one-on-one encounter.

Deflecting his son's multiple accusations, Phillip insists that he's done sufficient penance and declares himself redeemed: "I'm a man today. I prayed for Him to make me a man, and He made me a man. I can stand today. I have a voice today" (102). Phillip's claims of redemption barely camouflage his own deification. However, such a misappropriation of godhead, where one can both rationalize serious infractions and declare himself forgiven, clearly has a calamitous impact on Robert X and the family Phillip has denied. Moreover, Phillip's presumption of divinely endowed authority and refusal to account for his stained personal history microscopically encapsulates America's own moral affliction: a failure to reconcile and atone for its original, most abominable crime. Though Gaines sets the novel more than a hundred years after the official end of slavery, its specter permeates *In My Father's House* and is personified by Phillip's discarded family and the trials and tribulations to which it ultimately succumbs.

A Son's "Cancer of the Soul"
Slavery's Long, Unbreakable Chain

Given that *Father's House* dramatizes the personal and collective plights of African Americans in a small southern town still reeling from venomous Jim Crow beliefs and practices, one might question the thematic relevance of slavery. However, the tissue connecting all of Gaines's fiction is an abiding concern with history in its many iterations—national, racial, personal—and the interconnectedness of the forms which history takes. He elucidates this point in a signature 1976 interview:

> A pet theme I deal with in so much of my fiction (and I just think I took it a little bit farther in this particular book) is that blacks were taken out of Africa and separated traditionally and then physically here in this country. We know that on the slave block in New Orleans, or Washington, D.C., or Baltimore, or wherever the slave ships docked, families were separated from their children, husbands from their wives, fathers from their sons, mothers from their daughters. And I feel that because of that separation they still have not, philosophically speaking, reached each other again. I don't know what it will take to bring them together again. (Rowell, "'This Louisiana Thing That Drives Me'" 40)

Slavery and its putrid legacy are inarguably the dominant subject of his first literary hit, *Jane Pittman*. However, while Gaines doesn't directly situate the "peculiar institution" as the novel's dramatic impetus, *In My Father's House* represents the historical and personal consequences of slavery more *indirectly* and *implicitly* through themes of sexual license, expulsion, geographic exile, and dispossession—all of which he raises in the interview quoted above. By structurally centering Reverend Martin's multiple offenses and his inability to forestall their consequences, Gaines deftly and subtly calls attention to America's attempt to gloss over, rationalize, and even deny its malignant racial history. Ultimately, for Phillip Martin like the nation itself, redemption is only possible if he undertakes the wrenching but necessary journey back, resurrecting, reencountering, and accounting for his personal past. What Gaines identifies as the most regrettable aftershock of slavery, the rupturing of the African American family, is pivotal to fully grasping the author's deceptively complex fourth novel.

A central paradox underlying *Father's House* is that the very rights and privileges African Americans doggedly pursue as their inalienable rights as *American* citizens do not automatically heal slavery's psychic and spiritual lacerations and the suffering they continue to inflict. Specifically, while the social integration and economic parity that Reverend Martin so vigorously champions are worthwhile goals, the novel insists that the ability to, say, eat at a Woolworth's lunch counter would do little to repair a father-son relationship that may be irreparably damaged (*Conversations* 163). This belief might account for his decision to foreground the wayward, enigmatic Robert X, who is introduced long before our first glimpse of the titanic, influential Phillip. The novel's first four chapters unfold through various characters' encounters with and perspectives on this mysterious stranger, whose sudden appearance at once startles and frightens. These happenstance meetings with several St. Adrienne residents establish not only Robert X's pivotal role in the novel's plot, but, more gravely, they encapsulate the invisible and unaddressed suffering that scores of southern native sons still endure—suffering that no number of marches and sit-ins and legal statutes can alleviate.

In the opening scene, Virginia Colar, who reluctantly rents him a room, hones in on his disheveled state: "little twisted knots of hair on his face that passed for a beard"; "He look sick"; "His jaws were too sunken-in for someone his age"; "deep-set bloodshot eyes" (*Father's House* 3–4). His ramshackle appearance takes a more sobering and potentially foreboding turn when other residents share their own glimpses of Robert at various outdoor locations, including "sitting behind Reverend Martin's church" (11). Another reveals seeing a man "standing under one of the big oak trees in the cemetery" and declaring that, if it wasn't "Virginia's new tenant," "then it was a ghost wearing a long overcoat and a knitted cap pulled way down to his ears" (11). Still another places him "on the bank [of the St. Charles River], among the hanging branches of the weeping willow, oblivious . . . to everything around him except the swift-flowing river" (12). These various gazes fix Robert as physically destitute and rootless but, more importantly, they establish him as a spectral presence; these various recollections commingle his father's ministry, his spiritual dis-ease, and a gothic-tinged sense of gloom and impending death. The despair that seems to ooze from his very physical and spiritual pores is best articulated by "the tenant" himself, when the aptly named Shepherd arrives to take him to the celebration at Reverend Martin's: "'My soul don't feel good,' he said as he stared down at the alley that ran alongside the building. 'Like garbage, broke glass, tin cans. Any trash'" (25).

It is equally fitting, then, that Shepherd (though unaware of their kinship) should speak on behalf of Robert X and try to lead Reverend Martin to a deeper understanding of the spiritual alienation that envelops his long-abandoned son: "But I do know he says some strange things. The other day in his room he told me that he had cancer of the soul or something" (82). This composite sketch illuminates a wrenching pain which nearly defies description. It is at once specific to a young man whose needs his father willfully neglected but also representative of so many young African American men whom society has reduced to "trash"—discarded scapegoats onto whom it can project its own worst traits (for example, savagery, sexual brutality). Robert X's soul-sickness is irremediable; the cheap wine he consumes on a regular basis brings no relief, leaving him alternately screaming and crying alone in his room on a nightly basis (22). At once individual and collective, Robert X's incurable "cancer" afflicts generations of native sons who've been failed on multiple fronts by multiple people, places, and institutions. Orphaned and neglected on so many levels, he will take an inevitable plunge into "Big Man Bayou," suicide becoming his pungent testimony to a world utterly incapable of recognizing, let alone affirming, his full humanity.

Damaged and Degraded Daughters
The Shackles Unbroken

The revelations regarding Phillip's past and Robert X's embittered refutation of Phillip's interpretation of it bring into sharp relief an equally core issue potentially lost in the novel's focus on the frayed father-son bond: the plights of the figurative daughters of slavery, the degraded women who continue to pay an exorbitant cost for male domination. Just as the actual accuracy—dare one say, truth—of slavery and the magnitude of its atrocities are always subject to debate, Gaines dramatizes the potential discrepancies of one's personal history through Phillip's own conflicted memories of his past and, subsequently, in Robert X's wildly divergent reinterpretation of Phillip's pre–Reverend Martin life. Indeed, in addition to his presence as the unacknowledged, psychically damaged first child Phillip *bore,* Robert X functions as *bearer* in his own right: he carries the knowledge of his family's harrowing post-Louisiana life and the psychological dues paid by his mother, who, according to him, "is grieving herself to death" (97).

On the one hand is Phillip's version of his past life with Johanna Rey, whom he fondly remembers as "a beauty" with "That good, light-brown café-au-lait color," so good, in fact that "She never had to put makeup on that face; no iron in that hair" (67). His memory having been jarred by Robert X's unsettling reappearance, he begins the process of reassembling the episodes of a past he's blotted out—an arduous remembering that occurs neither sequentially nor comfortably. His present reencounter with this tortured personal history takes the form of a dream: he reimagines that final encounter, which occurred in his bedroom, with Johanna and six-year-old Etienne (Robert X) on the day that she and their children departed. In the dream, the nearly forty-year-old Phillip gave Johanna three dollars; she in turn placed it into the "small hand" of Etienne, who at first takes it but then returns it. The present, fully awake Phillip must now confront the discrepancy between the more comforting, "dream" version of the past and the unpleasant reality of what actually transpired on that day:

> When he [Etienne] left the second time, Phillip got up from the bed and ran after him. In the dream it happened like that, but twenty-one years ago he hadn't run after the boy at all. He had sat on the bed looking down at the floor until he was sure the boy had gone, then he went to the woman who was still clutching the money, tore it out of her hand, and threw it into the fire.

When the woman tried to get the money out of the fire with her bare hands, he slapped her so hard that she fell halfway cross the room. She came back, not for the money, the money had burned, she came back fighting. This time he hit her with his fist. (53)

Just as many Americans attempt to downplay the aftereffects of slavery's barbarism—physical, emotional, economic—Phillip too is forced to confront his sanitized version of a malicious past. Fully awakened, he must face head-on two contemptible but irrefutable character traits displayed on that fateful day: his passivity portends his lifelong failure to meet his children's needs—financial, emotional, spiritual— and his chilling chauvinism, exhibited in the blow he delivers to a woman he considered little more than his concubine.

Unlike her biblical namesake whom Christ cures and who ultimately witnesses his resurrection, such a life of restoration does not await the woman Phillip abandoned. On the contrary, Johanna's lot more closely approximates the bondwoman Hagar's: like her, Johanna will be cast aside after a man's needs are satiated, she and their offspring relegated to seeking a more hospitable homeland.[3] Phillip himself speaks to Johanna's multiply degraded positions and, inadvertently, discloses his own exploitation of her, which foreshadows her and their children's wretched fate:

The boy was what now—twenty-seven? twenty-eight? Twenty-seven, because he was born the winter of '42. Cane cutting— grinding. Because she had cut cane all day Saturday, and the boy was born on Sunday. He didn't see him for a week, because he wasn't living with her. He lived with his parents in one house, and she lived with her mother and sister farther down the quarters. He saw the baby a week later when she brought him to the gate wrapped in a blanket. A year later there was another boy, and a year after that a little girl. They still lived separately. He had no time for marriage, for settling down. There were too many other things to do; there were too many other women in his life. (63)

That she must perform field work as a means of survival mirrors the lives of many rural southern blacks, who eked out meager livings either as sharecroppers or field hands on former slave plantations. Though it isn't made explicit, the narrative suggests that Phillip by way of his family's status was spared this economic neo-slavery. Further, the physical exploitation of black southern women's bodies as laborers is compounded by an attendant and seemingly inevitable sexual exploitation, such women being susceptible to the sexual whims of any number of men—plantation owners, their sons, fellow field workers, and others. While Robert X's accusations—"You treated her like a common whore," "You raped her," and your "lust couldn't wait till you got to a bed"—may be a bit overwrought, they nevertheless signal the omnipresent threat of sexual violation such women faced.

Given slavery's noxious but enduring legacy, it is not surprising that Phillip would summon it to rebuff his son's charges and to explain his past recklessness, when he "wasn't a man": "I was some other brutish animal who could cheat, steal, rob, kill—but not stand.... They had branded that in us from the time of slavery" (102). Though Phillip's assertion is unassailable *historically* and contains more than a large measure of truth, his *personal* invocation of African American oppression typifies his proclivity for avoiding responsibility. Here he designates his sins as the byproduct of whites' perfidious behavior, which bestialized blacks and robbed them of any sense of respect for themselves both individually and collectively. Clearly, Phillip is neither an overseer nor a slave owner, but he's also oblivious to his apparent class and gender privilege. It is this unequal power dynamic that raises legitimate comparisons to men who had carte blanche with black women laborers forced to submit to their sexual demands. This scenario, coupled with the violence to which Phillip admits, casts him less as the powerless victim of the institution on which he blames his many misdeeds and more as one who perpetuates male sexual license and the attendant abdication of paternal responsibility. Her hardscrabble circumstances will compel Johanna to depart with her/their children. Though the circumstances do not exactly replicate those of her enslaved forebears, the South fails to offer sustenance to this native daughter; on the contrary, her deplorable situation is only exacerbated upon the family's journey westward, the cycle of poverty and violation seemingly uninterruptable.

While the "Great Migration," African Americans' mass exodus from the South to the North, has been well documented, many also sought refuge in frontier spaces such as Kansas and Nebraska (known as "Exodusters"), while others resettled in places such as Tulsa, Oklahoma, where they established thriving communities and businesses.[4] But just as the North offered only slightly less racial hostility—it was by no means the Eden many had imagined it to be—the West also fell far short. Regrettably, western metropolises such as San Francisco, to which Johanna and her unrecognized family migrated, proved as disillusioning as their urban northern counterparts. A bit of information about the Rey family background foreshadows the subsequent tragedy that will befall the family after its ostensibly voluntary exodus. When Phillip must finally divulge Robert X's lineage during a meeting of the St. Adrienne Civil Rights Committee in his home, he and fellow committee members piece together the Rey history: Boot Rey, Johanna's uncle, "Went North back in the thirties"; it is then revealed that he "Got in trouble with them Cajuns on the river and had to go. Had to go fast" (120). Though Boot's specific offense goes unspoken, his forced expulsion reflects a history of Cajuns menacing the rural blacks with whom they shared physical space but whom they reviled. And while Phillip will get a much fuller history of what befell his shunned family through a reunion with Chippo Simon, the best friend from his self-indulgent, pre-saved life who aided his shadow family's flight twenty-one years ago, Robert X brings to light the act (if not the underlying details) that led to the family's ultimate disintegration—and the reason behind Robert X's quest to confront the unrepentant father he holds responsible.

Robert X provides fragments of the event that prompted his return. In answer to his father's query regarding the source of his discontent, he reveals that his sister, Justine (the youngest of Phillip and Johanna's children), was "viciously raped" (102), we later learn, by one of Johanna's many no-'count lovers. As the older of the two male siblings, it was thereby incumbent upon him to avenge the attack; he laments that his younger brother, Antoine, "brought the gun to me" and "pushed it on me three times." But instead of performing his socially mandated responsibility, Robert X laments, "I took her in my arms and called on God." Casting his older brother's refusal to avenge their sister's rape as an unforgivable dereliction of masculine duty—like father, like son, perhaps?—Antoine kills Justine's attacker as retributive justice. Antoine serves a brief sentence, after which he and Justine migrate to the North (re: their great-uncle Boot Rey). These revelations bring into sharper focus a conversation Phillip had with a sullen, shame-ridden Robert X, who now seeks to assuage his own guilt by confronting and possibly killing the father whom he blames for the multiple horrors visited upon his now splintered family. Phillip tries to help ameliorate Robert X's shame of emasculation, reassuring him that he needn't have avenged his sister's rape because "that's what the law is for. That's what the law's there for" (103). Robert then offers his father a primer on America's a racial-sexual history, of which Phillip, as a son of the Jim Crow South, should be well versed: "'Law?' the boy asked, as if the word were foreign to him. 'There ain't no law. Why should the law protect us when the father won't? You think the law should care more for the family than the father? By law she wasn't even raped. Black girls don't get raped, black girls entice their rapist. Like Mama musta enticed you'" (103).

The tables now turned in terms of voice and authority, Robert X preaches a brief but sniper-accurate sermon on the dreaded history of sexually violated and voiceless black women—women who for centuries have been denied judicial recourse for the sexual terrorism to which they have been subjected. His sister's very name, *Justine,* ironically dramatizes the inability of black women to attain justice. From the time of slavery, when their bodies were legally unprotected and thereby permissible sites of white male domination and pleasure, to mid-twentieth century and beyond, black women are judged as inherently lascivious and thereby immune to sexual brutalization and the legal protection afforded to their white counterparts.[5] As well, this grotesque reality is compounded by the fact that women like Justine—

and for that matter her mother, Johanna—don't have the privilege of voicing their own tragic stories, instead having to rely on men like Robert X (and subsequently Chippo Simon) as surrogate witnesses to testify to the horrors they've undergone, horrors not experienced by the men themselves. Only by exhuming such accounts of the excruciating pain to which he has contributed—whether directly or obliquely—and acknowledging his complicity in this long-denied personal history can Phillip, like the nation itself, move toward spiritual and psychological restoration.

"He Will Bring Him Back to You if You Have Faith"
On the Road to Redemption

Although Gaines has insisted that he could never set any of his works in San Francisco, it is that city which provided him the necessary creative space/distance to recuperate the Louisiana past, the marrow of his now acclaimed body of fiction. Thus, though he always retained spiritual/emotional ties with the hamlet of Oscar, in which he was reared, the physical journey was imperative to his germination as a writer. While Johanna's excursion to the city by the bay proved catastrophic, the novel nevertheless highlights the potential benefit of geographic movement if not relocation. Phillip must physically move beyond the comforting but confining milieu of St. Adrienne, revisiting and reconnecting with places and people from his native black Baton Rouge community who predated his life of prestige and prosperity. Gaines's depiction of Phillip's journey evokes literary forms as diverse as the epic and the folktale, where the questing figure encounters a bevy of obstacles as well as a motley array of black folk vastly different from the middle- and upper-class black St. Adrienne dwellers. Those with whom he has chance encounters—some former acquaintances, others strangers—may not lead him directly to the person most familiar with his original family's fate. But most importantly, they provide Phillip with an invaluable education on a mélange of topics—social, racial, spiritual—that is crucial not only to his attempts to unlock his family's past, but more importantly, to Phillip's personal redemption.

Only by seeking out people from his former community can Phillip begin to restore the damaged relationships with both his biological and communal black families. His search for Chippo will entail a number of diverse persons: his godmother Angelina Bouie, who chides him for not informing her immediately of his "fall" and subsequently commands him to "kneel down here" as she caresses him (115); "two Catholic women" who share news of "the killing," which casts a pall over the entire black community: a young black Vietnam veteran who police claim was "going for a gun," a conclusion belied by his being "shot in the back" (144); Billy, so embittered by time spent fighting in Vietnam that he is now a radicalized guerilla hell-bent on "Burning this country down" by spearheading a racial Armageddon (162); and Adeline Toussaint, a siren-like former paramour to whom Phillip admits "I'm at war with myself" even as she tries to seduce him (178). Of even greater import in his spiritual revitalization, however, is an unlikely source: a possibly "jackleg" preacher he meets in a less-than-beatific setting.

The waitress at a rundown neighborhood café at which Phillip stops warns "Reverend Peters" that "this ain't no church" as he approaches Phillip. But a woebegone Phillip retorts, "I'm glad to have the company," which speaks to his chronic emotional isolation and thirst for connection. Donning an "old black overcoat" that was "much too big and hung too far to one side," Reverend Peters is described further: "He was a thin, brown-skinned man who could have been in his seventies or even eighties.... A Bible of wrinkled brown leather was stuck under his right armpit" (150–51). While his shabby countenance conjures images of the character who induces Phillip's spiritual crisis, Robert X, Reverend Peters also evokes John the Baptist, another itinerant disciple of Christ whose unkempt appearance and unconventionality ("John wore clothing made of camel's hair, with a leather belt around his waist, and he ate locusts and wild honey" [Mark 1:6] didn't impede his commitment to spreading the Good News.

Whether this man is actually a licensed man of the cloth or whether the title "reverend" is a communally bestowed, even mock nickname is irrelevant; what is clear is that Reverend Peters senses not just the deficit of faith that has left Phillip spiritually discontent, but, more profoundly, Phillip's lack of a community to which he can admit his doubt and attendant agony. This insight leads Peters to initially minister to Phillip rhetorically: "You asked Him to help you?" Unconvinced by Phillip's affirmative response, Peters refrains from replying verbally (his first inclination); instead, "He looked down at the table [where Phillip is sitting] and began to draw little marks on the cup with the tip of his finger. The marks he drew looked to Phillip like small crosses" (152–53). In an African American religious tradition known for its richly exuberant rituals/practices—from electrifying sermons and the "call-and-response" exchanges between preacher and congregation, to soul-stirring gospel music and "shoutin'" and "testifyin'"—Peters's unassuming gesture encapsulates the power of silent ministry as a potential spiritual balm, as an alternative vehicle for reaching a parched soul. Peters's comforting, measured approach has now laid the groundwork for Phillip to express/confess the genesis of the personal failing which has now plunged him into a spiritual abyss: "'There's a gap between us and our sons, Peters, that even He,' Phillip said, nodding toward the Bible, 'even He can't seem to close'" (154).

The earnestness of his few words, his muted sacred gestures, his receptiveness to Phillip's need to utter what ails him—all cast Peters as a healing presence, a quasi-shaman who administers to a Reverend Martin whose previously unspoken sins and ensuing guilt have left him spiritually bereft. Ultimately, the hope he held out to the despairing Phillip that God might reunite him and Robert X—"He will bring him back to you if you have faith"—is shattered. Though Reverend Peters cannot completely lift Phillip's burden, he nevertheless plays an essential role on Phillip's path to redemption. If only momentarily, he converts a dilapidated space where everything "seemed too old and worn" (152) into a sanctuary where one is not condemned or punished for his sins and ensuing doubts—the true enactment of Christian mission. His transformation of "Dettie's Dinette" casts the novel's title in a slightly different light: at least temporarily, Reverend Peters serves as surrogate "father" who provides a comforting port—a "mansion"—for an adrift "son" seeking a harbor amidst his churning spiritual storm.

In My Father's House is somewhat atypical in Gaines's body of fiction, given his unwavering commitment to excavating and chronicling the stories of bayou-dwelling blacks who endure and often overcome through their grit and resourcefulness, their make-a-way-out-of no-wayness. Exemplary of such characters is Miss Jane Pittman who, in the final scene of the 1974 film version of Gaines's breakthrough third novel, defiantly strides to and drinks from the public water fountain from which she had been barred almost her entire life. But the comforting "we shall overcome" narrative of black heroism amidst insurmountable odds, the familiar struggle and ascendance of the beloved community, is glaringly absent. The novel's ambiguous and decidedly non-triumphal conclusion, in which a dispirited and crestfallen Phillip laments to his wife, "I'm lost, Alma, I'm lost," belies uplifting notions of closure and personal restoration his readers may have come to expect. This deceptively complex novel, as much philosophical, moral, and existential as it is racial, may have appeared overly ambitious—perhaps even category-defying—given the scope of the author's previous works. Consequently, this assessment from the venerable literary critic Bernard Bell was representative: "*In My Father's House*—the story of a Southern civil rights leader's sins resurfacing in his vengeful, unacknowledged son to shake the father's faith in himself, his community, and his God—is the least compelling of his six novels examining the theme of African American male identity" (*The Contemporary African American Novel* 200). For his next novel, however, Gaines will return to more recognizable turf: the porches, fields, and ditch banks where he soaked in the voices and stories that have become his creative reservoirs.

7

A Gathering of Old Men

In 1982, over a decade removed from his first major literary achievement, Ernest Gaines was in a precarious place. His latest novel, *In My Father's House,* didn't come close to matching in critical or popular acclaim that of its predecessor; quite the contrary, it was greeted with lukewarm reviews and no solicitations from networks looking to adapt it for television. Further, Gaines was, by his own admission, "as broke as I could be," this on top of requiring knee surgery (*Conversations* 190, 295). But during this relative ebb, he would receive an opportunity that would affect him both personally and professionally over the next several decades: an invitation to teach at what was then the University of Southwest Louisiana. The following year, the university not only invited him back, but also offered him a tenured position and the key to his own home. Gaines would retire from teaching at what is now the University of Louisiana at Lafayette in 2004. Thus, though the years following *Father's House* may have been a bit fallow, the lifeline that USL cast in 1983 occurred alongside a marked resurgence in Gaines's popularity with the publication of a work the *Village Voice* praised as "the best-written novel of Southern race relations in over a decade."

One way to consider what Gaines titled in its nascent stages "The Revenge of the Old Men" is as a companionate work to *The Autobiography of Miss Jane Pittman.* Gaines noted the works' common creative chord in a 1993 interview: "I guess the easiest way to explain why I wrote *A Gathering of Old Men,* is now I had to write a book about men because I had written about Miss Jane Pittman" (271). Both novels trace the lives of elderly African Americans, though this male-centered novel is presented through the lenses of several community members, as opposed to the single focus of a formerly enslaved woman. This stylistic choice actually dates back to 1962, where Gaines first utilized multiple points of view in the story "Just Like a Tree." While these men haven't endured the horrors of slavery that left Miss Jane indelibly scarred, their pasts and presents are nevertheless impacted by a ruthless Jim Crow regime that has stripped them and their families of land, livelihoods and, too often, their very lives. As he did for *Jane Pittman,* Gaines ventured back—this time, literally—to the voices from the fields and porches of his youth, which he cites as the book's matrix. He recalls conversations with Mr. Walter Zeno, an elder/ancestral figure, "who died on that plantation . . . who had known my grandparents" ("A Gathering of Old Men," louisiana.libguides.com). He expounds upon his interactions with Mr. Zeno and other long-suffering men who knew firsthand the travails of living Jim Crow:

> Most of these men, and so had he—but he less than others—had taken all the insults that a black could have taken from the turn of the century until he died. He was born before the twentieth century. He died in '82 I think it was, and he was in his 90's at that time. I used to talk to him and there were other old men who would gather on the porch sometimes and I'd just talk to them all. . . . I was just talking to these old men and they were all talking about how brave someone else was. They were all talking about how brave their grandfathers were. That was a man then, that was a man then, he had done things. But I doubt that their grandfathers had done anymore than they had done, but they always talked about other men. I thought how could I, how could I make, get something that would bring these men together who really want to do something who wanted their one day in the sun, just one day because *A Gathering of Old Men* takes place in only one day. (*Conversations* 272)

Note the common strand between what Gaines describes and the origins of *Jane Pittman*: porches, people, stories. These conversations provided Gaines the grist that he would mold into a novel in which the principal action would be this: old men talking and testifying, embarking upon a painful journey to retrieve, relive, and retell brutal experiences that drained them of the very manly dignity they associated with their progenitors.

As Gaines's outline of its genesis suggests, the eponymous old men and the stories they weave constitute the novel's predominant action. However, a mysterious murder sets the stage for the ensuing action. Told from the perspectives of fifteen narrators, the novel opens in medias res, through the eyes of the youngest, "George Eliot, Jr., aka Snookum." He has been ordered by Candy Marshall, the niece of Jack Marshall, who now owns one-third of the plantation, to inform several residents who live on or near Marshall Plantation that they should gather at the home of Mathu, who resides in the plantation's quarters. Though she refuses to reveal the reason for her directive, the child quickly comes upon the scene that explains Candy's distress: "So when I came up even with his house, I ran in the yard, and that's when I seen Beau. Beau was laying over there in the weeds all bloody" (*A Gathering of Old Men* 6). Beau Boutan, a member of a Cajun family that leases land from the Marshalls, has been murdered, and the panic it unleashes in Candy will soon spread throughout the entire community. Beau is the son of William "Fix" Boutan, the patriarch of a ferocious family with a history of inflicting violence and mayhem upon the black community. Everyone in the community assumes that Mathu has killed Beau, given his reputation as the only black man refusing to cower to Fix or any other white person. Further complicating matters is Mathu's near-paternal relationship to Candy, whom he helped raise since she was a child as he worked on the plantation.

One of the old men soon reveals Candy's scheme for shielding Mathu from persecution: "She wanted us to get twelve-gauge shotguns and number five shells and she wanted us to shoot, but keep the empty shells and get there right away" (28). In her mind, that so many men might have possibly killed Beau will not only spare Mathu, but it will allow *her* to assume responsibility for the murder, Candy fully understanding that a southern white woman killing a Cajun man in self-defense would not be convicted by an all-white jury. She is adamant and undeterred in her scheme to protect Mathu, which she imagines as part of her broader calling of watching over the African Americans who've faithfully served her family: "No, I won't let them harm my people. . . . I will protect my people. My daddy and all them before him did, and I—. . . . I'll stand alone. . . . Before I let them harm my people, I'll stand alone" (19).

Once the old men learn that they've been called, many express not only fear but also guilt for failing to defend themselves and their communities against past attacks from Fix and other white thugs. Thus, this potential gathering at Mathu's amounts to a first stand in which the men can atone for decades of cowardice, evidenced when another child character derides two of his elders: "Y'all can go and do like she [Candy] say or y'all can go home, lock y'all doors, and crawl under the bed like y'all used to" (28). However, the men collectively consider Candy's command as something approaching a divine intervention that will enable them to expiate for past sins of passivity, and they answer her call, albeit not without trepidation. As one of them explains to his wife, "He works in mysterious ways. . . . Give a old nigger like me one more chance to do something with his life" (38)—the prospect of retributive violence potentially cleansing the old men of lives suffused with victimization and shame.

One of the men, Clatoo, sets the gathering in motion, picking up his fellow "soldiers" in his truck. Since he has to make several trips, he instructs each group to "wait for them at the graveyard, and we would all walk up to Mathu's house together" (42). Once assembled, the men begin their pilgrimage in a quasi-military formation. Upon reaching Mathu's, they are met by several people who have congregated on the porch: in addition to Mathu, Candy, and "Louis Alfred Dimoulin aka Lou Dimes" (her newspaper reporter–boyfriend), the collective includes some of the men's wives and grandchildren. Significantly, though the men's decades of inertia animate their stand, the gathering is inclusive in gender and generation: the women will not only offer moral support, but at least one, "Rooster's big wife, Beulah Jackson," will assert her willingness to lay down her own life for the cause of black resistance in the face of white vigilantism. The lone naysayer is Reverend Jameson, "the only man there who didn't have a gun," who beseeches the old men—unsuccessfully—to retreat to their homes as they've done in the past to avert a standoff with Fix's clan. The embodiment of the men's decades of faintheartedness, the quivering minister is ridiculed by his fellow blacks, reduced to tears when they refuse to even look at him. Seeing through Candy's false claim of responsibility for Beau's murder, Lou derogatorily utters a nevertheless unassailable fact: "Fix is going to demand a nigger's blood, Candy" (63).

Shortly thereafter, Sheriff Mapes arrives with his deputy Griffin, both men aware of the gravity of the situation and potential for bloodshed upon Fix's imminent arrival. In order to forestall this, Mapes has sent another deputy to Fix's home; in the interim, he hopes to end the old men's stand and arrest Mathu, whom Mapes regards as "[t]he only one with nuts enough" (72) to have killed Beau. As the prototypical southern sheriff—"big, mean, brutal" (84)—who has no qualms about beating blacks into submission, Mapes is caught off-guard when one of the more decrepit old men, "Uncle Billy," nevertheless claims "I did it" in response to his demand to know who killed Beau. To Mapes's shock and amazement, Uncle Billy withstands the sheriff's blows and continues to insist that he murdered Beau. This scene is repeated when other men refuse to flinch in the face of Mapes's brutality. On the contrary, not only do the porch-sitters refuse to back down, but after witnessing the obsequious Jameson's willingness to absorb Mapes's blows, "suddenly every last person in the yard and on the porch, whether he was sitting, squatting, or standing, began forming a line up to Mapes. Candy was at the head of the line" (71). While Mathu will privately confirm Mapes's presumption that he in fact is the culprit, he refuses Mapes's "man-to-man" appeal that he implore the old men to end their stand. In fact, Mathu, who heretofore harbored contempt for men he considered cowards, refuses to infantilize them and defends their pluck: "A man got to do what he think is right, Sheriff" (85).

Buoyed by their ability to withstand Mapes's blows, the old men wrest control of the encounter from him, and he is forced to accept that the gathering will not conclude until they have shared their individual stories about a past that Mapes cannot comprehend despite his claims of "I see." In the novel's middle and longest section, narrated by "Joseph Seaberry aka Rufe," several men retrieve and recount harrowing memories of countless indignities and atrocities. These stories don't merely catalog a history of black victimization, but they also present the men as complicit in that victimization. Subsequent sections introduce additional central characters, through either plot or narration, including Fix Boutan and his youngest son, Gil (Gilbert or "Gi-bear"), who is a budding football star at Louisiana State University and part of a running-back tandem that includes an African American teammate ("Salt and Pepper"). Hosting his own "gathering" of white men, Fix convenes a meeting that includes his family as well as Luke Will, a well-known hoodlum who, like the Boutans, has terrorized the black community with impunity. Though Fix is bent on avenging Beau's murder, young Gil sharply dissents, imploring his father to end a violent legacy that threatens to derail his football career. Stunned when Gil declares, "Papa, I won't go along" (138), Fix chooses not to seek vengeance, since he would only do so with his sons' unanimous consent. However, Gil's own principled stand comes with an exorbitant price, as Fix banishes him from the family: "Leave, Gi-bear.... I don't wish to see you in this house, or at that cemetery. Go. Go run the ball" (146). Undeterred, Luke Will disregards Fix's decision, organizing his own mob to avenge Beau's death.

Once Mapes learns of and shares Fix's decision with the army of old men, he pronounces the arrival of a new, less racially volatile day reflected in the integration of college football, a religion unto itself in the South. Though this presumably bloodless outcome is preferable to one of Fix's notorious "rides," the old men's desire to atone for the past through battle is thwarted, leaving them dispirited. As Mathu turns himself in to Mapes, Candy and the old men offer conflicting though revelatory responses. When Clatoo asks Mapes if "Just the men with guns" can meet briefly inside of Mathu's house, Candy asserts her sense of racial and territorial domination: "Like hell. . . . This is my place"

(173). In effect, her ownership of the plantation includes the quarters and Mathu's domicile, her reputed devotion to him notwithstanding. She amps up this display of "white power," posing an even more grievous threat—eviction—if the men accede to Clatoo's request: "'Y'all can go on and listen to Clatoo if y'all want,' she said. 'But remember this—Clatoo got a little piece of land to go back to. Y'all don't have nothing but this. You listen to him now, and you won't even have this'" (174). Completely oblivious to her inherited paternalism, she maintains: "I'm protecting them like I've always protected them. Like my people have always protected them" (174). Given that the novel is set in late-1970s—post–Jim Crow—Louisiana, this threat is especially callous, the ultimate power play enacted by a true daughter of the Jim Crow South. In a truly ironic twist, it is the Bull Connor–ish Mapes who notes the historical umbilical cord linking Candy to her plantation-owning forebears: "And you want to keep them slaves the rest of their lives."

The men do eventually convene inside of Mathu's, expressing a sense of pride derived from their willingness to act collaboratively; for the first time, they've had the audacity to meet the challenge of white vigilantism. But there's also a sense of deflation, Fix having denied them the opportunity to put their words into action; as one states, "I don't feel like going back home empty-handed" (180). However, Mathu reassumes his role as the men's model of uncompromising self-possession and fortitude. Heretofore seeing himself as the only true man among a cadre of supine black men, he not only extols the men's courage, but he exclaims that their bravery has occasioned his own spiritual though secular revival: "'I been changed,' he said. 'I been changed. Not by that white man's God. I don't believe in that white man's God. I been changed by y'all. Rooster, Clabber, Dirty Red, Coot—you changed this hardhearted old man'" (182).

Yet, in a dexterous plot twist true to the conventions of the murder-mystery genre, Beau's actual killer emerges from hiding: Charlie, a fifty-year-old field worker described as "the quintessence of what you would picture as the super, big buck nigger" (186). But unlike his godfather (*parrain*) Mathu, Charlie belies the stereotypical "big buck" prototype he outwardly projects: on the contrary, he shares the older men's history of cringing before whites. Charlie offers Mapes a comprehensive description/confession, detailing what sparked the fateful faceoff that left Beau lying dead in front of Mathu's house. Charlie's redeemed self is reflected in a declaration he directs to everyone, Mapes in particular: "I'm a man ... I want the world to know it. I ain't Big Charlie, nigger boy, no more, I'm a man. Y'all hear me?" (187). But before Mapes can arrest him, Luke Will arrives and demands that Mapes "Hand him over" (193).

Charlie now joins forces with the old men in a battle royal against Luke Will's ragtag mob which, symbolically apropos, uses Beau's tractor as its fortress. When Charlie proclaims, "This my fight," Clatoo speaks for the battalion of old men: "This everybody fight ... It ain't go'n be no lynching here tonight" (195).[1] The ensuing battle is simultaneously curative and cathartic, all of the old men now bearing arms for the express purpose of fending off not only Luke Will's specific threat, but symbolically defending their families and communities against years of oppression that has taken multiple forms. After Luke Will shoots and kills Charlie, the old men direct a hail of bullets toward the tractor, avenging Charlie's death by killing the "son of a bitch" who murdered Mathu's godson. Just as the men encircled Beau's corpse at the outset of their gathering to mark a unified front against their actual and symbolic enemy, the battle's denouement involves another ritualistic gesture in honor of the now-martyred Charlie: According to Dirty Red, "After I touched him, the rest of the men did the same. Then the women, even Candy. Then Glo told her grandchildren they must touch him, too" (210). This tribute is especially fitting given Mathu's own denunciation of the "white man's God": Charlie's apotheosis embodies black men's willingness to atone and bleed for their own sins, which has the power to cleanse and renew their entire community.

"I Ain't Used to No Niggers Talking to Me like That"
Rewriting the Southern Racial Script

Though the obvious place to begin with respect to the work's core themes/concerns might be the tapestry of stories the old men embroider, I want to bring attention to another facet of the novel that might seem insignificant. Though set in the late 1970s, the Marshall Plantation and the town of Bayonne are still enshrouded by the shadow of Jim Crow, evidenced by the number of blacks tending the Marshalls' fields and occupying the plantation's former slave quarters. And undeniably, there has been a modicum of progress, emblematized by the popularity of "Salt and Pepper" on LSU's integrated football team and the shuttering of the "nigger room" at the local bar patronized by white men such as Jack Marshall and Luke Will. Still, the "New South" heralded in metropolitan areas like Atlanta doesn't capture the ethos of the rural hamlet, where centuries-old hierarchies of race and class still consign blacks to the lowest rung. Gaines's friend and fellow writer, the late James Alan McPherson, described his native homeland thus in 1988: "I have learned that most of the smaller towns still maintain a narrow range of acceptable ideas and through this process have refined a simplified code of behavior that is considered 'correct.' This code allows little deviance for *anyone,* white or black, male or female. There is little room for the complex human being" (203). Historically, these entrenched dictates of racial—and as McPherson rightly notes, gendered—conduct mandated white dominance through voice and authority and black deference through silence and acquiescence.

Put in a slightly different manner, these codes are reinforced through prescribed racial scripts, in which blacks *performed* deference and obsequiousness while whites *performed* the power and privilege that accrued to them solely on the basis of pigmentation. But one vital element of this seemingly immutable rural South that Gaines reimagines is not only the old men's redemption of themselves through armed resistance, but black characters' willingness to interrupt, disrupt, and remap the very core forms of interracial interaction. Thus, the response of Griffin, Mapes's Barney Fife–ish deputy, to one of the old men deriding him as a "little no-butt nothing"—"I ain't used to no niggers talking to me like that" (95)—signals a challenge to previous protocols governing racial engagement. Many characters breach the previously unequal terms of white-black interaction, in effect inverting the racial script. Such modes of resistance take both overt forms—

verbally subverting and contesting white displays of authority—and more subtle forms through nonverbal displays of fortitude and resilience.

If Charlie's willingness to talk back/black to Beau after decades of silent obedience dramatizes overtly the plantation's shifting racial dynamics, several earlier moments and scenes presage his verbal self-assertion. Indeed, the stage for challenging the prevailing modes of racial interaction is set early in the novel. Though a seemingly fringe character, "George Eliot, Jr., aka Snookum" maintains a key place as both the novel's opening narrator as well as its youngest. In response to Candy's directive to summon everyone to Mathu's, Snookum reaches the Marshall House and waits for the cook, Janey Robinson, to meet him at the gate. His offhand remark, "But I knowed Janey woulda killed me if she even thought I was thinking 'bout coming in that yard" (8), bespeaks how black children are taught from an early age not to violate seemingly infinite and impermeable boundaries of race, space, and class. Nevertheless, this curt encounter between black child and black domestic is telling and implicative, beginning with Janey's scolding query:

> "What's the matter with you?" she said, at the gate.
> "Candy want you to call Lou," I said.
> "You say 'Mr. Lou,' and you say 'Miss Candy,'" Janey said, looking down at me from the other side of the gate. "I don't care how libbel they is, you still a child. You say Mister and Miss round me. You ain't too old for me to tan your butt, you know." (8)

Though not as overtly offensive as the stalwart plantation mammies who chided other blacks on behalf of the whites they slavishly worshiped, Janey "looking down" from her perceived superior, "gated" vantage point as a domestic attempts to instill in Snookum the same respect bordering on reverence for white authority figures that governs her own behavior, going so far as to threaten violence in its promotion. Conversely, in a southern historical context in which "boy" was an epithet whites routinely spat at black men regardless of age or stature, Snookum's omission of titles of respect/authority, and thereby his willingness to call white adults "out of their name," mark an ironic reversal of that demeaning southern custom. Gaines underscores this point allusively, invoking the name of the English author—George Eliot—who dared to defy custom and a chauvinistic literary establishment by donning a masculine pseudonym.[2] Snookum's seemingly innocuous but consequential "misnaming" might nevertheless prefigure a larger shift in the collective attitudes of black Bayonneans: that acts of self-empowerment can occur through their willingness to assert voices they've muzzled for far too long.

If Snookum embodies the potential of black disobedience and defiance, the old men themselves enact a seismic shift in the racial scripts that have rendered blacks silent and powerless. Stymied in his attempt to elicit from the old men Beau's actual slayer, Mapes will resort to a stratagem that has always worked: unbridled blunt force. When he asks Griffin to bring him an old man to interrogate, the deputy selects an especially decrepit, eighty-year-old "Uncle Billy" ("uncle" another everlasting southern epithet for black men): "He looked up at Mapes a second; then his eyes came down to Mapes's chest. He had a nervous twitch that made his bald head bob continually as if he were always agreeing with you. He was quite a bit shorter than Mapes, maybe even a foot shorter" (67). When the old man dares to proclaim "I kilt him," Mapes strikes an initial blow that he assumes will bring the desired result. But on this newly dawning day of racial defiance, Uncle Billy will repeat his claim of guilt, again eliciting Mapes's wrath: "*Pow* went Mapes's hand again. Blood dripped from Uncle Billy's mouth, but he would not wipe it away" (68).

The increasingly befuddled sheriff now directs his coercive battering onto another old man, Gable. But whereas Uncle Billy "never raised his eyes higher than Mapes's chest," Gable "looked him straight in the face" (69). When Mapes delivers a blow in response to Gable's "I shot him," "Gable's face jerked to the side, but came right back. His eyes watered, but he stared Mapes straight in the face." Withstanding a second whack, Gable repeats the taunt spoken by the defiant college student in "The Sky Is Gray": "'Not the other cheek?' Gable asked. 'Both times you hit the same one—not the other one?'" Taken together, the men's gestures entail acts of physical resistance, their bodies absorbing painful wallops but not rendered prostrate by the pain. To further magnify their stand, Gable ridicules Mapes, subverting the biblical injunction stipulated in Matthew 5:38 to establish a willingness to endure prolonged physical battering. Gable here reimagines Christianity, a tool whites have historically used to conquer or placate; alternatively, he repurposes it as a muscular tool for self- and collective assertion. In effect, both old men land hefty blows without landing a single punch, rewriting a script in which white thuggery had heretofore brought about black compliance and submission. Rufe subsequently describes the utter futility of Mapes's violent intimidation: "So now he just stood there, a big fat red hulk, looking down at the ground" (93). From this anemic position, his downward gaze recalling that of southern black "uncles" prohibited from looking directly at whites lest they consider themselves equals, the humiliated Mapes is reduced to the lowest rung on the southern ladder: that occupied by a "nigger."

"'Cause This Is the Day of Reckonding, and I Will Speak the Truth, Without Fear"
Storytelling and Story-Listening as Acts of Resistance

Given the sanctity of the spoken word in Gaines's creative formation, his centering of old men telling stories—figuratively as well as literally—is more than apropos. While Gaines has dramatized the dilemmas and challenges black men undergo through singular characters—from Jackson Bradley, Marcus Payne, and Copper Laurent in his 1960s fictions, through Jimmy Aaron and Phillip Martin in his 1970s novels—the author departs sharply from this mode in *Gathering*. This stylistic shift deemphasizes the trajectory of a single man's life, as Gaines instead situates the group of old men as the novel's collective protagonist (*Conversations* 167). The section in which many of the assembled old men will speak their individual stories, "Joseph Seaberry aka Rufe" becomes an oral history recording racial degradation and terror that takes myriad forms: bodily, psychological, spiritual, economic, even environmental. Anchored in the black folk and oral traditions, the "Rufe" section becomes a storytelling tour-de-force, as the collective protagonists excavate wrenchingly painful experiences while simultaneously holding themselves accountable to the entire community. Comparable to the nonviolent stands Uncle Bill and Gable mounted, the speech community that the old men formulate enacts a form of nonviolent verbal resistance. Alternatively, voices and stories become viable weapons, enabling the tellers to stand up to the white hegemony that had heretofore silenced them. Though the men will ultimately engage in violent confrontation, the stories they fashion are a necessary precursor. Their willingness not only to speak truth to power, but to confess their own complicity in their victimization, is the first step in restoration of self and community. Subsequently, these individual acts of self-expression will embolden them to act collectively when given the opportunity to face down the violent threat that had historically rendered them impotent and bowed.

The predominantly—though not exclusively—male speech community that has congregated on Mathu's porch signals a shift in terms of verbal control and power, with Mapes's presumed position of authority being undermined and destabilized. Gaines employs one of African American literature's dominant metaphors—vision/blindness—to capture the shadowed, silent history of black degradation that fails to register on whites' radar, a failure which Mapes most egregiously embodies.[3] Witness this tense encounter that opens with yet another of the old men, Ding Lejeune, claiming to have killed Beau, followed by a testy exchange between Mapes and Johnny Paul:

"I kilt him," Ding said, thumping his chest. "Me, me—not them, not my brother. Me. What they did to my sister's little girl—Michelle Gigi."

"I see," Mapes said, looking at Ding and [his brother] Bing at the same time. "I see."

Johnny Paul grunted out loud. "No, you don't see."

He wasn't looking at Mapes, he was looking toward the tractor and trailers of cane out there in the road. But I [Rufe, the narrator,] could tell he wasn't seeing any of that. I couldn't tell what he was thinking until I saw his eyes shifting up the quarters where his mama and papa used to stay. But the old house wasn't there now. It was gone like all the others had gone. Now weeds covered the place where the house used to be.

"Y'all look," he said. "Look now. Y'all see anything? What y'all see?"

"I see nothing but weeds, Johnny Paul," Mapes said. "If that's what you trying to say." (88)

Flustered by Johnny Paul's cunning wordplay, Mapes finally begins to grasp that only upon permitting the men to recount their stories will he be allowed to arrest Beau's murderer:

"I see," Mapes said. "Either I stand here and let you talk about things you don't see, and the things the others don't see, or I take you in? I see."

"Yes, sir," Johnny Paul said. "But you still don't see. Yes, sir, what you see is the weeds, but you don't see what we don't see."

. . . .

"I see," Mapes said.

"No, you don't," Johnny Paul said. "No, you don't. You had to be here to don't see it now. You just can't come down here every now and then. You had to live here seventy-seven years to don't see it now. No, Sheriff, you don't see. You don't even know what I don't see."

"Do you know what you don't see?" Mapes asked him.

"Ask Mathu," Johnny Paul said.

"No, I'm asking you," Mapes said. "I'll get back to Mathu later."

"Ask Glo," Johnny Paul said. "Ask Tucker. Gable. Clatoo. Ask Yank. Jameson there. Ask any of them, all of them what they don't see no more." (89)

This verbal tussle provides the interpretive template for understanding the men's forthcoming stories. Mapes repeatedly reasserts his presumed superior ways of knowing—"I see"—only to have them resoundingly deconstructed by Johnny Paul. It takes another member of the community, the narrator Rufe, to reveal the substance of Johnny Paul's ruminations: while Mapes can only "see" weeds, what his slanted perspective doesn't reveal is the tangible evidence that blacks once inhabited this land—flesh-and-blood people who occupied homes and created families and cultivated gardens and congregated on porches and told stories. Johnny Paul's distinctly *black* ways of seeing and knowing starkly contrast with Mapes's whitewashed vision—his myopic focus on only what's visible and not what's been razed and erased, the *invisible* evidence that blacks previously existed in these now weed-strewn spaces. Johnny Paul's upending of Mapes's attempts to control this exchange sets the stage for the collective story montage to which several old men contribute. In so doing, they replace the visual absences of Mapes's limited sightlines with recollections of the people who once resided here, people who endured incomprehensible acts of racial hostility and whose relatives will now offer verbal testimonials in the name of keeping their histories alive.

Tucker best captures the imperative and fervor compelling the old men to speak what has so long been unutterable: "I'm stating facts," he exclaims, "Facts. 'Cause this is the day of reckonding, and I will speak the truth, without fear, if it mean I have to spend the rest of my life in jail" (94). In literary critical parlance, the stories that comprise the "Rufe" section might cumulatively be described as multivocal or polyphonic. While each is uniquely chilling, it is the cumulative power of the stories that gives the section its texture and forcefulness. The recollections encompass a range of atrocities, beginning with Tucker's tale of his indestructible brother Silas who, with just two mules, wins a race against the tractor-owning Boutans in John Henry fashion. As a result, Tucker laments, "They took stalks of cane and they beat him and beat him and beat him" (96). Not sparing himself blame, he ends with this condemning confession: "And I didn't do nothing but stand there and watch them beat my brother down to the ground" (97). The remembering and retelling of this story are crucial, as it reiterates a core theme in Gaines's works: how plantation owners like the Marshalls distributed the most fertile land for sharecropping to Cajun farmers, while blacks long tied to the land were given the least harvestable. Also noteworthy here is Tucker's willingness to hold himself accountable for failing to intervene on his brother's behalf. Thus, the very act of daring to give voice to the violence suffered marks a first step in the men's atoning for a past of passive acceptance of a dehumanizing status quo; they are finally freeing themselves of the fetters that had bound their tongues and allowed white brutality to have gone unspoken, let alone unanswered.

While the content of the story is compelling in and of itself, of vital importance is the dual act of storytelling *and* story-listening, the communal reaction to the story being an integral part of the ritual. Once Tucker acknowledges that "I ain't been able to talk about it before," struck silent by "Fear. Fear," though this repressed memory has "been boiling in me" (96), the following occurs: "He turned to Glo. Glo nodded her head. She knowed what he was talking about. We all knowed what he was talking about." Though the men dominate the story-sharing ritual, women figure centrally in it: here, Glo Hebert offers wordless acknowledgment and confirmation, which buoy Tucker. This passage also highlights the black community's investment in the story: though Tucker begins by acknowledging that those listening "don't know" the story "'cause y'all wasn't there," this doesn't prevent the community from grasping its essential truth: the unrelenting degradation of its members—physically, economically, and spiritually. Therefore, all "knowed" the story and can thereby claim it as their own; it is as much the property of each listener as it is the teller, notwithstanding the listeners' absence regarding the actual events narrated. Thus, the storytelling ritual is a reciprocal one in which the listeners inhabit the crucial role of both corroborating its content and affirming the speaker. As relates to Gaines's grounding of his work in the oral tradition, another way to consider this two-pronged storytelling dynamic is its proximity to call-and-response, a core component of African American expressive culture: the "caller," whether a minister or gospel singer, solicits input from her or his audience—for example, "Can I get a witness?"—their participation an indispensable part of the encounter.

Though too numerous to explicate, some of the more affecting stories entail such catastrophic realities as black men wrongfully convicted, state-sponsored torture, and the degrading racial politics of war heroism. Bolstered after daring Mapes to strike the other cheek, Gable reveals a bleakly familiar southern story: a black male—actually, a teen in this tale—condemned to die for allegedly breaching the sexual color line. Despite his age, sixteen, and impaired mental state, Gable's son is condemned to "the 'lectric chair on the word of a poor white trash. They knowed what kind of gal she was. Knowed she had messed around with every man, black or white, on that river" (101). Though the lethal punishment far outweighs the purported offense, what makes Gable's story ghastlier is the *execution* of his son's execution. He recalls the story as related to him by Monk Jack, a "colored trustee" at the jail who witnessed it:

Saying how they hit that switch and hit that switch, but it didn't work. And how when they unstrapped him and took him back to his cell, how he thought he was already dead and in Heaven. . . . [Monk Jack] Said he [Gable's son] said: "Thank the Lord it's over with. And it didn't do no more than tickle me some. Didn't hurt at all." Monk Jack they told him: "No, nigger, you ain't dead yet. But give us time."

The malfunctioning electric chair has resulted in a grisly botched execution, patently violating the U.S. Constitution's mandate against "cruel and unusual punishment." Not to be deterred, the officials return the chair to Baton Rouge for repairs—note the State's complicity in this merciless act of savagery—and subsequently *re*-execute Gable's son: "Monk said after it was all over with, them white folks walked out of that room like they was leaving a card game" (102).[4] Gable will admit to Mapes that Beau wasn't responsible, "but the same blood run in all their vein," Gable logically equating the venomously antiblack Boutans with a virulently sadistic justice system that would subject a black child to a double execution. Collectively, then, the stories embroidered by Gable, Tucker, and others are representative of individual and communal pain. In this multivocal tapestry of a chapter, Gaines masterfully layers story upon story. Though the tellers cannot change the outcomes, it is the very utterance of these heretofore unspoken histories that indeed transform this into "the day of reckonding," and the stories' retrieval, corroboration, and affirmation propel the tellers' and hearers' journey toward liberation and self-empowerment.

"Stand Your Ground, Honey"
Southern Womanhood in Black and White, Old and New

As its title indicates, the novel highlights and centers male action, whether verbal or violent. This masculine focus is reflected in the text's configuration: of the fifteen narrators, only two brief sections are narrated by women ("Janice Robinson aka Janey" and "Myrtle Bouchard aka Miss Merle," both peripheral characters). However, the author's own reflections about gender in the novel offer an opportunity to consider the instrumental role of women despite their sparse number as narrators. In response to a question about manhood functioning metaphorically in his fiction, Gaines offers this: "You [the interviewer] use the word 'manhood' because you associate it with most of my male characters rather than with the female characters, but it's that moment in life when you stand. Manliness is that moment when it is necessary to be human—it's that moment when you refuse to back down" (*Conversations* 242). Given this more elastic, malleable conceptualization of "manhood," one can imagine women like Aunt Augusteen Jefferson and Jane Pittman also comfortably inhabiting that gender identity given that their entire lives are marked by a refusal "to back down" in asserting their full humanity. Thus, while the novel is populated by scores of black men along with an ample number of white men (Mapes, the Boutans, Lou Dimes, Luke Will, Frank Marshall, and so on), two of the women characters merit discussion given conventional representations of black and white southern womanhood. Their attempts to stand—to assert their own individual personhood in overwhelmingly white- and male-dominated environments—offer a compelling snapshot of rural southern culture that might be described as "the changing same"; that is, how the vestiges of the old South still endure amidst an emerging, more modern "new" South, embodied in Gil Boutan's wildly popular integrated LSU team.

Outwardly, Candy is the antithesis of the prototypical, romanticized southern belle who populated plantation spectacles like *Gone with the Wind*. Abandoning the constraining gender roles and the stereotypically "feminine" ways in which women were expected to act and dress, Candy strikes a much more progressive, gender-bending pose. In the novel's opening pages, young Snookum offers this nonbiased physical description: "Her hair was light brown and dark brown and cut short, almost short like a man's hair" (5); Clatoo's subsequent description buttresses Snookum's: "She was a little, spare woman, not too tall; always wearing pants and shirts, never dresses" (50). This "masculine" countenance dovetails with her willingness to claim responsibility for Beau's murder and willingness to go verbally toe-to-toe with Mapes. Clearly, she represents a more liberated, even transgressive enactment of southern womanhood that doesn't tether women to the home and the attendant confining roles of helpmate and mother. Candy's willingness to chart a different path in terms of gender performance is noteworthy, given that a more traditional gender ethos shaped her upbringing. As related by Lou Dimes, with the death of Candy's parents and the inability of her guardians—her uncle Jack Marshall and his wife, Bea, both now faded alcoholics reminiscent of Blanche DuBois—to "bring her up properly," Candy's rearing fell upon (white) Miss Merle and Mathu, respectively: "One to raise her as a lady, the other to make her understand the people who lived on her place" (129). Clearly, Miss Merle failed; in stark contrast to antiquated conceptions of "a lady," the gun-toting, pants-wearing Candy commendably violates the stifling expectations enforced by Miss Merle and other representatives of a genteel, less-enlightened South.

Nevertheless, though the Louisiana of the late 1970s reflects a loosening of parochial gender roles for women, Candy still chafes under a patriarchal ethos, predictably reflected in older southerners such as Mapes and Miss Merle but also in the oldfangled attitudes of younger ones such as her lover, Lou Dimes. As the standoff is drawing to a close, Candy remains undeterred, now standing guard in the threshold of Mathu's front door in her presumed role as her surrogate father's protector—this despite Mapes's admonitions and Lou's entreaties that she "stop making a spectacle of herself" (175). Candy does garner the support of one of those present, Beulah Jackson: "'Stand your ground honey,' she said. 'Just stand your ground.'" Though laughing while doing so, perhaps Beulah sees in Candy a white, younger version of herself, willing to face down seemingly insurmountable male pressure—thus the interracial shout-out of sisterly support. Once Mathu lovingly coaxes her to step down, Lou assumes his socially mandated male authority and forces Candy back into her proper "place" in the South's still relatively restrictive gender constructs: "Lou picked her up, under his arm, and came with her down the steps. Candy was cussing him, hitting at him, cussing Mapes, kicking, but Lou didn't pay her any mind. He took her out to the road, throwed her into her own car, and slammed the door. Then he stood there with his back against the door, looking at us in the yard" (177). Its humorous elements notwithstanding, Candy's literal and figurative manhandling here places her in a seemingly paradoxical role. Earlier I discussed her own racial paternalism (re: threatening the old men who dared to caucus inside of Mathu's house without her). In further display of her own "old South" mindset, Candy appeals to Mathu's long tenure in service to her family, which entails his remembrance of "The first Marshall . . . from the [Civil] war" (176); she then waxes nostalgic about what she assumes is her and Mathu's shared sense of a halcyon past that she refuses to relinquish: "'You knew them all,' Candy said. 'Grew up with my grandpa. Raised my daddy. Raised me. I want you to help me with my own child one day'" (176).

Just as Mapes's racial blindness doesn't permit him to "see" past evidence of black community but only "weeds," Candy's vision is similarly obscured. Like many southern whites, she is "attracted [to blacks] out of a liberal paternalism that guides them to those less fortunate than themselves or a nostalgic longing for the maternal figure of a comforting black mammy" (Abernathy, *To Hell and Back* 13). In her myopia, she imagines the seamless continuation of plantation life replete with black servants obediently and blissfully rearing white children; in effect, she envisions Mathu as little more than a male version of Margaret Mitchell's "Mammy." However, in a show of solidarity with his elderly brethren who've challenged previously demeaning racial scripts, Mathu enacts his own declaration of independence on the novel's final page, refusing her offer of a ride home following the trial: "He told her no; he told her Clatoo was there in the truck, and he would go back with Clatoo and the rest of the people" (214). Ultimately, then, Candy is both victim and perpetrator, bumping up against the glass ceiling of southern patriarchal domination represented by Mapes and Lou while simultaneously attempting to preserve a mythical but inequitable Old South of beneficent white plantation owners and contented black servants.

In contrast to Candy's severely limited conception of Mathu and the hamlet's other blacks as anything other than her charges, "Rooster's big wife," Beulah Jackson, embodies a self-possessed, independent model of new black southern womanhood. A descendent of Big Laura from *Jane Pittman,* as well as evoking images of the indefatigable Mississippi civil rights activist Fannie Lou Hamer from the 1960s, Beulah departs from standard depictions of elderly southern black women—pious churchgoers, obedient mammies, long-suffering wives.[5] She flashes her fierce demeanor at the outset of the men's siege, when Reverend Jameson unsuccessfully begs the assembled old men to return to their homes as they have so timidly done in the past: "Reverend Jameson, just shut up.... Just shut up. Nobody listening to you; so just shut up. Go on back home, like Candy said. Nobody listening to you today" (56). Rejecting Jameson's flaccid Christianity which mandates black capitulation to white reign, Beulah unashamedly embraces protest over prayer. (She even challenges him to a fight later.) More consequentially, Beulah refuses to censor herself in Mapes's presence, despite his threats. In the pivotal Rufe section, which is dominated by the men's stories, Beulah caustically responds to the sheriff's taunting question, "You mean y'all run out of stories?" once the men have finished: "'Nobody run out of nothing,' Beulah said. She went on looking at Jameson a while before she turned to Mapes. 'You want any woman here to start? I can tell you things done happened to women round here make the hair stand on your head. You want me to start? All you got to say is yes. All you got to do is nod'" (107).

Beulah's bare-knuckle rejoinder is especially lethal because she directs it to the southern sheriff, historically endowed with the power to subdue, lock up, and kill black people with impunity. As well, her outrage takes a distinctly black feminist turn, as she dares to unearth and utter the history of sexual abominations that black women have endured even prior to the nation's founding. When Mapes resorts to his default option—the threat of jail—Beulah replies without hesitation or trepidation: "I ain't no stranger to buckets and mops . . . Hoes, shovels, axes, cane knives, scythe blades, pickets, plows—and I can handle a gun, too, if I have to. I been in the pen before" (109). Recalling Candy's flouting of gender roles and expectations, Beulah ultimately fashions herself as the anti-mammy, insinuating herself—in words and, if need be, deeds—into the men's gathering not only as an advocate for their cause, but as someone willing to take up arms herself in defense of her community.

Beulah's woman-to-man verbal combat with Mapes is also contested on the battleground of racial memory. In cataloging the litany of crimes Fix has committed against the black community, Beulah accuses him of carrying out a decades-old drowning of two children. However, when Mapes chastises her for ascribing such a heinous act to the Cajun patriarch based solely on his villainous reputation—"And you got no proof Fix was mixed up in that"—Beulah ardently contends: "'Now, ain't that just like white folks?' *Beulah said to us, but still looking at Mapes.* 'Black people get lynched, get drowned, get shot, guts all hanging out—and here he come with ain't no proof who did it. The proof was them two little children laying there in them two coffins. That's proof enough they was dead. Least to black folks it's proof enough they was dead'" (108; emphasis added). Reminiscent of the

episode where Johnny Paul exposed Mapes's racial-historical blindness ("No, you don't see"), the sheriff's shortsightedness is again exposed, for he can't envision how decades' worth of antiblack crimes
renders specific perpetrators of those crimes irrelevant. Contrary to
the sheriff's *evidentiary*-based racial memory, Beulah offers a sort
of *blood* memory based on the accumulation of black corpses, bodies
whose murders have gone unpunished by a corrupt justice system
epitomized by the type of unprovoked beatings Mapes himself earlier
administered to the old men.

Conversely, in Beulah's reimagining of communal history, the reality of racial violence is measured in mutilated bodies and the devas-
tated families left in their wake; of less importance are quantitative
facts which are routinely ignored by a criminal justice apparatus
which at best winks at white-on-black violence and at worst abets its
perpetrators. In Beulah's distinctly black-centered way of knowing
and remembering, accurately affixing blame is unimportant; instead,
Fix becomes a surrogate for countless whites whose wanton crimes
against black bayou-dwellers have gone unacknowledged, let alone
punished. As indicated by the italicized words in the above quotation,
Beulah in effect conducts an impromptu trial, where she trains her
laser-like gaze on Mapes in the court of *her* peers. In this porch-side
courtroom, the only definitive "proof" required is the testimonies
of black survivors of the carnage left by unrepentant whites like the
sheriff and the Boutan clan—for all intents and purposes one and the
same. Though far apart in age, race, and status, Candy Marshall and
Beulah Jackson interject themselves into this overwhelmingly male
gathering, their presences simultaneously recalling a romanticized
southern landscape and offering flickers of a more liberated, less
gender-confining Dixie.

For all of the progress embodied in the old men's stand, an anecdote
Gaines shared validates Beulah's claim that "Things ain't changed that
much round here" (108). Gaines in a 1994 interview recalled an encounter involving himself, white director Volker Schlöndorff, and a
local resident during the filming of CBS's 1987 televised version of *A
Gathering of Old Men* in his native New Roads. Seeing a woman "hang-

ing a dress out on a rack in the front of a store," Gaines "approached her, saying 'Excuse me madam, can you tell me where we can get some coffee?' She was short and kind of stocky, and her face was very white and powdered; she looked at me and just turned away from me and spoke to Schlöndorff, who was standing aside" (*Conversations* 310). The indignity of invisibility, as it were; or, a distinguished writer is not without honor, except in his own hometown. Ten years would elapse between this novel of black resistance and white comeuppance and the work that would cement Gaines's reputation as a preeminent American author. In fact, the critical and popular plaudits that 1993's *A Lesson before Dying* would eventually receive ultimately exceeded those garnered by his first literary smash of twenty-plus years earlier.

8

A Lesson before Dying

If the early 1980s represented something of a personal and professional valley, Ernest Gaines's fortunes had risen meteorically by the next decade. Indeed, 1993 would prove to be a red-letter year on multiple fronts. Though he still felt as passionately about the writing life as ever, he nevertheless ended decades of singledom, marrying Dianne Saulney, an attorney from New Orleans whom he met at a Miami book festival. His financial fortunes rose as well; though it took several attempts for officials to reach him at the University of Southwest Louisiana, he eventually received news that he was a newly minted MacArthur Fellow. The so-called "genius" fellowships the MacArthur Foundation annually awards expanded his account balance by $375,000; he was officially no longer "as broke as I want to be," as he'd complained some twelve years earlier. Lastly, he probably could not have anticipated that the novel he'd been working on the previous seven years about a young, borderline-illiterate African American man awaiting execution in 1948 rural Louisiana would earn him a second Pulitzer nomination and his first major literary prize. In fact, *A Lesson before Dying* would bring the expanded readership few writers of "literary" fiction enjoy: it has become a staple on college syllabi and a mainstay in local book clubs; it has been the featured text in the National Endowment for the Arts' annual "Big Read" program, which promotes a single book to be read by local communities nationwide; it has been adapted for the stage; and fittingly, it was made into an HBO film featuring Cicely Tyson, exactly twenty-five years after her breakout role as the 110-year-old Jane Pittman in 1974. Indeed, *A Lesson before Dying* has eclipsed his 1971 novel as his most renowned work of fiction.

As he did for *The Autobiography of Miss Jane Pittman,* Gaines scrupulously researched the details that would inform the setting, plot, and characterization. Though he'd initially planned to set the novel in 1988, he settled on 1948 for a couple of reasons. First, it was a watershed year personally, as the fifteen-year-old who'd never set foot in a public library joined his mother and stepfather in California and spent countless hours devouring books in that state's desegregated reading hubs. Secondly, and more germane to the novel's expository details, Paul Nolan, Gaines's colleague at the University of Southwestern Louisiana, informed him about a shocking event from the 1940s that would become lodged in the author's creative sinews:

.. something had happened about a year or so before that [1948]—this young man had been sentenced to the electric chair twice—I think it was in 46 or 47. Because the chair had failed to work properly the first time. And so I was working around those years—I use those years, a lot, the thirties and forties—I didn't want to put it in 47 because I didn't want anyone to compare those two stories. And I have received letters from different people—attorneys and even ministers—who remember that execution in 1947, and they have asked me if I had it in mind when I was writing the book. What I *did* learn from that incident was that the state had had a portable electric chair that they could run wires through for the night before. I wanted to work the story itself into the frame of a semester for black school children of that time, which was about five and a half to six months if you lived out in the country. (*Conversations* 307)

The specific execution to which Gaines refers was that of Willie Francis, a seventeen-year-old black adolescent sentenced to death for robbing and murdering a white pharmacist in St. Martinville. Ironically, according to Gaines, the events of the Francis case occurred "only a few miles from where I was now teaching and no more than seventy miles from where I had lived as a child and the area where most of my previous stories had taken place" (*Mozart and Leadbelly* 53). The case has in the ensuing years drawn attention and outrage, not necessarily for the apparent miscarriage of justice: the evidence against Francis was scant; the jury all-white; and his two lawyers called no witnesses and presented no evidence. Sadly, such heinously wrongful convictions were unremarkable in the Jim Crow South.[1] But this case was stupefying for its barbarity: the potentially innocent young man experienced the mental and physical torture of being electrocuted in an apparatus that malfunctioned; as a result, he was subjected to a second, "successful" execution following the U.S. Supreme Court deciding that doing so did not violate the Constitution. Some forty years later, in 1986, an attorney enrolled in his creative writing class would introduce Gaines to Bertrand LeBlanc, who argued Francis's case before the high court. Gaines described him as "a Cajun fellow, probably in his seventies, bent, frail" (58).

Additionally, because visitations to the condemned character's cell constitute the novel's nucleus, Gaines sought expertise from those knowledgeable of correctional facilities' inner workings. He first wrote to the warden at Louisiana's infamous Angola prison, inquiring whether someone other than a blood relative, lawyer, or clergyman would be permitted to visit a prisoner (*Conversations* 306). Though the warden answered his initial query, he didn't respond to Gaines's subsequent requests for information (mistakenly assuming that Gaines wanted to visit the prison himself). Having reached a seeming dead end, Gaines was aided by a University of Southwestern Louisiana colleague, who introduced him to a former sheriff of a small town. Gaines posed the same question regarding who would be permitted to visit a condemned inmate: "The sheriff told me that in the case of a parish jail it would be entirely up to the discretion of the sheriff. He told me that the sheriff of the jail was totally in charge and that he made all the decisions" (*Mozart and Leadbelly* 55–56). Supplemented with extensive background material, Gaines was now ready to flesh out what he described in its formative stages as a novel about "a young man being in the wrong place at the wrong time, and he was charged with murder" (53).

Though Gaines drew loosely upon the Francis case for the novel's scaffolding, his story of a condemned young man, Jefferson, is not a nonfiction, historical novel in the vein of Truman Capote's classic *In Cold Blood* (1966). Therefore, *A Lesson before Dying* is not "based on" the Francis case, a point about which the author is clear: "The stories are different, still I would use some of the information from the previous case. Both young men are black. Both nearly illiterate. Both were involved in the murder of a white man. My young man would maintain his innocence to the end. No defense witnesses were called in either case. Only white men served on the juries" (53–54). Whereas a racially charged murder trial comprised the climax of *A Gathering of Old Men, Lesson* opens with Jefferson's trial, the details of which are conveyed by the novel's narrator, Grant Wiggins. Slightly older than Jefferson, who is in his early twenties, Grant opens the novel with this rather enigmatic assertion: "I was not there, yet I was there" (*A Lesson before Dying* 3). Though he did not attend the trial, he is apprised of its proceedings firsthand by his Aunt Louise ("Tante Lou"), who accompanies her stalwart friend and Jefferson's godmother, Miss Emma Glenn. We subsequently learn that Tante Lou reared Grant in the absence of his parents, who had moved to California. Grant elucidates the details about Jefferson's purported crime, which set the novel in motion. Innocently accepting a ride from two other young black men, Jefferson accompanies Brother and Bear to a convenience store where they hope to get alcohol. When the Cajun proprietor, Alcee Gropé, refuses to extend credit to the armed but moneyless two men, a gunfight ensues that leaves them and the storeowner (also armed) dead. An unwitting accomplice, Jefferson panics and, after gulping a swig of whiskey, stuffs his empty pockets with money from the register, only to be met by "two white men [who] walked into the store" (6).

In the trial that follows, the prosecutor and defense attorney make parallel arguments: the former contends that Jefferson's vicious attack and robbery can be explained by all blacks' seemingly genetic predisposition to violence, while the latter insists that their concomitantly innate intellectual deficits would not permit Jefferson to concoct such a diabolical crime. In fact, according to the defense, "Why, I would just as soon put a hog in the electric chair as this" (8).[2] Aside from the obviously dehumanizing swine metaphor, also telling here is the lawyer's use of a demonstrative pronoun in lieu of Jefferson's name, the so-called "defense" attorney semantically objectifying him and thereby magnifying the near-illiterate young man's silence and veritable invisibility in a situation where his very life is at stake. The guilty verdict a foregone conclusion, the judge pronounces "Death by electrocution" at the sentencing hearing. While an elderly southern black woman such as Miss Emma was perhaps shocked but not surprised by the sham trial, what she found more distressing and unacceptable was her godson's public, verbal bestialization: "Called him a hog" (12). It is that designation that fuels the novel's central action.

Though powerless to reverse his death sentence, Miss Emma is nevertheless determined to elevate him from the designation as one of nature's filthiest creatures: "'I don't want them to kill no hog,' she said. 'I want a man to go to that chair, on his own two feet'" (13). Hearkening back to the esteemed designation of "the One," Grant like *Jane Pittman*'s Jimmy Aaron is the rural folk community's "great black hope." His superior education endows him, in "Talented Tenth" fashion, with the responsibility to uplift those denied the privilege of a formal education. Therefore, Grant is the natural choice to instill in Jefferson a sense of self-worth. However, given that he staunchly "hated this place and all I wanted to do was get away" (15), Grant ardently rebuffs the task that Miss Emma, with pressure from his aunt, expects him to accept. He pointedly counters that, although he is in fact the teacher at the church which doubles as a single-room schoolhouse, he is no miracle worker: "'Yes, I'm the teacher,' I said. 'And I teach what the white folks around here tell me to teach—reading, writing, and 'rithemtic. They never told me how to keep a black boy out of a liquor store" (13). Further, Grant insists, visiting Jefferson is an ultimately futile enterprise because, in his estimation, "Jefferson is dead . . . he's already dead"—Grant here speaking to Jefferson's spiritual if not physical state. However, the entire project to rehabilitate Jefferson rests on the approval of Sheriff Guidry, whom the women plan on lobbying for permission. Despite Grant's unwillingness to accompany the women to the home of Henri Pichot—his sister, Edna, is married to the sheriff—his aunt issues this ultimatum: "'You going with us up the quarter,' my aunt said, as though I hadn't said a word. 'You going up there with us, Grant, or you don't sleep in this house tonight'" (14). This brief but revelatory encounter foregrounds several salient issues: Miss Emma's unflagging commitment to establishing black humanity despite the insidiousness of Jim Crow; the women's formidable sisterly bond; Grant's own ambivalence if not hostility regarding his place in the community; and finally, how his aunt's threats might affect Grant in terms of agency and his ability to chart his own life's course.

The women's next maneuver is to convince Guidry to allow Grant access to Jefferson to facilitate the lesson his godmother wishes him to learn before his execution. We soon learn of both women's ties to the Pichot house and the grounds for Miss Emma's appeal. During Grant's childhood, Miss Emma worked as the Pichots' cook, his aunt their laundress. Moreover, Grant's young age did not spare him from the rigors of plantation life. Though now a young man, standing in the Pichot kitchen triggers memories of all the time he spent there as a child, when he had to "bring in wood for the stove, to bring in a chicken I had caught and killed, eggs I had found in the grass" (18). After repeating the bestial epithet that sparked her outrage, Miss Emma declares, "I need you to speak for me, Mr. Henri" (20); in effect, Mr. Henri will become her proxy, convincing Sheriff Guidry to facilitate her objective: "I want the teacher to talk to my boy for me." Though lacking financially, Miss Emma is not without currency; unbowed, she asserts, "I done done a lot for this family and this place, Mr. Henri. . . . All I'm asking you talk to the sheriff for me. I done done a lot for this family over the years" (21).[3] Both flustered by and taken aback at what he considers his former cook's insolence, Pichot grudgingly agrees to speak to Guidry and turns his back to leave. Making a subsequent visit on his own, Grant endures a wait of over two hours in the same kitchen before Guidry informs him that he may in fact visit Jefferson, though he expresses his own qualms: "And I'd rather see a contented hog go to that chair than an aggravated hog" (49). Guidry's regurgitating of the defense attorney's hog metaphor reinforces how every entity within the southern judicial network—lawyers, judges, sheriffs, deputies— regards African Americans as feral and worthy of eradication.

Although Tante Lou appears to be a domineering force stymieing Grant's autonomy, his love interest emerges as an equally influential woman in his life. Separated and seeking a divorce, Vivian Baptiste is a teacher and the mother of two children; other key details about her include her complexion, which is described as "very fair" (104), and that she hails from the nearby town of Free LaCove, which evokes a suspicious response from Tante Lou: "I hear they don't like dark-skin people back there" (114). Vivian's personal history confirms Tante Lou's accusation: Vivian was summarily shunned by her family because she married a dark-skinned fellow student at Xavier University in New Orleans. As it did in *Catherine Carmier,* intra-racial skin-color prejudice thus emerges as a prominent theme in the novel, as Grant will encounter mulatto characters such as his former schoolteacher Matthew Antoine as well as engage in a brawl with a group of brick-layers who similarly despise darker-complexioned blacks. However, Vivian plays an even more instrumental role in that she seconds the elderly women's wish for Grant to facilitate Jefferson's reeducation. Grant and Vivian frequently meet at what serves his alternative home, the Rainbow Club, a restaurant/bar where other teachers regularly congregate.

After dropping off Tante Lou and Miss Emma following their initial visit to the Pichot home, Grant flees there, expecting Vivian to support his wish not to become involved. But Vivian's response spotlights another central facet of the novel: though the title might ostensibly signal the consequential lesson of self-worth and obligation that Grant will provide Jefferson, equally significant is the instruction that Grant himself receives from various characters throughout the novel. In addition to the women closest to him, other quasi-instructors will include Matthew Antoine; Dr. Joseph Morgan, the white school superintendent; Reverend Ambrose, who attends to Jefferson's soul at Miss Emma's behest; and even the unschooled Jefferson—all will proffer invaluable lessons for the formally educated but emotionally disconsolate young instructor. Thus, Grant is caught off guard when Vivian offers a lesson on community and obligation. Not only does she claim that "We're teachers, and we have a commitment" (29), but she will echo the elderly women's desire that he intervene on Jefferson's behalf: "I want you to go up there," a point she reiterates in even more personal and collective terms as she continues, "I want you to go for me . . . For us" (32). This early lesson will eventually compel Grant to rethink his subsequent claim that "He's no kin—" (77) as a legitimate basis for denying the women's collective hope that he embrace Jefferson as a spiritual if not biological brother, and not disclaim him as disposable and Other.

The initial visit to Jefferson's cell proves fruitless, his grim fate leaving him despondent, even nihilistic. Though his godmother has prepared his favorite foods, he refuses to eat and barely interacts with her; he only repeats in various forms that "Nothing don't matter" as he stares blankly at the ceiling. However, Jefferson does train his gaze on "Professor Wiggins," perhaps incredulous that someone who'd shown no interest in him before would now accompany his godmother to his segregated dungeon "at the end of the cellblock" (71). Quite tellingly, Jefferson aims accusatory questions at the man his godmother has chosen—unbeknownst to him—to instill the self-value that has eluded him his entire life. In response to Grant's confusion about the first question Jefferson flings toward him, "You the one?" Jefferson follows up with a more piercing query: "Go'n jeck that switch?" suggesting the Grant will pull or "jeck" (jerk) the lever that will emit the fatal dose of electricity.[4] Seeing that their two subsequent visits are failing to bring about her desired goal, Miss Emma feigns illness before the scheduled fourth visit. Lest Grant think this will relieve him of this unwanted chore, however, Tante Lou declares that "He's going," alone. Deftly, Miss Emma has retooled her plan, hoping that the men will be forced to bond in her absence. Though Grant ultimately yields to his aunt's demand, he can no longer hold his tongue and berates the woman who raised him:

"Everything you sent me to school for, you're stripping me of it,"
I told my aunt. . . . "The humiliation I had to go through, going
into that man's [Pichot's] kitchen. The hours I had to wait while
they ate and drank and socialized before they would even see
me. Now going up to that jail. To watch them put their dirty
hands on that food. To search my body each time as if I'm some
kind of common criminal. Maybe today they'll want to look into
my mouth, or my nostrils, or make me strip. Anything to hu-
miliate me. All the things you wanted me to escape by going to
school. Years ago, Professor Antoine told me that if I stayed here,
they were going to break me down to the nigger I was born to be.
But he didn't tell me that my aunt would help them do it." (79)

Grant's stand (tirade?) encapsulates not only his heretofore sup-
pressed rage, but the outrage shared by other black young southern
men who harbor latent feelings of emasculation. His reference to
being stripped and inspected is especially evocative, the language
here purposely conjuring images of the auction block and scenes of
sexual violation; in effect, Grant perceives his treatment as a type of
rape, the most debased form of male humiliation. Finally, in putting
the nail in the verbal coffin he's assembling with his barbed words,
Grant accuses his aunt of the most heinous act of betrayal: conspiring
with the very white power structure that seeks black men's total degradation and annihilation. I've juxtaposed Grant's excoriation of his
aunt with Jefferson's accusatory questions to him, however, to illus-
trate Grant's own shortsightedness. In effect, Jefferson's misdirected
accusation, in which he ascribes malevolent, racist motivations to
Grant's presence—re: "[you] Go'n jeck that switch?"—echoes the understandable yet misplaced anger Grant projects towards Tante Lou.
Both young men, more alike perhaps than the intellectually superior
Grant would care to admit, have been so battered in a virulently supremacist South that they misdirect their ire toward those within
their orbit: their black brothers and sisters.

An important person Grant encounters during his frequent visits
to the jailhouse is the "young deputy" who escorts him to and from

Jefferson's cell. Described by Grant as "nearer my age, and he seemed better educated than the chief deputy or the sheriff," Paul Bonin represents a relatively enlightened white authority figure who's not driven by racial animus. In fact, Paul insists, "We might as well call each other by our names" (126), a seemingly innocuous suggestion that nevertheless breeches the convention in the 1940s' South that required all black men to address all whites as Mr., Mrs., or Miss, irrespective of that person's age. This relatively convivial relationship across racial lines figures prominently in the novel's denouement, where Paul will recount for Grant his pupil's final moments on death row.

Professor "Higgins" and "the Big Mulatto from Poulaya"
A Tale of Two Educators

Inarguably, black teachers, especially in places like rural Louisiana in the 1940s, were almost exalted in their communities, their formal training elevating them intellectually above the "peasantry" who'd been denied such opportunities. As the honorific "professor" infers, Grant was assumed to be the natural choice to effect Jefferson's hog-to-man conversion—this point borne out in Tante Lou's reply when Grant accuses her of aiding and abetting whites' dehumanization of him: "And I wished they [the community] had somebody else we could turn to. But they ain't nobody else" (79). Paradoxically, this rarefied position also spoke to the severely limited opportunities for educated southern blacks whose communities expected them to "uplift the race." Gaines has remarked upon the unique burden shouldered by black educators, whose advanced education confines them almost exclusively to teaching given the South's professional glass ceiling; such pigeonholing fosters a strong resentment among those who choose to remain and not flee like many of their educated counterparts (*Conversations* 198). Grant reinforces this to Jefferson: "I teach because it is the only thing that an educated black man can do in the South today. I don't like it; I hate it" (*A Lesson before Dying* 191).

Fuming over his aunt's unilateral decision casting him as Jefferson's mentor, Grant takes out his frustrations—verbally and corporally

—on those lacking even less autonomy than he: the students in his K-6 church school: "I slashed him hard across the butt with the Wescott ruler" (35); "I brought the Wescott down into his palm" (36); "She was so terrified by my voice that she jerked around to face me, then staggered back against the board" (37); "... and when I got in good striking distance of his shaved head, I brought the Westcott down on his skull, loud enough to send a sound throughout the church.... [The other students] seemed petrified" (38). While multiple informal teachers instruct Grant on personal and communal obligations, his encounters with two actual educators will prompt him to reconsider his simmering rage and the hardhanded way he engages those most vulnerable: poor black southern children.

The first educator is Dr. Joseph Morgan, the parish school superintendent who has just arrived for his annual trip to the "colored" schools: "The superintendent was a short, fat man with a large red face and a double chin, and he needed all his energy to get out of the car" (52). Realizing that he has no clue of his name despite having visited the school numerous times, Grant greets him thusly: "'Grant Wiggins,' I said," to which Dr. Morgan immediately responds, "How are you, Higgins?" (52). This demeaning misnaming bespeaks the dubious nature of Dr. Morgan's once-a-year visit. (He visits the white schools twice annually.) Dr. Morgan then orders each grade to stand as a unit; from each group he selects individual students to come forward for inspection and quizzing. He examines the students' bodies, a routine for which Grant was prepared, though he now realizes that one of the summoned children's palms he'd checked for cleanliness were now "as black and as grimy as if he had been pitching coal all day" (55). Though he clearly sees himself as working on his students' collective behalf, one might criticize "Higgins" on grounds similar to those on which he assailed his aunt: Does Grant's role in this deprecating exhibition exacerbate the children's objectification? Of course, the white-controlled education system renders Grant relatively powerless, so noncompliance might mean that his already poorly resourced school might be deprived of the hand-me-down supplies they get from their well-equipped white counterparts.

As the inspection becomes even more invasive, Grant does arrive at an awareness of the children's—and by extension, his own—degradation: "And besides looking at hands, now he began inspecting teeth. Open wide, say 'Ahhh'—and he would have the poor children spreading out their lips as far as they could while he peered into their mouths. At the university I had read about slave masters who had done the same when buying new slaves, and I had read of cattlemen doing it when purchasing horses and cattle. At least Dr. Joseph had graduated to the level where he let the children spread out their own lips, rather than using some kind of crude metal instrument. I appreciated his humanitarianism" (56). The inescapable plague of slavery surfaces here as it does throughout Gaines's fiction. Moreover, one wonders if Gaines has named the character allusively, given that the novel is set not long after World War II: "Dr. Joseph Morgan" audibly approximates Dr. Josef Mengele, the Nazi physician whose incalculably barbarous "experiments" on Jews often involved "inspections" of their bodies as well. Subsequently, Dr. Morgan will offer Grant faint "praise": "Higgins, I must compliment you. You have an excellent crop of students, an excellent crop, Higgins. You ought to be proud." Gaines makes this cogent point without subtlety.

The same immoral enterprise, known as American slavery, that reduced African Americans to natural resources and commodities has resurfaced in a less odious form: a predatory sharecropping system that limits black children's schooltime to three or four months while the bulk of the year is spent assisting families in harvesting crops for paltry sums. Perhaps Grant now grasps that Dr. Morgan's *thingification* of his pupils, coupled with his own misnaming, is all of a piece: in the same vein as Jefferson's mistitled "defense" attorney, powerful whites such as Dr. Morgan regard all blacks as less-than-human entities—"hogs," "crops"—to be executed or worked like mules and cotton gins for the enrichment of whites. Though this self-proclamation will occur much later in the novel (during the climactic execution scene), Grant ultimately reaches a fuller understanding that his plight, along with that of Jefferson and his students, reflects the perpetuation of enslavement, in slightly more palatable social forms: "Because I know what it means to be a slave. I am a slave" (251).

Infusing humor at often unexpected moments (re: the climactic trial in *A Gathering of Old Men*), Gaines leavens this racially weighty episode with a humorous interlude that nevertheless makes a profound point about race, education, and citizenship. When one particularly bumbling student, Louis Washington, sheepishly asks Dr. Joseph, "Want me go stand outside and s'lute flag?" the benevolent superintendent—overseer?—instructs him to do so in the classroom. Louis complies, raising his hand to his chest and reciting, "Plege legen toda flag. Ninety state. 'Merica. Er—er—yeah, which it stand. Visibly. Amen" (56). Gaines here raises a question as apropos during slavery as it is in the timespace of the novel: Why should disenfranchised African Americans of any age commit to memory a pledge to a land that shows them no allegiance? Eliciting a grunt from the superintendent and chuckles from classmates, Louis's mangled rendition is nevertheless pregnant with meaning. His omission of the concluding phrase, "with liberty and justice for all," explicitly highlights the novel's dramatic sparkplug: Jefferson's wrongful arrest, conviction, and the travesty of a trial that followed. Another botched phrase, "one Nation under God, indivisible," speaks to an enduringly fragmented nation; it couldn't be any less divided on matters of racial equality if it were in fact "Ninety state[s]." Louis's omission of the divine in his rendition points to the moral hypocrisy of a country—especially its Bible-thumping southernmost region—that considers itself a "Christian nation" despite its centuries-long denial of full rights and privileges that American citizenship purports to guarantee to all regardless of hue. Ultimately, Louis's deceptively unintelligible version of a foundational creed eloquently bespeaks the plight of black children being groomed for lives of servitude in fields or substandard classrooms—or worse, as Jefferson grimly describes what awaits him after weeks of consuming the southern delicacies his aunt has so lovingly prepared: "Just a old hog they fattening up to kill for Christmas" (83).

In the following chapter, Grant relates a memory that has had an enduring impact on his views on race and the usefulness of education given the bleak outlook young southern blacks face. He connects his pessimistic perception of his role to a lesson gleaned from his own childhood teacher, Matthew Antoine, whom he dubs "the big mulatto from Poulaya" (62). Antoine has consistently preached to Grant—both during his tenure as Grant's teacher and when Grant reaches adulthood—that the only feasible option for a black man in a racially asphyxiating South is "to run and run"; this admonition, then, helps explain Grant's own indestructible hatred of his homeland and comparable desire to vanish. Compounding matters is Antoine's mulatto identity, which has thrust him into a racial limbo: simultaneously black and white, but exclusively neither. However, he makes unassailably clear which race he regards as superior, though he can never attain membership. During a visit to his now retired and ailing former instructor, Grant recalls, "Once, as I sat at the fireplace with him, he said to me, 'Nothing pleases me more than when I hear of something wrong. Hitler had his reasons, and even the Ku Klux Klans of the South for what they do'" (63).

What might be considered Antoine's hyper-racist views, in which he sympathizes with the most depraved perpetrators of genocidal violence, are clearly meant to compensate for his nonwhiteness; harboring such views, he believes, will be looked upon favorably by whites while cementing his own disassociation from the black community—and the black self he clearly abhors. Grant even remembers Antoine's expression of these toxic views when he himself was a student of "Professor Antoine": "There was nothing but hatred for himself as well as contempt for us. He hated himself for the mixture of his blood and the cowardice of his being, and he hated us for daily reminding him of it" (62). Instead of racial enlightenment, Antione's lessons, then as now, amount to a type of endarkenment that has clearly left its imprint on Grant, evidenced in his own resentment of fellow blacks, feelings of disconnection from family and community, and ambivalence about whether his teaching can appreciably improve the lot of children in a chronically discriminatory South.

Given Antoine's misanthropy and maleficent racial attitudes, one might wonder why Grant seeks him out, as he even visits him one last time shortly before he succumbs to an unspecified illness. Grant is keenly aware that "There was no love there for each other. There was not even respect" (64). Such an acknowledgment makes another assertion all the more vexing: "I didn't like him, but I needed him, needed him to tell me something that none of the others could or would." I conclude that Antoine serves as a cautionary presence for Grant, his spiritual deadness and implacable hatred of self and black people indicative of what awaits Grant lest he imbibe his ex-teacher's contaminated—and contaminating—philosophy. Gaines indicates the potentially corrosive impact of such hatred through Antoine's physical appearance on Grant's last visit: "He looked terribly frail that day"; "His hand was large, cold, and bony. He was coughing a lot" (65–66). The incurably afflicted Antoine projects here a death-in-life presence, his emotional and spiritual deadness embodied in his atrophying body. Put another way, the malignant ethos that has consumed him his entire life now manifests itself in his decaying, skeletal appearance; even Grant placing another log in the fireplace fails to warm a man who can only grouse, "I'll still be cold. I'll always be cold." Just as Grant came to realize his complicity with a white educational apparatus that demeans and devalues black children, he perhaps intuitively understands that he needs to be exposed to Antoine to apprehend the hatred that renders his former instructor isolated, diseased, and even cadaverous ("cold"). Indeed, Grant does eventually, over the course of time, arrive at a more enlightened and redeeming view after his encounters with Jefferson, realizing "I am still part of the whole" (194). Inarguably, Antoine's negative lesson before dying was indispensable, illuminating for Grant that he too was stumbling down the same dark path that led his teacher to an early grave.

"This Go'n Be My Place"
Improvised Familial and Communal Spaces

When one thinks of interior spaces in African American men's writing, several come to mind—Bigger Thomas's prison cell, Invisible Man's subterranean "hole," the Boston prison where Malcolm Little was transformed into Malcolm X. And while Gaines has spoken of love for his rural native land—the bayous, cane fields, and rivers of New Roads to which he faithfully returned—interior spaces in his works have been metaphorical incubators, sites of emotional and spiritual rebirth and transformation. Recall, for instance, Procter Lewis's brief exposure to Hattie Brown and Munford Bazille in "Three Men," where the older incarcerated men functioned as role models who disabused the young killer of believing that violence bestows *true* black manhood. Similarly, Jefferson's cell functions as a pedagogical space for both teacher and student, both rejuvenated through their exchanges in what could be a suffocating, life-negating hell of a place. Moreover, within the confines of the jail, Gaines depicts how African Americans have improvised in transforming ostensibly uninviting structures into nurturing, even familial ones.

Though seemingly only a slight improvement over Jefferson's cell, where he'd hosted visitors, the alternative space's very name, "The Dayroom," implies a type of openness and luminousness, where a looming death sentence or confinement to the southern hellhole might be temporarily if not permanently mitigated. Recall the heavily monitored and restrictive conditions of Grant's visits to Jefferson, constricting conditions that are exacerbated when Jefferson's entire supporting posse—Reverend Ambrose, Tante Lou, and Miss Emma—comes calling. Picture Miss Emma trying her best to recreate the comforts of home during these visits, bearing what Grant calls "enough food to feed the entire prison" as the five of them balance plates on their laps in the cramped, decidedly un-homey jail cell. Here the elderly women's resourcefulness, their make-a-way-out-of-no way-ness, comes through when they petition for less austere, more amenable surroundings. In advocating for a more sociable milieu, Miss Emma and Tante Lou call upon Edna Guidry, whom they target as yet another surrogate voice in their quest for better dining quarters. Edna is initially reluctant to get involved in her (white) man's business. Thus, Miss Emma's complaint about the cramped cell and their desire to commune with Jefferson in the more spacious dayroom is immediately met with skepticism: "What's wrong with the cell," "Wasn't it big enough," Edna rejoins. "Yes, but they couldn't all sit down. Was it necessary that they all sit down at the same time? Couldn't they take turns?" "I'm sure that Reverend Ambrose didn't mind standing. And maybe Jefferson could stand up too, and let Tante Lou and Miss Emma sit down" (133).

The women are taken aback by Edna's non-solution, given that she has dared to break with southern racial protocol by having her maid serve them coffee in her living room. Edna's initial reticence demonstrates that her willingness to breach racial and spatial boundaries has its limits. However, Miss Emma is relentless in reminding her former "mistress" of her decades of service and sacrifice as the family's domestic, a long-standing historical situation in which African American women have played essential roles in the white families whom they serve and even prioritize over their own (think Dilsey Gibson in Faulkner's *The Sound and the Fury* or the perpetually headkerchiefed Hattie McDaniel in *Gone with the Wind*). But Miss Emma and Tante Lou shatter the mammy mold in demanding more humane treatment for themselves and their own family members.[5] Their lobbying via their white sister-intercessor eventually brings the desired outcome, their segregated sisterhood helping to chip away at seemingly ironclad racial dividers.

Once they gather in the dayroom, Miss Emma converts this space of transitory respite into a hallowed gathering ground, which Grant describes: "The large room contained three tables, made of steel, with benches attached on either side, also of steel. There were no other visitors in the dayroom, and Miss Emma selected the center table. She took out the food and placed it on the table. She set four places, two on either side of the table. My aunt and Reverend Ambrose stood back, watching her. My aunt would say later that Miss Emma went about setting the table the same way she would have done at home, humming her 'Termination song to herself" (136). Assigning places at her table—"This go'n be Jefferson's place, and this go'n be my place"—Miss Emma becomes the architect of a poignant, inspirational moment, the dining table being the pillar of familial and communal engagement. This seemingly pedestrian venue is vital, the sharing being only a small part of the jail's overall importance as a crucible where stories are told, memories recollected and passed down, philosophical differences debated, and wisdom imparted. The dayroom, the surrogate and provisional home secured through Miss Emma's canniness and persistence, becomes an extension of Grant's unofficial classroom— Jefferson's cell—where lessons before dying will be transmitted and absorbed.

Like the jail, the "Rainbow Club" also serves a dual function as black-owned restaurant-bar in the rigidly segregated Bayonne and simultaneously as Grant's surrogate home, a refuge from his aunt's demands as well as a rendezvous spot for him and Vivian. (Though separated, she's still married and trying to attain both a divorce and custody of her two children.) The combination bar-café, owned by married proprietors Joe and Thelma Claiborne, will take on far more consequential meaning, serving as an unofficial classroom where Grant will be taught the worth of community and one's unshakeable responsibility to it. One indispensable lesson occurs in the club's bar, where men routinely congregate as bartender Joe serves up adult beverages. (Thelma cooks and oversees the café section.) Three (wise?) men "stood talking baseball," specifically about a young Jackie Robinson, who "had just finished his second year with the Brooklyn Dodgers" (87). As he is throughout the novel during various intimate gatherings, Grant is simultaneously within the men's proximity but, tellingly, outside their brotherly circle: the space he occupies, "halfway down the bar," symbolizes his emotional disconnection, his frequent self-imposed relegation to the community's fringes.

The men's pantomiming of Jackie's baseball moves sparks Grant's recollection of another African American sports legend, Joe Louis, and his first fight—a loss—against German Max Schmeling in 1936. This outcome casts a pall over the entire quarters community, Grant recalling that there was even an accompanying "period of mourning" (88). However, the Brown Bomber would ultimately redeem himself— and more importantly, provide collective esteem for the millions of black Americans who saw him as their conquering hero in a nation which relegated them to second-class status. That all of the residents jammed into two homes to listen to the broadcast on the only radios in the quarters signifies Louis's exalted status. Grant captures the community's cathartic, jubilant response to the redemptive rematch:

> And there was nothing but chaos. People screamed. Some shot pistols in the air. There were mock fights. Old men fell down on the floor, as Schmeling did, and had to be helped up. Everybody laughed. Everybody patted everybody else on the back. For days after that fight, for weeks, we held our heads higher than any people on earth had ever done for any reason. I was only seventeen then, but I could remember it, every bit of it—the warm evening, the people, the noise, the pride I saw in those faces. (88–89)

Though Grant can't fully glean the momentousness of this occasion for those with whom he shares physical *place* but not connective emotional *space*, his memory of it does transport him to more familiar terrain: the academic world of formal education, specifically where he received what might be classified as the "book learning" that has both elevated him in the community but simultaneously estranged him from it.

Grant recalls "The little Irishman," a visiting professor who by chance lectured to students at the historically black college Grant attended, and the work on which he spoke, James Joyce's "Ivy Day in the Committee Room." Even after his African American professor acquires and lends him a copy of *Dubliners* (the volume in which the story appears), the meaning behind Joyce's depiction of men gathered to commemorate their political beacon (legendary nineteenth-century Irish nationalist Charles Parnell) remains elusive:

> I read the story and reread the story, but I still could not find the universality that the little Irishman had spoken of. All I saw in the story was some Irishmen meeting in a room and talking politics. What had that to do with America, especially my people? It was not until years later that I saw what he meant. I had

gone to bars, to barbershops; I had stood on street corners, and I had gone to many suppers there in the quarter. But I had never really listened to what was being said. Then I began to listen, to listen closely to how they talked about their heroes, how they talked about the dead and about how great the dead had once been. I heard it everywhere. (90)[6]

The "years later," the time that elapses between his initial engagement of the story and his comprehension of its meaning, attests to the indispensable role of lived experience: the acquisition of life lessons not printed in books but undergone in the "school of hard knocks," where one pays one's dues by surviving and witnessing various struggles. Only after years of spending time in/on various communal milieus—bars, barbershops, churches, street corners, clubs—can Grant experience something comparable to a Stephen Dedalus–like epiphany: his proximity and exposure to "his people's" everyday lives—their stories of personal strife and agony, joy and triumph, which by extension become the community's connective tissue—provide vital ways of knowing and being. Only with time can Grant fully grasp and meld his formal and informal educations, acquired respectively from the university and the community. These separate but equally enlightening classrooms provide him the necessary, incalculable wisdom that will undergird his subsequent engagement with Jefferson, and, ultimately, underscore his place *within* the communal circle, and not on its outskirts.

Jefferson's Blues
From Voiceless Object to Writing Subject

Perhaps more so than any other work in the African American literary and historical canon, Frederick Douglass's 1845 *Narrative* is a testimony to the rejuvenating potential of voice. This is revealed when he describes "the valuation," where he, his fellow enslaved, and other property are to be divided between the son and daughter of the recently deceased slaveowner. After the animate and inanimate property has been appraised, Douglass describes the ensuing "division":

"*I have no language* to express the high excitement and deep anxiety which were felt among us poor slaves during this time. Our fate for life was now to be decided. *We had no more voice* in that decision than the brutes among whom we were ranked" (90; emphasis added). The grotesqueness of human inventory warrants no discussion, but what also stands out here is Douglass's emphasis on language—or more precisely, his figurative inability as writer to summon any words that could possibly convey the enslaved persons' emotional trauma. As chattel, he and his counterparts are literally denied voice, the capacity for speech conferring humanity and distinguishing men and women from the "brutes" with which Douglass and his peers are equated. The opening chapter of *Lesson* clearly hearkens back to Douglass, as Jefferson too is consigned to the category of beast, a "hog" robbed of the ability to speak on his own behalf. A careful explication of *Lesson*'s opening chapter elucidates how Jefferson's plight approximates Douglass's in that he, too, is denied language and voice, relegated to the silenced category of object whose worth or lack thereof is determined by whites.

Gaines masterfully captures the depth of Jefferson's voicelessness through the manner in which he constructs the expository chapter, which outlines the murder of store-owner Gropé, the ensuing trial, and the verdict. Instead of having Jefferson testify firsthand about the catastrophic but accidental murder he witnessed but had no part in carrying out, Gaines uses the first-person narrator—subsequently revealed to be Grant—to present those events. Gaines's decision to position Grant (himself absent from the trial and who presumably received specific details from Miss Emma and Tante Lou) as the purveyor of Jefferson's story dramatizes the extent to which Jefferson has probably been denied a voice throughout his entire existence. This reality is confirmed much later in the novel, once the now-incarcerated Jefferson divulges the details of his life to Grant shortly before his execution: "I went in the field when I was six, driving that old water cart. I done pulled that cotton sack, I done cut cane, load cane, swung that ax, chop ditch banks, since I was six. . . . Yes, I'm youman [human], Mr. Wiggins. But nobody didn't know that 'fore now. Cuss for nothing. Beat for nothing. Work for nothing. Grinned to get by" (224). This thumbnail sketch captures what Martin Luther King denoted in his anguished "Letter from Birmingham Jail" as a "degenerating sense of 'nobodiness'" (597).

It's not difficult to imagine a lifetime of having no voice, given Jefferson's virtual peonage from a desperately young age. By having Grant recapitulate the events of the murder, punctuated with his concluding assertion, "That was his story" (6), Gaines effectively signals Jefferson's silence if not total absence, both within the confines of a biased courtroom and over the course of a lifetime where he fared marginally better than the beast-of-burden Douglass. Further, Gaines's investing of Jefferson's story with Grant effectively connects two lives that, on the surface, appear vastly incomparable on the basis of class and status—but *not* race. However, if Grant is an objective surrogate for Jefferson's version of events, two subsequent voices dramatize how pernicious racial attitudes magnify Jefferson's silence, objectification, and invisibility.

Though serving wildly different functions within the criminal justice system, those entrusted with determining Jefferson's guilt and innocence expose the grave consequences of putting black defendants' lives in the hands of persons who see them as expendable. Again related by Grant, the prosecutor presents a crude but historically familiar case based on America's interminably venomous racial suppositions: "When the old man and the other two robbers were all dead this one—it proved the kind of animal he really was—stuffed the money into his pockets and celebrated the event by drinking over their still-bleeding bodies" (6–7). Black men were seen as genetically feral brutes, no more capable of compassion than the animals from whom they have yet to evolve. In response, Jefferson's lawyer crafts this glossily eloquent "defense" to the "twelve white men" who comprise the jury: "Mention the names of Keats, Byron, Scott, and see whether the eyes will show one moment of recognition. Ask him to . . . quote one passage from the Constitution or the Bill of Rights. Gentleman of the jury, this man planned a robbery? Oh, pardon me, pardon me, I surely did not mean to insult your intelligence by saying 'man'—would you please forgive me for committing such an error?" (8). This line of argument deems Jefferson innocent by reason of racially predetermined imbecility, a "non-man" who skulks around the lower rungs of the hierarchical Great Chain of Being. Gaines astutely invokes another racially tainted practice of the Jim Crow South here: the attorney deems Jefferson intellectually inferior on the presumption that he can't recite passages from our nation's sacred documents, conjuring images of bogus "literacy" tests pervasive in southern voting precincts, where African Americans were required to recite such passages as a condition for exercising their "right" to vote. When he augments this defense by designating Jefferson a "hog," it becomes starkly clear that he and the prosecutor are operating from the same rancid racial playbook—blackness as depraved, blackness as deprived, blackness as deficient. Taken together, these complementary renditions of Jefferson's alleged crime render him a silent witness to the assassination of his very personhood, akin to the language-less and voiceless status Douglass described as his plight as living inventory.

Having so convincingly established Jefferson's voicelessness, Gaines was nevertheless determined to resuscitate his voice and have him speak on his own behalf, in his own words. Though he had no idea how he would achieve this when sketching out the characters' respective arcs, he ultimately resolved his narrative dilemma: in addition to a radio, Grant suggests to Jefferson that "I could bring you a little notebook and a pencil. You could write your thoughts down" (185). With this was born the novel's second-to-last chapter, the only titled one among its thirty-one: "JEFFERSON'S DIARY." In his 2005 essay "Writing *A Lesson before Dying*," Gaines comments further on the outlet through which the "barely literate" Jefferson ultimately comes to speak for himself: "He has never written a letter in his life. He was barely able to write his elementary school assignments. But now, with his pencil and his notebook, he tries to define his humanity—in the few days he has left to live" (*Mozart and Leadbelly* 61).

Many of the novel's thematic threads come together in this chapter. Written entirely in his voice in what might be considered "ungrammatical" English, the diary is Jefferson's unedited meditation on an amalgam of topics: his past, his sentence, religion, his relationships with the people in his life, the depth of his pain that comes with a lifetime of neglect, and the rebirth he experiences through connection with Grant and his many other visitors. It culminates with his declaration of his unreserved, unqualified humanity—thereby revising and countering the dehumanizing narratives which opened the novel: "good by mr wigin tell them im strong tell them im a man good by mr wigin im gon ax paul if he can bring you this" (*Lesson* 234). This enlightened perception of self corrects his own earlier assertions that he was not "youman." Even more, it reflects the same conclusion at which Grant too will arrive about himself, that he is still "a part of the whole" (194). Despite his few remaining hours spent in isolation, Jefferson too reconnects, thereby fulfilling his aunt's desire that he achieve manhood status and be forever conjoined to the beloved community, a community that transcends barriers of race, class, gender, and education.

Describing what he considers the overall impact of the novel's most affecting relationship, Gaines concludes, "Grant converts Jefferson, and Jefferson converts Grant, and the whole thing comes back to probably help us—I should hope so—also, Paul has been changed, and he is going to make some points—at least I hope so" (*Conversations* 307). Indeed, Gaines captures the individual and collective curative possibilities of the two young men's relationship, men ostensibly separated by chasms of education and fate. Even more, the author imagines an inspiriting and inspirational camaraderie that extends beyond the novel's pages and encompasses readers as well. From this wholistic perspective, Jefferson's martyr-like death has the potential to help bridge barriers between characters and readers separated by race, region, history, and experience. Gaines would reap immediate benefits from the publication of what has subsequently become his most enduring literary achievement (re: the National Book Critics Circle Award for Fiction and the MacArthur "genius" award in in 1993). But perhaps the truest measure of the book's wider cultural resonance was its 1997 selection as an "Oprah Book Club Selection," an honor attesting to the book's ability to also collapse barriers separating "literary" and "popular" fictions and readers. Those audiences would have to wait nearly twenty-five years for another book of fiction from the writer who in the twenty-first century has ascended to the pinnacle of southern scribes: a novella that dramatizes characters knitted together by the threads of race, violence, and history, occurring in the familiar if never-quite-pastoral landscape of his cherished rural Louisiana.

9

The Tragedy of Brady Sims

In 1970, twenty-six-year-old Alice Walker claimed that thirty-seven-year-old Ernest Gaines was "perhaps the most gifted young black writer working today." Now well into the twenty-first century, Gaines's literary eminence has proven Walker an astute appraiser of literary talent. Considering their luminous careers, one might legitimately pronounce Walker and Gaines the respective mother and father of contemporary African American southern literature. Moreover, Gaines invites comparisons to another literary dignitary: he and the renowned novelist/critic Toni Morrison are the rare authors of any race whose publishing careers have spanned over fifty years. Though Gaines retired from teaching in 2004, he retired neither his pen nor his zest for writing. *The Tragedy of Brady Sims,* his 2017 novella and eighth book of fiction, marks yet another signal moment in Gaines's distinguished career.

The work's origins date back to 1994, when Gaines expounded upon the then-titled work "The Man Who Whipped Children": "It's about—when did this start happening? That we blacks always whipped our children—is that an African tradition, or not? Is it a Germanic tradition where a certain discipline exists? I knew there was a man on that planation where I lived, who would, if the father was absent, whip the bad children, if one of them needed to be controlled in order to keep him from going to Angola [penitentiary] where he would be killed" (*Conversations* 327–28). In both content and style,

Brady Sims evokes comparisons to several works, especially *The Autobiography of Miss Jane Pittman, A Gathering of Old Men,* and his last novel, *A Lesson before Dying.* Like *Jane Pittman,* the story commences through the eyes of a young professional probing the life of an elder in the black community. While his occupation differs from that of the history teacher attempting to extract Miss Jane's story, journalist Louis Guerin undertakes research on Brady's life. Ambrose Cunningham, the editor of the *Bayonne Journal,* has tasked Louis with writing a "human interest story" on the man whose "face was the color of dark worn leather, and looked just as tough" (*Brady Sims* 5). The event that engendered Cunningham's request occurred in the opening courtroom scene, recalling the beginning of *Lesson,* where the demeaning appellation of "hog" by Jefferson's defense lawyer set the narrative machinery in motion. Once a young man—soon to be revealed as Brady's son, Jean-Pierre—has been sentenced and is led out of the courtroom by two white deputies, Louis describes what transpires: "I looked back over my shoulder and saw that the two deputies had stopped with their prisoner and were facing old Brady Sims. Next came the loudest sound that I had ever heard. I saw the prisoner fall back with blood splashing from his body, and both deputies let go of his arms at the same time. Brady Sims stood there in that old faded blue jumper, with the smoke still rising from the gun in his hand" (3). Assuring the deputies that he will turn himself in to Sheriff Mapes in two hours, Brady returns to his home.

Unlike *Lesson,* where the details surrounding the murder for which Jefferson is being tried and the resulting death sentence are revealed at the outset, *Brady Sims*'s underlying plot details—for what crime has Jean-Pierre been sentenced and what could possibly explain the ghastly public slaying of one's own child—are withheld until salient details about Brady's life and relationships have been revealed. In pursuit of these details, Louis will mine a culturally rich communal male milieu, the barbershop. While the novella doesn't specify its temporal setting, photographs of cultural icons adorning its walls—Muhammad Ali, Jackie Robinson, Malcolm X, and Mahalia Jackson, along with civil rights allies John and Robert Kennedy—suggest a 1960s *mise-en-scène.* Despite the wariness expressed by Frank Jamison, who retains extensive knowledge about Brady's past, regarding the formally educated Louis's objective—"You think he knows how to listen and choose, and don't write what he ain't suppose to write?"—Jamison is reassured by fellow barbershop habitués who vouch for the young reporter (26). Comparable to *A Gathering of Old Men,* where acts of storytelling and story-listening take precedence over violent confrontations, *Brady Sims* unfurls through the eyes of Brady's peers, who share firsthand information as well as heard-through-the-grapevine secondhand information. Through one of them, the pastor of the local black church, we glean the source of the novella's original title. In response to congregants exasperated by chronically uncontrollable children whose lives often dead-end at the carnivorous Angola, narrator Jamison explains: "[Reverend] Tyree told them that if they couldn't control the children—get somebody on the place who could. But who? Then they came up with Brady. Brady Sims. Brady could stop them. None of Brady's kids ever got into trouble" (38).

One significant departure from *Gathering* is the characterization of Mapes, whom Gaines recasts here as a much more sympathetic and racially enlightened figure than his original incarnation as the prototypical, Bull Connor–esque southern sheriff. Once Louis (through the voices of the barbershop occupants) has laid the foundation for Brady's life, Mapes assumes narrative control in a brief section in which he ruminates on his own relationship with Brady and reveals arguably the novella's most harrowing moment. In the novella's brief coda, Louis again resumes what has only been nominal narrative control: again, his voice is superseded by those much closer to Brady—Mapes and Jamison. Mapes's elegiac reflection, in fact, best encapsulates the titular character: "He was a man some people would say was too hard. He lived in hard times—and the burden we put on him wasn't easy. Yes, we. That includes myself. If we had done more, his burden wouldn't have been so heavy" (113). As he has done through the multifaceted men and women who populate his bucolic storyworlds, Gaines fashions Brady Sims as a man at once charitable and self-absorbed, reckless and sensitive—in effect, confoundingly human.

"All That Is Left Are the Old, the Very Young, and the Lame"
The Immortal Search for Home and Father

A cavalcade of male protagonists—Jackson Bradley (*Catherine Carmier*), Etienne Martin/Robert X (*In My Father's House*), and Grant Wiggins (*A Lesson before Dying*)—have expressed sentiments ranging from ambivalence to unbridled malice toward their native South. Grant's especially pungent reference to it as a "hellhole" epitomizes many black men's association of the South with multipronged violence—physical, familial, sexual, economic, psychological. That all of these men returned, however, speaks to their unbreakable connection to the place they reluctantly consider home. Given the interminable persistence of Jim and Jane Crow, two barbershop regulars, Jamison and Joe Celestin ("Old Celestin"), engage in a seriocomic debate on the reasons younger blacks have departed. Though they might both concur with Mapes's rueful observation in the climactic scene in which he goes to arrest Brady, "All that is left are the old, the very young, and the lame" (*Brady Sims* 103), each man offers a thoughtful hypothesis on this conclusion.

Their verbal showdown on the roots of young African Americans' exodus begins with Jamison retrieving a chair and plopping down directly in front of his verbal adversary. As Louis describes, "All of this was done cool and quietly, and everyone else in the place was as quiet as though they were at a wake. Then suddenly Jamison screamed, 'WAR, WAR, you old baldheaded bastard. WAR.'" Then this: "'TRACTOR, you old wooly head, wooly head—something else,' Joe Celestin tried to throw back the insult" (32–33). The old men's signifyin'—their antiphonal throwing of shade à la the dozens—and the listeners' responsive laughter lends the scene a comic, folkloric feel, comparable to a similar scene of male porch-sitters in Hurston's 1926 short story "Sweat." However, Louis summarizes the argument in sobering terms: "I had been hearing it ever since I had been coming to the barbershop. Jamison claimed that it was the Second World War that took the young men and women from the plantations to go into the military and to military plants up north for work. Those who went into the military had a chance to go to school to further their education and get good jobs. None of this could have been possible had it not been for the war" (33). From Jamison's vantage point, while the war and resulting out-migration might have been unfortunate, they ultimately paid dividends for a younger generation given the stark racial and economic realities of staunchly segregated rural Louisiana.

Conversely, Celestin "said because the white man had money to buy machines—the tractor—and the black man didn't have the money to buy machines, he couldn't compete with the tractor, and so he had to leave . . . the land kept the people together; the city didn't." Celestin further explodes the myth of the urban North as a racial Canaan: "And how 'bout all them out on the street? . . . Ain't trained for any kind of city work. Young ladies got to sell their bodies; young men drinking and on dope, 'cause they can't find any work to do. Eating all that old junky food; half of them skinny as a rail; young ladies fat and bloated up. The land gived them good food, kept them in good shape" (34).

To be sure, African American writers have taken up this North-versus-South, metropolis-versus-rural debate for over a century, from Booker T. Washington to James Baldwin to August Wilson.[1] We also witness here a recurrent motif: the tractor as a dominant trope throughout Gaines's fictive corpus signifying multiple things—the destruction of the land, the displacement of blacks as tillers of the soil, the deleterious effects of mechanization. Given that Celestin's extolling of the land's virtues aligns with Gaines's own reverence for the agrarian milieu that supplied his community a gracious plenty in terms of material and spiritual nutrition, I wound venture that his sympathies would lie with "Old Celestin." Nevertheless, his framing of this scene as a good-natured clash with equally compelling positions suggests that, like all multilayered social-racial phenomena, "The Great Migration" cannot be reduced to a simplistic "good-vs.-bad" argument.

In addition to the aforementioned novels, *The Tragedy of Brady Sims* calls to mind another Gaines work even more explicitly. *In My Father's House* remains Gaines's most direct and extensive treatment of the rupture separating black fathers and sons. He has reiterated his abiding concern with what appears an interminable, irreparable

breach: "Fathers and sons were brought here in chains and then separated on the auction block in slave-holding places. I don't think that
they've made a connection since. Too often our fathers cannot help the
sons" (Brown, "Scribe" 212). Like Reverend Phillip Martin's estranged
son Etienne, Jean-Pierre had been taken to California by his mother,
only to return to his native bayou in search of his long-absent father.
How thematically apropos, then, that Gaines spotlights this concern in a work published well into his sixth decade of writing fiction.

That none of Brady's children have ever been imprisoned prompts
the quarters' denizens to grant him the power to corporally punish
offspring they deem unmanageable and borderline incorrigible. They
presume that this draconian, spare-the-rod-spoil-the-child mentality will bring the desired result of sparing their sons from a veritable
living death. Jamison explains, "Some of the old people would rather
see their children dead than go to Angola. 'Cause if they ever came out,
they would be dead inside—just broken" (*Brady Sims* 26). However
understandable and legitimate this sentiment, Gaines adroitly problematizes the widely held assumption that might will make black children right through his depiction of Brady's relationships with his own
sons. Charlie, Brady's son with his first companion, Eula, was arrested
for stealing a "Pretty, shiny red-and-white bicycle—a Schwinn" (48).
Securing a ride from Sam Brown, Brady arrives at the jail, whereupon
Mapes assumes that he'll talk to his son (whose age is not given). However, Mapes continues, "No. Brady started in the cell, hitting the boy
across his back and his head with the buckle end of the belt. The boy
went down on the floor, Brady continue to beat him" (49). After Mapes
releases his son to him and the ride home commences, "Brady threw
the boy in the backseat and got in there with him and started beating
him again." When Brady quibbles about the cost of the trip to and from
the jail, Sam counters, "You see that blood on that seat back there?"
Here the issue of punishment befitting the crime is starkly displayed.

On the one hand, such severe discipline can be rationalized as a
reasonable deterrent, as a childhood criminal act might become a
gateway to an adulthood of lawbreaking. Better one's child suffer at the
hands of a corrective parent than be gorged by the maw of an ogre-like,

racist southern penal system. On the other hand, however, Gaines raises a thorny question: might such domestic violence, however "lovingly" intended, convey the unintended notion that such brutality can be deemed a legitimate response in *any* conflict—not only those involving one's own children, but also girlfriends, wives, other adult males, and even whites? Moreover, I raise another of Gaines's predominant thematic concerns: the debilitating legacy of slavery. That Brady *whips* and leaves Sam's car *bloodstained* calls forth images of a disciplinary instrument used to subdue African Americans during our nation's darkest historical moment.[2] Though an imperfect comparison, is the historical legacy of white-on-black barbarity nevertheless being perpetuated by black fathers seeking to discipline their sons, notwithstanding the righteousness of their intentions? Brady's intemperate violence, in fact, has undesirable consequences. Suffering their father's beatings well into their teens, his older two sons ultimately "volunteered for the service just to get away from Brady" (51). Correspondingly, the beating of young Charlie "helped [Eula] make up her mind to leave here" (48), the dissolution of Brady's first family caused by the corporal punishment the community has deemed potentially beneficial.

Unfazed by this calamitous result, Brady stays true to what Jamison identifies as his bedrock maxim, which would become a prophecy: "He swore that no child of his was going to Angola—he would kill them first" (51). One of the women he "takes up with" upon Eula's departure was Mika Leblanc, described as "a tiger" whom Brady would "slap" but who'd reply with her own fist. This serial domestic violence, which now predictably includes women, reemerges in his relationship with a son he has by yet another woman, Betty May. Jamison's description of Jean-Pierre is prescient: the son's "ways [were] just like Brady—stayed in trouble. Brady used to beat him, but that didn't do no good. Boy had too much of Brady's blood in him" (59). Now in his late sixties or early seventies, Brady hands his presumably teenaged son a shotgun and an order to "go out and get a rabbit for supper." Returning empty-handed, Jean-Pierre suffers his father's predictable wrath: when Brady informs that he's going to retrieve a bullet to see what he himself could hit, "Jean-Pierre bust out of the house, headed for the field. Brady shot, 'pow,' hitting a corn stalk on the next row." Though this story draws peals of laughter from the barbershop crew, Brady's hardcore ways bring about a familiar result: "Not long after that, Betty Mae left and took her [and Brady's] children to N'Awlens" (60). Not to be lost here is that Jean-Pierre is a chip off the old Brady: whether in New Orleans or their eventual destination, California, Jean-Pierre "stayed in trouble," a magnet for turmoil like the father whose brutality precipitated the demise of two families.

Having presumably if predictably descended into a life of unsavory behavior, to which his father's absence quite conceivably contributed, Jean-Pierre returns home, ostensibly because "I just wanted to see my daddy" (65). Though Brady perhaps attempted to compensate for his absence by giving his son lodging upon his return, he quickly sours when Jean-Pierre begins dating a white woman; that, along with their noisy bedroom gymnastics, leads father to summarily evict son. When two gangsters from the West Coast, Fee and Lawton, suddenly appear in search of "Louisiana Roy," it is revealed that Jean-Pierre's return wasn't necessarily spurred by paternal longing but by astronomical unpaid gambling debts incurred to "Too Tall," for whom Fee and Lawton work. As described by Jamison, a quarters' resident, Pugg, ran to Brady's house to inform him that the two strongmen have kidnapped Jean-Pierre:

> "Arthur told me come tell you two men grabbed your boy. Took him in a car somewhere."
>
> Pugg said Brady stuffed his pipe with his finger. "Figgered it was something like that," he said.
>
> "What you go'n do?" Pugg asked.
>
> Brady didn't answer him.
>
> "You want me go see if I can't get Fifty Cent to take me to see Mapes?"
>
> "Suit yourself. Long as you pay for it." (85)

One may certainly argue that Brady's refusal to insinuate himself into his son's illicit activities is justifiable—in fact completely reasonable given that the beatings he inflicted were in fact meant to prevent such behavior. Still, his silence and inertia are telling, his told-you-so demeanor smug and unsympathetic. That he refuses to lift a finger on his son's behalf suggests that the space dividing black fathers and sons, which Gaines insists stemmed from their separation on slavery's auction block, is as insurmountable as it is unscalable. With his father's unwillingness to intercede, Jean-Pierre's dismal fate is sadly sealed: the wayward son convinces Fee and Lawton to rob a bank, which leaves a white clerk dead and Jean-Pierre condemned to death. But unlike Jefferson, there will be no lesson before dying—only a quick, execution-style death. Jamison's somber observation on which Part One concludes, "Lawton was dead. Both Fee and Jean-Pierre was sentenced to Gruesome Gertie's lap. Brady cheated the chair out of one, when he killed his own boy" (96), raises a number of compelling questions—moral, racial, and judicial: Was the filial slaying a mercy killing driven by a father refusing to allow the state to sentence yet another black man to death in a South that does so disproportionately? Was it done to spare the child what the community's elders considered a living death behind Angola's nightmarish walls? Or was it motivated by the father's own misguided hubris—that he and only he, not the state's hell-on-earth penitentiary, would be responsible for his child's death in the ultimate, irreversible execution of corporal punishment?

With its spotlight on the elusive father-son relationship and its rippling injurious effects—shattered families, high-minded and detached fathers, alienated and desperate sons—*The Tragedy of Brady Sims* is yet another chapter in the author's faithful examination of black men wrestling with demons from within and without. The ruinous violence that leaves both father and son dead in its wake continues a vicious cycle of black male internecine violence that permeates the body of Gaines's work: from patriarch Raoul Carmier's orchestrating of his illegitimate ten-year-old stepson's death and the climactic physical battle between himself and Jackson Bradley in *Catherine Carmier*; to Marcus Payne's and Procter Lewis's senseless bar-fight murders in *Of Love and Dust* and "Three Men," respectively; to Etienne's brother's murder of the black man who raped their sister in *In My Father's House*; to Grant Wiggins's testosterone-induced melee with the "mulatto bricklayers" in *A Lesson before Dying*. Finally, one wonders whether Brady's truly tragic suicide, which hearkens back to Etienne's plunge into the St. Charles River, results from a similar inability to reconceptualize notions of authentic black manhood that depend less on violence and more on one's ability to form emotionally intimate relationships based on empathy, nurturance, and respect for self—the very same enlightened masculinity Munford Bazille preached to Procter.

Conclusion

A Secured Legacy

In 1976, Southern University English professor Charles H. Rowell founded a literary journal whose mission was to publish black southern creative writers as well as scholarship on their works. Now well into the twenty-first century, *Callaloo* stands as a premier journal in the field of African American literary and diasporan cultural studies. But long before, in the journal's inaugural year, Rowell conducted an interview with a forty-three-year-old Ernest J. Gaines, whose fiction hadn't yet become fixtures on course syllabi or the subject of extensive scholarly inquiry. Entitled "This Louisiana Thing That Drives Me," this expansive and richly substantive conversation showcased Gaines's artistic raison d'être: his commitment to portraying the lives of his fellow black denizens in a style that captured their language and lived experiences faithfully and unapologetically. This now landmark conversation was instrumental in exposing Gaines to a wider reading audience familiar with him primarily from viewing CBS's 1974 filmed version of *Jane Pittman*. The aesthetic principles and creative vision Gaines outlined have defined his body of fiction over the subsequent forty-plus years. That his last work, published forty-one years after that signature interview, is set in that same rural

Louisiana milieu attests to the fact that his native state continued to spark his creative gears.

In that work, *The Tragedy of Brady Sims,* an out-of-towner visiting Felix's barbershop for the first time—newspaper man Louis Guerin derisively labels him "the client with the new haircut"—complains that the old men's yarns about Brady's life are so spellbinding that he cannot leave: "Start telling you a story and they know you won't leave 'til you heard the end" (58). That feeling applies equally to readers of Ernest J. Gaines's fiction, which similarly has held audiences rapt from the 1960s to the 2000s in stories and novels that contain connective narrative threads that are freshly woven in each telling. With such inimitable characters as Copper Laurent, Jane Pittman, Candy Marshall, and Grant Wiggins and the works in which they appear indelibly etched into the American literary landscape, Ernest Gaines has secured his place as a distinguished and transcendent author whose works continue to appeal to readers of multiple races, ages, geographic/national origins, and education levels. In addition to the numerous accolades he's garnered, the Ernest J. Gaines Award for Literary Excellence was established by a Baton Rouge philanthropic organization in 2006 to encourage and recognize blossoming African American fiction writers. Cumulatively, this award and the creation of such institutions as the Ernest J. Gaines Center at the University of Louisiana at Lafayette bespeak the breadth of his rich and enriching legacy, one rooted in Gaines's panoramic fictive universe and unbounded imagination.

APPENDIX

An Interview with Ernest J. Gaines

*This interview took place at the home of Ernest
and Dianne Gaines in June 2014.*

Keith Clark: Mr. Gaines, several writers pinpoint a particular moment when they realized that they would become writers. Novelist Ann Petry, who we were just discussing, was a teenager when she read *A Tale of Two Cities,* and she said that that was when she knew. For playwright August Wilson it was a Bessie Smith blues recording. So for you, was there a similar moment, an epiphanic moment when you realized that writing was going to be your vocation?

Ernest Gaines: I used to write letters and read letters for the old people here on this plantation where we're sitting right now because they couldn't—many of them could not write or read because they had not gone to school. So I used to write their letters and read their letters. Later, I tried to put on a little play here, and right here in that church back there [in the back of their home] which was my school. I wrote a little dialogue and everything, and I was about thirteen or fourteen years old at the time. But I didn't know that all of this was preparing me to become a writer. I just thought, "Well, you know, I'm having fun."

I didn't have a library here because I couldn't—well, I mean, there were libraries, but I couldn't go to any of the libraries here. So after I graduated from the little Catholic school, graduated from the eighth grade, my folks, who had gone to California during the war, sent for me in 1948. And I went to Vallejo, California, just across the bay from San Francisco. And I went to a library for the first time. At fifteen or sixteen, my stepfather gave me three choices: the movie, the YMCA, or the library. I didn't have money for the movies, so I went to the YMCA and watched these guys play basketball or shoot pool or box, you know. And I never had done any of that—you know, I'm a country boy, fifteen years old. So one day this guy told me to get in the ring with him. And when he asked me, "You want to try some boxing," I said, "You know, I don't know." So I got in the ring and he beat the living hell out of me. I ended up trying it and then I went to the library.

KC: That was the end of that.

(Laughter.)

KC: And it's interesting that you mentioned when you were fifteen you were writing letters for your relatives, I remember, and it—

EG: I was younger than fifteen; I was about thirteen or fourteen.

KC: Oh, okay—and I remember you putting that in *Miss Jane Pittman* with Jimmy Aaron, who writes the letters.

EG: That's right.

KC: And then you said you put on a church play, and I remember in *A Lesson before Dying,* Grant puts on that church play.

EG: Oh, yeah.

KC: So I see you were mining your own life for some of those characters.

EG: Yeah. I never thought about those little things. Must have been something deep in my subconscious that came out, you know, at that time. Yeah.

KC: One of my favorite stories to teach—I probably have it memorized—is "Three Men" from *Bloodline.* Could you say a bit about it?

EG: "Three Men" is about this guy—oh, I think his name was—thrown in the jail cell with those—the brutish guy—

KC: Mumford and—

EG: Hattie.

KC: Hattie—right.

EG: I knew a guy just like Mumford. You know, you grow up around guys. And I've seen some Hatties around too, you know. When I was writing about Hattie, I think I had James Baldwin in my mind all the time and so that was Hattie. But Munford was based on a guy who was a tough guy.

KC: Right. You've mentioned that Muhammad Ali influenced Marcus Payne from *Of Love and Dust.* One of the things that I've always wanted to write about in your work but haven't yet is your frequent allusions to sports heroes. You refer to Joe Louis and Jackie Robinson in *A Lesson before Dying.* So what is it about these athletes?

EG: Because those were the only heroes that we had at the time. These are the only two that blacks could appreciate at that time. We had no other hero—didn't have any movie star hero, didn't have any political heroes. But they had Joe Louis and they had Jackie Robinson. They didn't know about anyone else. I'm writing about country people—that's all I write about.

Everyone needs a hero. We all need someone to, you know, to be proud of. And those were national heroes for blacks. And just like the Dodgers: the Dodgers will always be loved by black people. No matter how many white people are on that team, they're going to stick to the Dodgers because the Dodgers brought up Jackie Robinson.

KC: They went to California too.

(Laughter.)

KC: In *A Lesson before Dying,* there's a brief but truly fascinating moment that's quite revealing. I believe Jefferson has a dream about Jackie Robinson where he pleads with Jackie to intervene to stop the execution of a young black man but Jackie can't—

EG: I read about that happening in Orlando, Florida. Yeah, a young man being executed in Florida. As they were taking him to the chair, and he goes, "Please, Mr. Jackie Robinson, help me. Help me." Or was it Joe Louis?

KC: You're right; it was Joe Louis.

EG: He cries out, "Mr. Joe Louis, help me." So, yeah, I read about it.

KC: Fascinating. And so I think you make a truly significant point that, even though these heroes are lionized in the black community and that they have a great deal of influence, it's severely limited when it comes to—

EG: Yeah—that was an interesting chapter to write because Grant had gone to town to meet up with his girlfriend, Vivian, and he had to pass time because he got to town about an hour before Vivian gets out of school. So he'd go to this bar and he's sitting at the bar. And I'm thinking, "Now, what am I going to do with that hour? What's he going to do?" I just can't say he stood there for an hour. I've got to come up with something. So I come up with these old men down the bar talking about Jackie Robinson, you know, because my story takes place in '48 and Jackie had just come in '47. So that's all everybody talked about. So that's how I did, "Jackie Robinson, Jackie Robinson, Jackie Robinson's still okay now."

KC: The film version of *A Lesson before Dying* was highly regarded, though the film that I use most frequently in my teaching is the film version of "The Sky Is Gray."

EG: Oh, yeah?

KC: I think it's a beautiful film with Olivia Cole playing the mother. It's so affecting and poignant. When I was chatting with Mrs. Gaines, she pointed out that one of the things that she found most appealing about your work is your treatment of women, and so I think that story is representative of that, since you've got a woman ushering James into manhood. You recall the scene in the dentist's office where the white nurse says, "the doctor's not going to see any more patients"?

EG: Right, right.

KC: And Octavia stands up to her. Though she doesn't convince the nurse to change her mind, she at least shows James that just because somebody white says something, that doesn't mean you just have to just passively—

EG: Right. I've been criticized for the scene where Octavia slaps James when he couldn't—didn't want to kill, kill the birds he'd trapped. But what she's trying to do is show him, "You're going to have to do these things. If anything happens to me, you're the oldest son and your brother's about eight years old. But you're going to have to do it, you know, and so do it." So it's not the right way to get them to do anything, but that's the only way she knew how to—

KC: Survive—it's about survival, right?

EG: Right. That's what I'm saying.

KC: I'm going to move onto a different topic, Mr. Gaines. Many cultural critics have condemned what they deem the "Prison Industrial Complex"—I don't know if that's a phrase you've heard, but it gets used a lot: the deliberate, state-sponsored warehousing of black men in so-called "super-max prisons," which are often erected to revitalize economically depressed white communities. Like in my state of Virginia—

Dianne Gaines: And they're private.

KC: They're private and they're all about profits. But the incarcerated men in your works—obviously Jefferson in *A Lesson before Dying,* as well as Procter Lewis in "Three Men"—undergo profound, life-altering experiences while incarcerated. Could you talk about the importance of the prison in these characters' evolution?

EG: Well, I wish that was a question you didn't bring up. I don't know how to explain the role of Grant and the godmother—

KC: Miss Emma.

EG: Without those two people, I don't think that Jefferson would have been—would have changed. I don't think he could have changed without either one, had he not taken the advice of either one of them. But the story is really about Grant's changing. We know Jefferson is—we know Jefferson is going to die. We know that Grant must continue to visit, to talk to him, which Grant does not want to do.

And the sheriff tells him once that, you know, for his agitation, we don't want to let you come back anymore; it's better to let a hog die peaceful—you know, ignorant—than to keep agitating him, trying to change him because you can't, you can't change certain people. So he's mainly changed both of them: one who tells him to kneel, Miss Emma, and the other one tells him to stand, Grant. Sometimes that seems like it's a conflict between kneeling and standing, but both had to—he needed both in order to become a man.

And he had only one week, maybe one month, or a day, before he would completely, completely become a man. I think Grant was sitting there watching him at the window and he suddenly saw not somebody that's hunched over, but he saw someone with his shoulders back, you know, Jefferson's standing better. And Grant's finally felt that pain in that visit and that's what he had gone there to tell Vivian, but he got in a bar fight with those guys, but he told her that Jefferson was coming around. But by Jefferson's coming around, it's the same Grant because Grant was not going to be saved. Grant was going to—it wasn't until—what was that, the guy, the little deputy, Paul Bonin. Yeah. He came back to tell them about him [Jefferson] in the death room, that he knew that Grant had done something, that he had reached him, but Jefferson had also reached Grant, so that's why he [Grant] cries.

KC: That's interesting, Mr. Gaines. Obviously, we can focus on the literal, physical prison that Jefferson occupies, but from what it sounds like you're saying, Grant is also in a type of prison of his own mind and the way he thinks about race and black people in his world—

EG: Yeah, yeah, yeah. And you were saying about the other person?

KC: I just wanted to ask you about Procter Lewis and his teachers, Hattie and Munford.

EG: Yeah, Mumford. And that little kid, the fourteen-year-old. It wasn't the prison itself that changed them. It's the characters who come into their lives while in that prison, because Procter would have, if he'd gotten out in a month or so, would likely do the same thing again tomorrow, you know, the very same thing. So Munford says, "Don't let him" [don't allow the white man who owns the plantation on which Procter works to bond him out of prison]. And then Procter says, "Yeah—just like the old people, you're always telling people what to do, but look what you're doing." But Munford says, "That's what I'm doing, but I'm going to be back in here at the end of the next weekend or the weekend after next. I'll be back in prison because I don't know how to act outside of here."

KC: So he's telling them, "Don't become me, don't let this happen to you."

EG: Yeah, yeah. So it's not the incarceration; it's the people you meet in that cell, where you have time to redeem yourself. There's a place where you can't run away, you *have* to listen to advice, you have to, you know, listen to advice, which Procter never would have done on the outside.

KC: And you used the word "redeem." So the prison in a way is almost like a sacred kind of—not church—but a sacred kind of space where lessons and issues of morality can be dealt with. And we wouldn't even think about a prison with respect to morality, but it becomes a sort of space where these men help other men to redeem themselves.

EG: And another thing about *A Lesson before Dying*; I hope you noticed that the time that Grant began to visit Jefferson parallels the semester that he teaches, which lasts about five months.

KC: That's right.

EG: So he's gone from school to school, from one school to another school, classroom to classroom, you know.

KC: Indeed.

Let me ask you this, Mr. Gaines. Before the critical acclaim garnered by Toni Morrison's *Beloved,* and, more recently, the financial success and mass appeal of the film *12 Years a Slave,* one of your masterpieces, *The Autobiography of Miss Jane Pittman,* appeared at a time when relatively few authors imagined that our nation's "original sin," slavery, might contain a wellspring of gripping topics, themes, characters, and narrative possibilities. In *Miss Jane,* as you do in other works, you draw upon American history—slavery, the civil rights movement—and its compelling subject matter. Why has history been such an integral part of your work, and why do you think slavery specifically has captured the imagination of so many writers over the past few decades?

EG: Well, I suppose history has only showed me how—what I am today because of my past history. So where I come from, it shows me—without the past, you don't have a future; and by studying the past—not living in the past but studying the past—you can work towards creating a future. I didn't start with the past when I first started writing. I started *Catherine Carmier* with more of the '60s in mind, but then I realized that I had not said enough in that book. So I went back in *Of Love and Dust,* which was about the '40s. And then I noticed I still had not said enough to explain Marcus or the rest of the people, so I must go further and further back.

So it was then that I decided to go back to *Miss Jane Pittman* to try to say something about our present because at that time when I was writing *Miss Jane Pittman* was the time when all these demonstrations were going on in, you know, in the South here. I remember someone asked me once, out in San Francisco, "Gaines, what are you doing?" I said, "Oh, I'm writing a story about an ex-slave. She lives to be 110." "Gaines, man, people are writing about revolution and you're writing about an old slave? Man, come on, Gaines." I said, "Well, you know, I have to explain: I think by understanding her position or what happened, it ex-

plained this world and the conditions we're in today."
"Oh, man, Gaines. People are writing about the revolution; nobody's interested in an old lady that lived to be 110 years old." I said, "Well, okay. I was going to write about it anyhow," so I went and wrote about it.

KC: So you were really trailblazing because now we've had several writers who've gone back and written about it, but you did it at a time when slavery wasn't on the books.

EG: Yeah.

KC: And it sounds like you took a lot of heat for that.

EG: I did, I did. They cut me up and they cut me up.

KC: Your decision to write about slavery reminds me of something I learned in doing research for my book on Ann Petry. She said that she was interested in young people's learning, so she visited schools; this reminded her of when she was a student. She observed the similarity between the books she read and those currently being used in how they represented slavery, which always depicted slaves singing and happily content in their subjugation. This compelled her to write a book on Harriet Tubman for young people to show them that slavery was being misrepresented in their textbooks—that even in slavery there were many enslaved people who resisted, like Miss Jane Pittman, right, who spoke up.

EG: Yeah, but now a lot of white students have to read those same types of books and then they read *The Autobiography of Miss Jane Pittman*. Then they'd tell me, "We have never been taught any of this. We never read it," and they never had to read anything about it until reading this. And you know, *Miss Jane* is required reading in France.

(Laughter.)

KC: I'm just fascinated because the topic is still so relevant. *12 Years a Slave* is important. *Beloved* is important. But you know, it's important for us to know that there's a history of people who were writing about these things before it was popular to do so. There's such an interest now in slavery and trauma and memory, and those things are absolutely important, but we still need to go back.

EG: You know, there's this actor who I used to—I respected him a lot before I read about him just the other day. This guy's name is Oldman, Oldman—

KC: Gary Oldman?

EG: Yeah. I liked his acting and everything. But I read an article—was it yesterday or the day before—where he says he agreed with— what's that guy who insulted the Jewish community that one time, that very successful actor?

KC: Mel Gibson?

EG: Mel Gibson, right. And he says, "We can't say anything about anybody. We're too politically incorrect to criticize anybody." And he said that if you didn't vote for *12 Years a Slave* for the Academy Award, you were considered a racist. You know, you still have those kind of people running around out here.

KC: Oh, absolutely.
Let's see, Mr. Gaines. Where are we? Here's something I want to ask you. Many of your most celebrated counterparts—Chester Himes, Wright, Baldwin—found America so racially hostile that they migrated to Europe. Though you didn't take this route, most of your works—and you correct me if I'm wrong—but most of

your works were written while you were on the West Coast, and
several of your protagonists are "prodigal sons"—most famously
Grant in *Lesson,* but also Jackson in *Catherine Carmier.* Would
you say that you were a sort of "domestic expatriate," that you had
to leave the South in order to embroider the stories and conflicts
of your fellow southerners? Did leaving fuel your ability to recreate your native soil in all of its heroism, horror, and tragedy?

EG: I left the South because my people wanted me to be educated because nobody in the history of our families had ever gone beyond
high school on either side. So that's why I left the South. I think
the greatest thing from my life was leaving the South when I was
fifteen years old. I think there's a reason, that there's a reason that
could have happened to me. The next greatest thing was returning to Louisiana because that helped me with my writing. I could
not have written if I had not come back. I was—I hadn't been back
permanently when I wrote *Miss Jane* or *Of Love and Dust* or *A
Gathering of Old Men,* but I was constantly coming back. I was
always coming back. I never thought I was an expatriate. I always
felt that only the body had gone to California, but everything, the
soul, stayed—remained in Louisiana.
I never felt that I was ever going to give up Louisiana for California. I think I could have survived in California. I could have survived. But it would not have been the same as being here, because
this sixty acres of land here is home, and I never felt that any part
of California was home. I just thought that was a temporary place
for me, because I felt that eventually I would have—eventually I
would have come back here to die here. I didn't know when I was
coming back. I came back when I was in my fifties.

KC: And that's when you started teaching at Lafayette?

EG: Teaching at—yeah. But leaving in '48 was the biggest move to
save my life. Coming back and fifteen years later, in '63, to spend
six weeks—six months—in Baton Rouge was the greatest move to

help my writing. Yeah, those two dates; but first I had to go. I had to leave in order to come back, you know. I saw some of these expatriates, and we spent a year in France. I taught the first course in creative writing in the history of France at the Rennes, University of Rennes.

KC: And what year was that?

EG: That was 1996. And we were able to—we lived there about four months, five months, and then the rest of the year we lived in Paris. I used to run into these expatriates. I didn't see all of them, but I didn't see anyone who was really happy. They—I just had a feeling that they wished they could—and I wish they could—they wished they could come back, but they had been gone so long that they were now ashamed to return. Do you guys know this guy, Emmanuel something, something Emmanuel?

KC: Is he a writer?

EG: Yeah, a writer. He put that book together, that collection of stories by—oh, I have it somewhere, they're probably in my office—by Negro writers. He put that together in the '60s, I think. Anyway, he just seemed unhappy. What was Emmanuel's name, honey, his first name or last name? James Emmanuel?

DG: James Emmanuel.

KC: Right, right.

DG: He's a poet.

KC: Your comment made me think about a couple of things. I remember August Wilson talked about how black people leaving the South was a real mistake. He believed that all of our communities and institutions were in the South. And then your observation about expatriates made me think about Baldwin. People always assumed that he considered Paris his home instead of the United States, but he said, "You don't ever leave your home. You take your home with you—you better, otherwise, you're homeless." And so it's interesting that he was echoing your sentiments about where you're from being important in terms of who you are, and you can't get away from that.

EG: Right.

KC: Let's see. I just have a couple more things. In several interviews, you've been asked about how major American male writers have influenced your writing. But your work, as far as I read it, belongs to a rich tradition of southern women writers as well—Zora Neale Hurston, Margaret Walker, the recently departed Maya Angelou, Alice Walker. Though I don't recall you having read women writers as an adolescent and as a blossoming writer—you've talked about not having read any black writers—but are there any women writers whose works you subsequently discovered and admired?

EG: I admire all of their work, but I've never been influenced by any one, any; to be honest, I've not been influenced by any African American writer. I have been influenced by our music, especially our blues and especially our rural blues. Those are the—that's the great inspiration in my life. A friend of mine wrote me from Washington, DC, a lady friend of mine whom I knew and had known at ULL [University of Louisiana at Lafayette], and she told me that every morning a young African American man would get on the elevator whistling Mozart, whistling Mozart, to distinguish himself from any other African American. To say, "You know, I'm not—"

Well, I wrote her back and said, "You know, I like Mozart." I said, "I like Mozart. I like Haydn. I like Brahms," I said. "But I also like Leadbelly, Lightnin' Hopkins, Big Bill Broonzy, all of them," I said, "I really"—and he could have whistled one of those tunes as well. I said, "That's where I get the title from, [Gaines's collected volume of essays and stories] *Mozart and Leadbelly.*"

KC: Yes.

EG: I said, "Mozart taught me how to build a house—that is, having read white writers, the only literature we were always taught at school from junior high school to high school, college." I said, "They showed me how to construct the stories, how to—your subconscious is able to do all these things." But Leadbelly told me what to put into the house, see? I think all of our literature is like that. We draw from both sides. So this young man can draw as much from Leadbelly as he can from Mozart. I said, "Well, the answer to that is because we—everything we do is, we're drawing from the white man as well as our own African American experience. Combine the two."

KC: Absolutely. I like the architecture metaphor that you used. And it's interesting when you talk about locating the blues as such an inspiring artistic force. I remember Baldwin saying that he couldn't finish *Go Tell It on the Mountain* while he was in France. But he said listening to a Bessie Smith record while he was in Switzerland—not France—and listening to her and Mahalia Jackson took him back to Harlem. And August Wilson has said, again, listening to Bessie Smith, that was when he knew he was going to be a writer. So it was something about that blues that was transformative.

EG: Oh yeah.

KC: Well, it's funny. What you just said sort of anticipated my next question, "Are there specific musicians who may have stimulated your imagination?" And you just named a whole bunch of them, so that was the answer to that.

Just a couple more things, Mr. Gaines, on "The Writing Life."
So critics have always foregrounded—and I would say often
exaggerated—writers' critiques of each other: Wright and Baldwin, Wright and Ellison, you and Wright and Ellison, right? But
what receives far less attention is the convivial, heartfelt relationships amongst some writers. So for example, Baldwin was
very close to Lorraine Hansberry and Maya Angelou. Have you
developed any literary friendships that might counter what often
seems writers' dismissal of each other?

EG: I didn't understand all of it.

KC: So in other words, have you developed any friendships with
other writers? I'm sorry—editors have always told me that I use
ten thousand words when I could use ten, so forgive me.

(Laughter.)

EG: All right. I wouldn't say I have any strong relationships with any
other writers, but I've had contact with some writers. What is it,
like, Michael Harper, the poet.

KC: Yes, he taught at Brown for years.

EG: Right, right. Ishmael Reed, I've known. Al Young, I've known. Alice—

DG: Alice Walker.

EG: Alice Walker, yeah.

KC: So you've had contact with Alice Walker?

EG: Oh, yeah. Quite a few times, yeah. But it's nothing like—we don't
send each other Christmas cards or anything like that or call one
another on the phone. We don't do anything like that, but now

that I don't get around much anymore, I very seldom see or go to these gatherings where writers are.

KC: Your mentioning Alice Walker reminds me of a quote from the writer Gayl Jones. I remember she said in an interview that was published in a volume called *Chants of Saints* from the late '70s, "When I think of Ernest Gaines, I think of voice and story." And I thought, boy, that is—that's it. That's the heart of it. I think of people talking and think of them weaving their narratives.

EG: I never did read anybody say that about me, but I think that's what I try to do. Yeah, if I believe in the character and the story, I—someone had asked me how do I write, get into the mind of a character. I said, "Well, you first, you have to hear the voice, hear the voice of the character. Then I can see how to make that a child or an older lady or just a tough guy or somebody. I said I have to get that voice and once I get that voice down, I said I can make it work." So I forgot who I was talking to, some group somewhere. The next morning, I read in the newspaper, "Writer hears voices."

(Laughter.)

I said, I didn't say that—

KC: This person just didn't hear your voice.

EG: Good thing he didn't ask me how'd you get this old lady's voice or how'd you get the little boy. You have that voice down. You have to get that voice. You have to hear it every day over and over and over. "Writer hears voices."

KC: So Mr. Gaines, it's funny. You've created probably over a hundred characters. Is there any one that you would say stood out that gave you particular trouble in terms of trying not just to find their voice but fill in their life story or history, or not?

EG: I had a lot of difficulty writing *In My Father's House*. I tried to
write it from a first-person point of view, but I couldn't get one
character who would know everything. I couldn't put it into
Phillip Martin's narrative or what's his name, Robert X's. Or that
other guy who ran around—what's his name?

KC: Chippo Simon?

EG: Chippo. I just couldn't ever get a voice for him. Never got a single
voice which would carry the story. I could have done it in multiple
voices, but I went back and did the best I can. I've been reading
parts of *In My Father's House* recently, and I've been really pat-
ting myself on the shoulder, yes, you know, some of this is pretty
good.

(Laughter.)

KC: You deserve to pat yourself on the shoulder. But of all of your
books, that one has gotten the least attention. Why do you think
that is? I mean, I've just recently reread it and it's so rich.

EG: Yeah, yeah, yeah. It has got the least attention. I remember
[interviewer] Pat Rickles said that it was the—not coldest, but
the darkest book she'd ever read. Maybe that's it. I felt that people
didn't see that vibrant movement and characters, so they end
up with *A Gathering of Old Men* or *Miss Jane* or something like
Of Love and Dust, they'd say the same thing, it's slow. It takes
place in winter too, you know, and it's omniscient. It's cold and—
everybody's cold around the place.

KC: One of the things that fascinates me about Reverend Phillip
Martin is how he's so focused on the political and the civil rights
movement that he's almost foreclosed or tried to erase the personal. But you show in the novel vividly and movingly that you
can't erase the personal. The personal is political in some ways or

is more important than the political. And you can try to erase it or move it out to California or whatever, but ultimately, you've got to deal with the personal.

EG: Yeah, yeah, yeah. I think Phillip questions God when he let these two white men hold him down on the floor when he falls and then the white liberal stuff, you know, and he goes and he asks God, "Why'd you let me do this? You know, why? Why? I could have knocked their hands away in a way that's easy as knocking away a fly. Why'd you let me stay down there?" He's questioning God.

KC: Mr. Gaines, I've got just a few more things I wanted to ask you. Looking back on your five decades as a preeminent voice in American literature, do you think you've paid a price for your success? Has there been a cost for becoming a successful writer?

EG: A cost, yes. I was determined to become a writer; I was determined to become a writer, so I sacrificed much. I sacrificed family. I didn't get married until I was sixty, because I didn't want to. If I had gotten married earlier, I would have had a broken family, I know, because I didn't want that. I didn't want any child of mine to grow up without a parent. Asking me about the thing that I regret most that I can—I worked only hard enough to keep myself going. I didn't make [enough] that I could give gifts at Christmas or birthday presents or things like that. Those are the kind of things that, well, I regret—but had I not done it, made the sacrifices, I don't think I would have written what I've written.

KC: I talk so much about Baldwin because he's an important writer to me as well. And I remember one documentary in which his mother was interviewed and she said, "Well, he *had* to write." And it sounds like what you're saying is that, despite the cost you paid, you had to write.

EG: Oh, yeah. I don't think writers write unless they have to write. I don't know why—yeah, you have to write because you have to get that monkey off your back or whatever it is. You have to do it.

KC: So it sounds like you wouldn't have done anything any differently, even knowing the cost now that you paid; you wouldn't have done anything any differently—or would you?

EG: No, I don't think so. You're asking me, would I, knowing what I know today, have gotten married and raised a family—

KC: Right, and not chosen the writing life or focused on it so much.

EG: Right. No, no, no—I don't think so. I have a book in there by Duke Ellington, *Music Is My Mistress.* My writing was my everything. I've had a few ladies in my life, but I wasn't—as soon as it became serious, I started sneaking away.

(Laughter.)

KC: Back to the typewriter—oh, that's funny. You know, there's one thing I think people miss in your fiction, Mr. Gaines, is that there's a lot of humor, truly funny scenes and situations. Like *Of Love and Dust* with Aunt Margaret banging on that door, "What's going on in there?" when she knows that Louise and Marcus are having sex—that's funny.

(Laughter.)

EG: And moving back and running.

KC: Right—she's determined.

EG: She said, "Boy, I hope you're not doing what I think you're doing."

KC: Right. So it's somewhat unfortunate that people focus so much

on the heavy and the ponderous and the difficult so much that
they miss the—

EG: Right, right, right. And they miss the humor.

KC: As your writing shows, it's a vital part of our southern experience.
Okay, Mr. Gaines, one last question. James Baldwin said in
the late '70s that "America has not changed" fundamentally.
But perhaps he could not foresee the seismic election of Barack
Obama in 2008, not to mention his reelection. So, clearly America
has progressed regarding its treatment of and attitudes about its
native sons and daughters. Some have gone as far as to say we're
living in a "post-racial" moment, right—that Du Bois's declaration
that "the problem of the 20th century is the problem of the color
line" is now an outdated notion. What is your assessment of our
current racial landscape?

EG: Some things have changed; some things never will. You know,
I live as well as 99 percent of the people, white or black, in this
state where I live. You know, I have things and share a camp down
there by the river and a church in the backyard, a guest house over
there, pecan trees, apple trees, all that stuff around here. But who-
ever's living that same way—and everyone knows us—Mr. Gaines
and, you know, the police or the banker or the postal people, they
all know Mr. Gaines or "Mr. Ernest," they call me, and "Miss Dianne." But at the same time, my brother would not get that same
kind of treatment. I don't think it's changed to the point where
racism is "post"—that we're post-racism. I don't think that. But of
course, things are better today than they were when Baldwin was
here.

KC: Sure.

EG: Here in Louisiana, and especially in the southern states, I think
it's changed much more in the southern states than in those

other states. One of the most racist, I mean, segregated cities is Chicago. Chicago is segregated; Milwaukee is the same way, you know, it's segregated.

KC: There was just a documentary on the other night about how segregated Chicago is.

EG: Yeah, right. So you hear, you find out a lot of movement in places. You know, when we go to restaurants, white restaurants, you know, we're just going to the restaurant. We don't expect someone to, you know, not serve you.

KC: So the overt racism that you knew as a child has certainly dissipated, if not disappeared completely.

EG: At the same time, you know, you're having problems. I have a nephew who works for the government and he said he would see some hatred. He's come to my place where I work and mentioned Barack Obama's name and said, "Man, these people hate this man. They hate him. They hate Hillary." But it's changed. Yes, he became president of the United States, but look at those people out there now. And they want to cooperate with him? No matter what he tries to do, they can say, "Well, Obama didn't get this done. He didn't do this. He promised to do this. He didn't do this." How can he? You know, the government is—I mean, when he does something by executive decree, they criticize him for that, right? So our mayor here in Baton Rouge is black. The mayor of New Roads, our little town here, is black. But the truth is you still have some racist bastards around.

KC: And it's funny, we were talking about sports earlier, and I don't know if you heard about this, about six weeks ago, maybe a couple of months ago, Hank Aaron said exactly what you just said. He said that the way some politicians treat Obama is like, I don't know if he used the N-word, but he said they treat him really badly. And do you know that people starting emailing Hank Aaron, this is eighty-year-old Hank Aaron, and saying, "How dare you," calling *him* the N-word. "We're going to burn your jersey. We're going to—"; this is Hank Aaron. And they did that in '74 [when he broke Babe Ruth's home-run record], and the country was more racist in '74, but this is 2014 and they said these things to Hank, eighty-year-old Hank Aaron. So we haven't quite overcome.

EG: I don't think I'll see it in my lifetime. I've received the Medal of the Arts from—

DG: President Obama.

EG: No, no, Clinton.

DG: Oh, Clinton first.

EG: The National Art—

KC: You've gotten it twice?

EG: I think I'm the only person who's gotten both of those medals [National Medal of Arts and National Humanities Medal]. Like, when they called to tell me that I received the medal, the National Medal of Art, I said, "You know, I have received a medal already," and I said, "I received it from President Clinton." And they said that was the National Humanities Medal. I said, "Yeah." I said, "It's not the same?" And she said—the director of the National Endowment of the Arts—and she says, "No, it's not the same." I said, "I don't want to be embarrassed if I get up there and they say, 'You have one already,' and I don't want to be embarrassed." Oh, she said, "Oh, no, we looked at all of that already." I said, oh, okay.

DG: We'd done our homework.

EG: Yeah, we'd done our homework. I said, okay, I'll show up.

KC: And Mr. Gaines, how did you feel when you won that MacArthur Award? That is so prestigious. I forgot, was it in the '80s or '90s?

DG: Nineteen ninety-three.

KC: 'Ninety-three—do you remember it? Can you say something about that, about how you felt when you learned that you had won a MacArthur?

EG: Oh, yeah. See, I didn't believe it. I was at [University of Southwest Louisiana]. Oh, I think I said, "Oh, are you sure I won it?" "Yes." I said, "Well, how much money is it?"

(Laugher.)

KC: Let's cut to the chase.

EG: Yeah, right. Talk about how much money it is. And she told me. I was, like, oh, okay.

KC: Do you remember how much it was? Do you mind saying, or no?

EG: $375,000. Today, it's over $500,000.

DG: But the dollar is worth less today.

EG: Yeah. $375,000, and they pay it off in five years. When I was going to Stanford, I got $2,500? [the Wallace Stegner Fellowship to study creative writing in 1958]. Anyway, Stegner gave us all our money at one time and he just got this guy, this Jewish guy, out of jail, and he gave him that money—this guy was a fellow along with me—and he bought a big old white Cadillac.

(Laughter.)

A Brief Post-Interview Riff: On Libraries, "Liberals," and Racial Climate Change

Like predecessors Richard Wright and James Baldwin, Ernest Gaines has never shied away from the public sphere, granting numerous interviews that have appeared in a range of outlets, popular and scholarly alike. Though some of the topics we discussed had been addressed in previous interviews (for example, his beginnings as the ten-year-old scribe on River Lake Plantation, the nineteenth-century Russian literary "masters" whom he emulated), I was struck by his ruminations on a range of topics: how adolescent reading was a portal to his lifetime work, the biases brazenly expressed by celebrated Hollywood actors, and our current racial landscape—his thoughts about the latter bringing to mind Amiri Baraka's oft-quoted phrase "The Changing Same," which he coined in his seminal writings on black music in the 1960s. I offer here cursory post-interview musings—a riff—on these disparate topics.

The Vallejo Public Library became a sort of crucible in young Ernest's budding literary imagination, the newly arrived teenaged transplant choosing it over the YMCA, where he'd been bludgeoned in the boxing ring. This bastion of learning, from which he was barred in 1940s Louisiana, conjures images of fellow black scribes from Wright and Baldwin to Malcolm X and James Alan McPherson—all of whom have similarly claimed libraries as both learning oases and creative wombs. Gaines's recollections brought back two particularly galling if illuminating episodes separated by more than a century: the violent reaction of young Frederick Douglass's master upon learning that his wife has been teaching the precocious young boy to read; and a white man slapping McPherson on an Atlanta street, the young man's offense being that he dared to appear in public carrying books he'd checked out from the just-desegregated public library.

I was a bit surprised when Gaines mentioned Mel Gibson and Gary

Oldman, though in retrospect this might not have been so unexpected given his protracted experiences with an entertainment industry that adapted several of his works for the small screen. Specifically, the author was referencing these actors' not-quite-post-racial utterances: Gibson's respective 2006 and 2010 rants—"The Jews are responsible for all the wars in the world!"; "You [his then girlfriend] look like a fucking pig in heat. If you get raped by a pack of niggers, it will be your fault"—elicited this defense from Oldman: "I don't know about Mel. He got drunk and said a few things, but we've all said those things" ("Caught on Tape"). Gaines's unprompted broaching of this topic and reaction to these lavishly praised actors' boorish, unenlightened views dovetail with recent controversies such as "#OscarsSoWhite," the hashtag engendered by the Motion Picture Academy's failure to nominate *any* people of color for acting awards in 2016 (ignored were the highly lauded films *Creed* and *Straight Outta Compton,* which featured African American actors in lead and supporting roles). Most recently, the feel-good biopic *Green Book,* despite earning the "Best Picture" statuette in 2019, was excoriated for sanitizing its racially complex subject matter and whitewashing the actual history of *The Negro Motorist Green Book*—a literal compendium of hotels, restaurants, and other businesses which catered to black travelers during the Jim Crow era.

Addressing my query on race relations in twenty-first-century America, Gaines sounded both personally buoyed but ultimately less than sanguine. Though grateful for the patina of respect that has accompanied literary celebrity, along with the accoutrements of financial success, he nevertheless strikes a far from optimistic chord regarding appreciable racial progress. As an addendum to our discussion, I'd proffer our current rancid racial-political climate as exhibits A through Z to lend credence to his perspective: the demonizing and scapegoating of immigrants, the barring of entire groups based on their religion from a land that trumpets its commitment to "religious liberty," the resurgence of white nationalism and the racial/ethnic violence that underpins it, and the shooting of African American Alton Sterling by two white Baton Rouge police officers in 2016.

These events conjure thoughts of Gaines's early story "The Sky Is Gray," where racial climate change was imminent but gnawingly variable and precarious, akin to the sun attempting to penetrate seemingly impenetrable clouds. Or to echo Gaines himself, America has never been and remains far from being "post" when it comes to racial animus, not quite having metamorphosed into the "Beloved Community" that Martin Luther King Jr. dreamed in his halcyon forecast for what our nation *could* become. I can only hope that his prodigious body of fiction (and nonfiction) will help foster our ongoing evolution, the lessons therein as vital in twenty-first-century America as they were in the decade in which Gaines published his first fiction, a decade marked by the tragedy of Emmett Till and the heroism of Rosa Parks.

NOTES

Introduction

1. The following sources were consulted for background material on Gaines: Lowe, "Chronology"; "Ernest J. Gaines," achievment.org/achiever; and Yon, "Gaines, Ernest J."

2. This quote appeared originally in the following, which was reprinted in Lowe's *Conversations with Ernest Gaines*: Ruth Laney, "Southern Sage Savors His Rise to Success," *Emerge*, May 1994, 66–67.

3. Perhaps most infamous is the case of Gaines's southern counterpart Walker: the film adaptation of her Pulitzer-winning *The Color Purple* reaped astronomical profits for everyone except its author. In *The Same River Twice*, she ruminates upon her futile efforts to obtain her share of the film's earnings. She also includes letters written seeking remuneration. Appealing to her own attorneys, she wrote: "I would settle for $3,000,000. I come to this figure based on my belief that at least 100,000,000 has been realized in profit and that 3% of that is due me based on my contract" (Walker, *The Same River Twice* 266). Considering this entreaty retrospectively, and with more than a twinge of resignation, she lamented: "Reading these letters now I see the humor in my willingness to 'settle' for three million. Though my lawyer was able to get a portion of the monies I considered due to me, as I understood my contract, in the ten years since the movie was released I have received a fraction of this amount" (266). Irony upon ironies: the novel was noteworthy for its unique epistolary style, the heroine Celie's "Letters to God" detailing her sexual abuse being the most moving.

1. Sugarcane, Railroad Cars, Prisons, Peoples: Dominant Themes and Topics

1. For specific scholarship on Gaines's treatment of African American masculinity, see works by the following critics in the reference list at the end of this volume: Auger, Clark, Crisu, Jones, Magill, Nash, Thompson, and Wilson.

2. For an incisive discussion of the historical and metaphorical meanings of space in Gaines's work, see Thadious Davis's "Parishes & Prisons: Ernest Gaines's Louisiana & Its North Carolina Kin Space," chapter 5 of *Southscapes: Geographies of Race, Region, and Literature*, 257–334.

2. Catherine Carmier

1. Incest recurs as a central theme in two of Faulkner's masterpieces. In *The Sound and the Fury* (1929), Quentin Compson's obsession with sister Candace's sexuality begins in their childhood and extends well into adulthood, perhaps one of the many psychological demons that impel his suicide during his freshman year at Harvard. The threat of sibling incest also looms even larger in *Absalom, Absalom!* (1936), where patriarch Thomas Sutpen fathers a son, Charles Bon, with his first wife who, unbeknownst to him at the time, is mixed-race. Disposing of her and the child upon learning this, Sutpen then marries a fellow white southerner who bears him two children, Judith and Henry. The adult Charles meets and befriends his half-brother at the University of Mississippi, and the castoff mulatto son becomes engaged to Judith to effect the ultimate revenge. However, Henry eventually learns of their common patrilineage, and with the threat of miscegenation being more egregious than incest, Henry murders his half-brother at the gates of their father's plantation.

2. In her study *Saints, Sinners, Saviors: Strong Black Women in African American Literature,* Trudier Harris charts the development of such characters in popular culture and literature, of which Hansberry's Lena Younger is a prototype. Though such domineering, uber-pious figures have been apotheosized in African American culture, Harris explores the overlooked downside of such cultural representations: "Seldom have we stopped to think, however, that this thing called strength, this thing we applaud so much in black women, could also have detrimental effects or consequences.... Strength frequently perpetuates dysfunctionality in literary families, where the strong dispositions and actions of black female characters have negative impacts upon the lives of their relatives" (10).

3. "What does Raoul mean?"

3. Of Love and Dust

1. In her biocritical study, Wilson scholar Sandra Shannon expatiates upon how the twenty-year-old budding poet embarked upon his artistic apprenticeship, much of which occurred in the same cultural spaces that shaped Gaines. Shannon writes about this informal but inestimable curriculum, especially so given that he'd dropped out of high school: "Without much of a fuss, Wilson moved out of his mother's apartment, took a job as a short-order cook, and began frequenting the tobacco houses, bars, and restaurants of Pittsburgh's Hill District. For Wilson, then known as 'Youngblood' among the older men around him, this education was just as valuable as that provided by the system he had recently abandoned. These usually male-dominated establishments took the place of the stuffy classrooms where he had been fed a steady diet of Eurocentric writers" (*The Dramatic Vision of August Wilson* 18).

2. Throughout the interviews collected in Lowe's *Conversations with Ernest Gaines,* as well as in copious critical treatments of "Three Men," Procter's name is frequently

spelled "Proctor." Since the name appeared as "Procter" in the original 1968 edition of *Bloodline*, I take that to be the correct spelling.

3. In all of these iconic works of American and African American literature, miscegenation is a prominent theme: Frederick Douglass, *Narrative* (1845); Harriet Jacobs, *Incidents in the Life of a Slave Girl* (1861); James Weldon Johnson, *The Autobiography of an Ex-Colored Man* (1912); Langston Hughes, *Mulatto* (1935); William Faulkner, *Absalom, Absalom!* (1936); Zora Neale Hurston, *Their Eyes Were Watching God* (1937); Richard Wright, "Long Black Song" (1938); and James Baldwin, *Another Country* (1962).

4. Even before DNA evidence proved incontrovertibly that Thomas Jefferson fathered several children by the enslaved Sally Hemings, writers such as William Wells Brown had conjectured as much; see *Clotel* (1853), the first novel to be published by an African American. For a contemporary fictive treatment, see Barbara Chase-Riboud's groundbreaking novel *Sally Hemings* (1979). For a historical examination, see Annette Gordon-Reed's definitive study, *The Hemingses of Monticello: An American Family* (2009).

5. Writing about interracial marriage in late-nineteenth and early twentieth-century Louisiana, anthropologist Virginia Domínguez asserts, "White legislators sought to prevent all forms of continued sexual contact between the 'pure' and the 'impure,' and it was clear by the turn of the century, if not before, that prohibiting interracial marriage alone would not achieve this goal. Thus, in 1908, the legislature passed a bill (Act 87 of the regular session, p. 105) making concubinage 'between a person of the Caucasian race and a person of the negro race a felony, fixing the punishment therefore and defining what shall constitute concubinage'" (*White by Definition* 29).

6. For background on Angola State Prison's history, see "Angola State Prison: A Short History," Voices Behind Bars, ccnmtl.columbia.edu/projects/caseconsortium/ casestudies/54/casestudy/www/layout/case_id_54_id_547.html.

4. *Bloodline*

1. Published in 1941 in *Atlantic Monthly*, Welty's story portrays an elderly black woman's strenuous journey from a rural town to Natchez, Mississippi, to purchase medicine for her grandson.

2. About his depiction of racial inequality in the story, Gaines explains: "I don't do it overtly, I don't show the racism and prejudice. I don't have to go kicking people out or saying awful things to people. However, during the entire day of 'The Sky Is Gray,' the people can't go into certain places.... although many things have broken down since the 1940s when 'The Sky is Gray' took place, but there are many of those walls that are still there, invisible walls to most people, but they're still there" (*Conversations* 257–58).

3. Two of the most famous biblical instances involving washing as a means of providing comfort and displaying genuine affection include Christ's washing of his disciples' feet in John 13:14–17 and a "sinful woman" washing Christ's feet with her tears in Luke 7:36–39.

4. Gaines clarifies any confusion regarding Copper's insistence that he's a member of

the armed services and a war veteran: "No, no no. He makes that up; there's no such thing as war. He created that whole thing himself. There is no army" (*Conversations* 260).

5. One of the defining moments in Invisible Man's coming-of-age occurs in the novel's first chapter in which his grandfather dispenses uncharacteristically radical advice on challenging white domination through dissemblance. By donning a figurative "mask" of docility and servility, instructs the grandfather, African Americans can engage in covert actions to disrupt white supremacy while appearing compliant—that is, acting in stereotypical ways (for example, the Sambo) to conceal subversive and liberating actions. On his deathbed the grandfather rails: "Son, after I'm gone I want you to keep up the good fight. . . . Live with your head in the lion's mouth. I want you to overcome 'em with yeses, undermine 'em with grins, agree 'm to death and destruction, let 'em swoller you till they vomit or bust wide open" (Ellison, *Invisible Man* 16).

5. *The Autobiography of Miss Jane Pittman*

1. *Lay My Burden Down* (1945), a WPA volume containing short interviews conducted with formerly enslaved persons during the 1930s, became Gaines's "Bible" as he was researching and writing the novel (*Conversations* 94). Further, he notes, "After reading so many of them (I forget how many [interviews] I read, maybe a hundred), I got a rhythm, a speech, a dialogue, and a vocabulary that an ex-slave would have had" (95).

2. Consider Jane's self-assertion in the context of this excerpt from Truth's oration: "The man over there says that women need to be helped into carriages, and lifted over ditches, and to have the best place everywhere. Nobody ever helps me into carriages, or over mud-puddles, or gives me any best place! And ain't I a woman? Look at me! Look at my arm! I have ploughed and planted, and gathered into barns, and no man could head me! And ain't I a woman? I could work as much and eat as much as a man—when I could get it—and bear the lash as well!" ("Sojourner Truth").

3. In the essay "Miss Jane and I" (1978), Gaines writes extensively about a 1967 visit to the home of friend and fellow Louisiana writer Alvin Aubert. During their wide-ranging discussion, Gaines shared his idea for writing a novel "about a 110-year-old woman who is born into slavery" (*Mozart and Leadbelly* 18). Gaines also writes that he and Aubert "talked about a black professor who had been killed in 1903 for trying to teach young African Americans to read and write and to look after their health. His grave is on the bank of the False River, about five miles from where I was born. My wife, Dianne, and I go by there all the time to stand in silence a moment" (19). This, clearly, became the basis for Ned's life and death.

6. *In My Father's House*

1. The positions King explicates in his momentous "Letter from Birmingham Jail" appear to have been guideposts for Reverend Martin's own thinking. Famously identi-

fying "two opposing forces in the Negro community," King professes about the second: "The other force is one of bitterness and hatred, and it comes perilously close to advocating violence. It is expressed in the various black nationalist groups that are springing up across the nation, the largest and best-known being Elijah Muhammad's Muslim movement. . . . I have tried to stand between these two forces, saying that we need emulate neither the 'do-nothingism' of the complacent nor the hatred and despair of the black nationalist. For there is the more excellent way of love and non-violent protest" (601).

2. "Father Divine" (around 1876–1965) was born James Baker and founded the "Peace Mission" in the 1930s, which still exists well into the twenty-first century ("Father Divine"). "The 'Honorable' Elijah Muhammad" (formerly Elijah Poole; 1897–1975) was a prominent leader in the Nation of Islam (the Black Muslims), from the 1940s until his death ("Elijah Muhammad"). "Reverend Ike" (Frederick Joseph Eikerenkoetter II; 1935–2009) was one of the first and most popular black "televangelists" in the 1970s, well known for his lavish lifestyle and gimmicky appeals for donations ("Reverend Ike"). The most recent of these hugely charismatic ministers, Eddie Long (1953–2017) pastored a "megachurch" in suburban Atlanta that, at its peak, had 25,000 members in the first decade of the new century. Long became embroiled in sexual scandal in 2010, which led to a precipitous decline in membership ("Controversial Megachurch Pastor Eddie Long Dies"). James Baldwin's Gabriel Grimes from his autobiographical first novel, *Go Tell It on the Mountain* (1953), is perhaps the most famous preacher in African American literature. Based partly on the author's own tortured childhood relationship with fundamentalist preacher/stepfather David Baldwin, the novel treats Reverend Grimes's emotionally abusive relationship with fourteen-year-old John Grimes, the stepson he torments as a "bastard" because Gabriel's wife Elizabeth never married John's father. Gabriel is himself the quintessence of Christian hypocrisy, preaching hell and damnation for "sinners" while secretly fathering a child with Esther, whom he deems a "harlot."

3. *Harper's Bible Dictionary* provides the following glosses: "Joanna: According to Luke 8:3, the wife of Chuza, Herod's (i.e., Herod Antipas) steward, and one of the women who accompanied Jesus. Along with Mary Magdalene, Susanna, and others who 'had been healed of evil spirits and infirmities,' Joanna gave assistance . . . to Jesus and the Twelve. In Luke 24:10, she is one of the women (with Mary Magdalene, Mary the mother of James, and others) who, having gone to anoint Jesus' body, find the tomb empty" (Shuler, "Joanna" 491). Hagar: In Genesis 16:1–16, "Sarai (Sarah) was barren and, in accordance with custom, gave her maidservant to her husband so that she could bear a child in place of her mistress. When Hagar became pregnant, she acted arrogantly toward Sarah and so Sarah, with Abraham's permission, dealt so harshly with her that Hagar fled into the Wilderness of Shur. There she met an angel who announced that she should return to her mistress and that she would bear a son, to be named Ishmael, from whom would spring many descendants" (Berlin, "Hagar" 365).

4. "Black Wall Street" is the popular name associated with Greenwood, Tulsa's successful black business district in the late 1910s and early 1920s. The community was

leveled in one of the deadliest acts of domestic terrorism to occur on American soil: "During the Tulsa Race Riot, which occurred over 18 hours on May 31–June 1, 1921, a white mob attacked residents, homes and businesses in the predominantly black Greenwood neighborhood of Tulsa, Oklahoma. The event remains one of the worst incidents of racial violence in U.S. history and one of the least-known: News reports were largely squelched, despite the fact that hundreds of people were killed and thousands left homeless" ("Tulsa Race Riot").

5. Saidiya Hartman explores sexual violence in nineteenth-century America in her study *Scenes of Subjection*: "The actual or attempted rape of an enslaved woman was an offense neither recognized nor punishable by law. Not only was rape simply unimaginable because of purported black lasciviousness, but also its repression was essential to the displacement of white culpability that characterized both the recognition of black humanity in slave law and the designation of the black subject as the originary locus of transgression and offense" (79–80).

7. A Gathering of Old Men

1. Though Gaines has never mentioned the Deacons for Defense and Justice specifically, he may have been influenced by this group of African American men formed to defend their community against white terrorism. Describing them as "an advocacy group for self-defense," historian Christopher Strain writes, "The group first organized in March 1965, as a nonprofit corporation in Jonesboro, Louisiana, after Klansmen had driven through Jonesboro with a police escort to distribute leaflets. A handful of local black men, all United States Army veterans, decided that if the white power structure would condone and abet such activity, they must do something to help themselves" ("We Walked Like Men" 365). One early instance of the deacons defending the black community occurred in Bogalusa in 1965, when a "cavalcade of cars driven by members of the Ku Klux Klan" invaded a black neighborhood: "When the Klansmen fired randomly into the homes of black Bogalusa residents, a fusillade of bullets met them in return. The unwelcome visitors quickly fled the neighborhood." Though Gaines may not have intentionally modeled his gathered old men after this group, the deacons' real-life actions presaged those of their fictitious brethren-in-arms.

2. George Eliot was of course the male pen name adopted by Mary Ann Evans, the pioneering Victorian novelist and author of such works as *Silas Marner* (1861) and *Middlemarch* (1871–72).

3. Visibility/invisibility has been an enduring and dominant metaphor in African American literature, the most profound examples appearing in two famed works. In *The Souls of Black Folk,* W. E. B. Du Bois originated his most enduring theoretical concept, "double-consciousness": "After the Egyptian and Indian, the Greek and Roman, the Teuton and Mongolian, the Negro is a sort of seventh son, born with a veil, and gifted with second-sight in this American world,—a world which yields him no true

self-consciousness, but only lets him see himself through the revelation of the other world. It is a peculiar sensation, this double-consciousness, this sense of always looking at one's self through the eyes of others, of measuring one's soul by the tape of a world that looks on in amused contempt and pity" (214).

As conceived by Du Bois, "the veil" acts as a murky partition preventing whites from seeing or even imagining African Americans beyond their own severely obscured, prescribed understandings. Analogously, the opening of Ralph Ellison's *Invisible Man* captures African Americans' nonexistence in the collective Anglo-American imagination: "I am an invisible man. . . . I am invisible, understand, simply because people refuse to see me. Like the bodiless heads you see sometimes in circus sideshows, it is as though I have been surrounded by mirrors of hard, distorting glass. When they approach me they see only my surroundings, themselves, or figments of their imagination—indeed, everything and anything except me" (3). Clearly informed by Du Bois, Ellison's protagonist articulates the paradox of African American identity through myriad images of sight/blindness.

4. Gaines drew heavily upon the tragic case of Willie Francis for *A Lesson before Dying*. The seventeen-year-old Francis was convicted of and executed for the murder of a white pharmacist in St. Martinville in what was little more than a kangaroo trial. However, in conceiving the story Coot recounts concerning his teenage son's double execution, Gaines focused on the most depraved and sensational facet of the 1946 case: that the mentally disabled, teenaged Francis was subjected to a second trip to the electric chair after the apparatus initially malfunctioned. The gruesome nature of the case led to an appeal to the U.S. Supreme Court. For further discussion of this miscarriage of justice, see Gilbert King's *The Execution of Willie Francis*.

5. Hamer was a civil rights activist in Mississippi in the 1950s and 1960s, heralded for her herculean efforts to register black voters. These activities landed her in jail, where she endured beatings so severe that they inflicted kidney damage and left her partially blind ("Fannie Lou Hamer").

8. *A Lesson before Dying*

1. Speaking to issues of dubious guilty verdicts in the Jim Crow South, Gilbert King writes in the introduction of his book on the Francis case: "It wasn't until I began talking to some of the older folks in St. Martinville, people who had been around during the 1940s, when the State of Louisiana sent the Negro teenager to the electric chair, that I began to get nods of recognition. With these folks, the name Willie Francis resonated. And time and again the responses I received were the same: 'Willie Frances didn't kill anyone,' or 'There are people in St. Martinville today who know what really happened,' or 'That boy was innocent'" (*The Execution of Willie Francis* xi).

2. Jefferson's description here recalls Wright's iconic 1940 novel *Native Son*. After Bigger Thomas is apprehended for the murder of white heiress Mary Dalton, a newspa-

per headline inaccurately labels him "a Negro sex-slayer" of monstrous proportions and describes him as such: "'He looks exactly like an ape!' exclaimed a terrified young white girl who watched the black slayer being loaded onto a stretcher after he had fainted. His arms are long, hanging in a dangling fashion to his knees. It is easy to imagine how this man, in the grip of a brain-numbing sex passion, overpowered little Mary Dalton, raped her, murdered her, beheaded her, then stuffed her body into a roaring furnace to destroy the evidence of his crime" (260).

3. Gaines pinpoints his motivation for having Miss Emma petition Henri Pichot on behalf of Jefferson, which relates back to the lawmen with whom the author corresponded: "... I develop this whole thing around what she had given to that family. ... You owe me one favor. And she keeps telling him over and over—so what I wanted was a sheriff who could not deny her having someone else visit her son. It was all based around that warden who wouldn't answer my second letter, who was saying 'forget it'" (*Conversations* 306).

4. A punctilious researcher, Gaines sought the assistance of one of his University of Louisiana at Lafayette students to help him draw as precise a portrait of the electric chair as possible: "He brought me pictures of the state prison, pictures of the electric chair—'Gruesome Gerty.' ... I asked him what kind of wood was the chair made of, how much does the chair weigh, how wide and thick were the straps that went around the arms and legs of the condemned. And I kept a picture of the chair on my desk, especially while writing the last chapters of the novel" (*Mozart and Leadbelly* 55).

5. Gaines relates in extensive detail the real-life models on which he based these two resolute women: "On the plantation where I was born, my maternal grandmother worked at the big house as cook for many years, and I myself had worked in the yard there on several occasions, collecting eggs from chickens that laid in the grass, gathering pecans, and picking fruit from the different trees. Now, suppose I made the sheriff's wife a member of the family where my grandmother had worked all these years. Wouldn't she, my grandmother, have done favors, extra favors, for members of that family? Would that be enough reason for her to feel that she could go to them for a favor, which I thought would be a better reason—and more convincing to the reader—to get the sheriff to allow the narrator to visit the prisoner? So I created two elderly women. They were Tante Lou, the narrator's aunt, and Miss Emma, the prisoner's godmother. And those two would apply the pressure" (*Mozart and Leadbelly* 57).

6. Throughout the collected interviews in Lowe's *Conversations with Ernest Gaines*, the author cites Joyce as a chief influence, singling out "Ivy Day in the Committee Room" as especially praiseworthy (76).

9. *The Tragedy of Brady Sims*

1. One of the most frequently quoted passages from Virginia native Booker T. Washington's 1901 autobiography *Up from Slavery* appears in the section "The Atlanta Ex-

position Address." In this speech, delivered to white southern businessmen in 1895, Washington made a heartfelt appeal, extolling the South's potential to uplift his fellow African Americans: "To those of my race who depend on bettering their condition in a foreign land or who underestimate the importance of cultivating friendly relations with the Southern white man, who is their next-door neighbor, I would say: 'Cast down your bucket where you are'—cast it down in making friends in every manly way of the people of all races by whom we are surrounded" (147). Non-southerner James Baldwin viscerally encapsulates the discrepancy between the dual, irreconcilable pastoral and pestilential Souths: "Florida, Georgia, Alabama, Mississippi, for example—there is the great, vast brooding, welcoming and bloodstained land, beautiful enough to astonish and break the heart" (*No Name in the Street* 68). In 1990, Pittsburgh-born Wilson bemoaned blacks' mass outmigration to the industrial but inhospitable northern United States: "One [regrettable historical decision] was the migration to the North. We were a land-based agrarian people from Africa. We were uprooted from Africa, and we spent over 200 years developing our culture as black Americans. And then we left the South. We uprooted ourselves and attempted to transplant this culture to the pavements of the industrialized North. It was a transplant that did not take" (qtd. in Rothstein, "Round Five for a Theatrical Heavyweight").

2. In one of the most searing passages from Douglass's 1845 *Narrative,* he describes a childhood episode that leaves an indelible emotional scar. As he cringes in a closet, he invokes the term "blood-stained" in recounting "this horrible exhibition" of viewing his aunt being stripped and beaten bloody by their master: "It was the blood-stained gate, the entrance to the hell of slavery, through which I was about to pass. It was a most terrible spectacle" (51).

WORKS CONSULTED

Abernathy, Jeff. *To Hell and Back: Race and Betrayal in the Southern Novel.* Athens: University of Georgia Press, 2003.

Ansa, Tina McElroy. "Women in the Movement, Women and Men." In *The Prevailing South,* ed. Dudley Clendinen, 186–93. Atlanta: Longstreet, 1993.

Auger, Philip. "A Lesson about Manhood: Appropriating 'The Word' in Ernest Gaines's *A Lesson Before Dying.*" *Southern Literary Journal* 27, no. 2 (Spring 1995): 74–85.

———. *Native Sons in No Man's Land: Rewriting Afro-American Manhood in the Novels of Baldwin, Walker, Wideman, and Gaines.* New York: Garland, 2000.

Baker, Houston A., Jr. "Incarceration." In *Keywords for Southern Studies,* ed. Scott Romine and Jennifer Rae Greeson, 9–21. Athens: University of Georgia Press, 2016.

Baldwin, James. *No Name in the Street.* New York: Dial, 1972.

Bell, Bernard W. *The Contemporary African American Novel: Its Folk Roots and Modern Literary Branches.* Amherst: University of Massachusetts Press, 2004.

Berlin, Adele. "Hagar." In *Harper's Bible Dictionary,* ed. Paul Achtemeier, 365–66. New York: HarperCollins, 1985.

Brasseaux, Carl A. *French, Cajun, Creole, Houma: A Primer on Francophone Louisiana.* Baton Rouge: Louisiana State University Press, 2005.

Brown, Anne Gray. "Scribe of River Lake Plantation: A Conversation with Ernest J. Gaines." 2006. Rpt. in *Personal Souths: Interviews from The Southern Quarterly,* ed. Douglas B. Chambers, 201–19. Jackson: University Press of Mississippi, 2012.

Bryant, Jerry H. *Born in a Mighty Bad Land: The Violent Man in African American Folklore and Fiction.* Bloomington: Indiana University Press, 2003.

Byerman, Keith E. "Ernest J. Gaines." *Dictionary of Literary Biography.* Vol. 33: *Afro-American Fiction Writers after 1955,* ed. Thadious M. Davis and Trudier Harris, 84–96. Detroit: Gale, 1984.

"Caught on Tape: Mel Gibson Race Rant to Girlfriend." www.independent
.co.uk/news/world/americas/caught-on-tape-mel-gibson-rac
e-rant-to-girlfriend-2017256.html (accessed May 23, 2019).

Clark, Keith. *Black Manhood in James Baldwin, Ernest J. Gaines, and August Wilson.* Urbana: University of Illinois Press, 2002.

"Controversial Megachurch Pastor Eddie Long Dies at 63." www.cnn.
com/2017/01/15/us/bishop-eddie-long-dead/ (accessed May 31, 2019).

Crisu, Corina Anghel. "'Tell Nannan I Walked': Reconstructing Manhood in Ernest J. Gaines's *A Lesson before Dying.*" *Zeitschrift für Anglistik und Amerikanistik* 55, no. 2 (2007): 155–72.

Davis, Thadious M. "Parishes & Prisons: Ernest Gaines's Louisiana & Its North Carolina Kin Space." Chap. 5 of *Southscapes: Geographies of Race, Region, and Literature,* 257–334. Chapel Hill: University of North Carolina Press, 2011.

Domínguez, Virginia R. *White by Definition: Social Classification in Creole Louisiana.* New Brunswick, NJ: Rutgers University Press, 1986.

Douglass, Frederick. *Narrative of the Life of Frederick Douglass, an American Slave, Written by Himself.* 1845. Rpt. New York: Penguin, 1982.

Du Bois, W. E. B. *The Souls of Black Folk.* 1903. Rpt. in *Three Negro Classics,* 213–389. New York: Avon, 1965.

"Elijah Muhammad." www.britannica.com/biography/Elijah-Muhammad (accessed May 31, 2019).

Ellison, Ralph. *Invisible Man.* 1952. Rpt. New York: Vintage, 1972.

"Ernest J. Gaines." www.achievment.org/achiever/ernest-j-gaines (accessed October 12, 2017).

Fairclough, Adam. *Race and Democracy: The Civil Rights Struggle in Louisiana, 1915–1972.* Athens: University of Georgia Press, 1995.

"Fannie Lou Hamer." www.womenshistory.org/education-resources
/biographies/fannie-lou-hamer (accessed December 14, 2018).

"Father Divine." www.blackpast.org/african-american-history
/father-divine-1879-1965/ (accessed May 31, 2019).

Gaines, Ernest. J. "Aunty and the Black Experience in Louisiana." 1982. Rpt. in *Mozart and Leadbelly: Stories and Essays,* 45–51.

———. *The Autobiography of Miss Jane Pittman.* 1971. Rpt. Evanston, IL: McDougal Littell, 1998.

———. *Bloodline.* 1968. Rpt. New York: W. W. Norton, 1976.

———. "Bloodline in Ink." 1989. Rpt. in *Mozart and Leadbelly: Stories and Essays,* 37–44.

———. "Boy in the Double-Breasted Suit." 1957. Rpt. in *Mozart and Leadbelly: Stories and Essays,* 87–96.

———. *Catherine Carmier.* 1964. Rpt. San Francisco: North Point Press, 1981.

———. "Christ Walked Down Market Street." 2005. Rpt. in *Mozart and Leadbelly: Stories and Essays,* 65–76.

———. *A Gathering of Old Men.* 1983. Rpt. New York: Vintage, 1992.

———. "Home: A Photo-Essay." *Callaloo* 3 (May 1978): 52–67.

———. *In My Father's House.* 1978. Rpt. New York: Vintage, 1992.

———. "Just Like a Tree." 1962. Rpt. in *Bloodline,* 221–49.

———. *A Lesson before Dying.* 1993. Rpt. New York: Vintage, 1994.

———. "A Long Day in November." 1964. Rpt. in *Bloodline,* 3–79.

———. "Mary Louise." 1960. Rpt. in *Mozart and Leadbelly: Stories and Essays,* 97–114.

———. "Miss Jane and I." 1978. Rpt. in *Mozart and Leadbelly: Stories and Essays,* 3–23.

———. "Mozart and Leadbelly." 1998. Rpt. in *Mozart and Leadbelly: Stories and Essays,* 24–36.

———. *Mozart and Leadbelly: Stories and Essays.* New York: Vintage, 2005.

———. "My Grandpa and the Haint." 1966. Rpt. in *Mozart and Leadbelly: Stories and Essays,* 114–28.

———. "My Uncle and the Fat Lady." *Callaloo* 30.3 (2007): 684–95.

———. *Of Love and Dust.* 1967. Rpt. New York: Bantam, 1969.

———. "Old Jack." *Callaloo.* 24.1 (2001): 69–70.

———. "The Sky Is Gray." 1963. Rpt. in *Bloodline,* 83–117.

———. *The Tragedy of Brady Sims.* New York: Vintage, 2017.

———. "The Turtles." 1956. Rpt. in *Mozart and Leadbelly: Stories and Essays,* 77–86.

———. "A Very Big Order: Reconstructing Identity." 1990. Rpt. in *Mozart and Leadbelly: Stories and Essays,* 32–36.

———. "Where Have You Gone New Orleans?" *National Geographic* 210.2 (August 2006): 54–65.

———. "Writing *A Lesson before Dying.*" 2005. Rpt. in *Mozart and Leadbelly: Stories and Essays,* 52–62.

"Gary Oldman Goes Off on Hypocrisy, Political Correctness, Gibson and Baldwin." www.cnn.com/2014/06/24/showbiz/celebrity-"news-gossip /gary-oldman-playboy-interview/index/html (accessed May 23, 2019).

"A Gathering of Old Men." louisiana.libguides.com/ernestgainescenter /a-gathering-of-old-men (accessed October 20, 2018).

Guterl, Matthew Pratt. "Plantation." In *Keywords for Southern Studies,* ed. Scott Romine and Jennifer Rae Greeson, 22–29. Athens: University of Georgia Press, 2016.

Hansberry, Lorraine. *A Raisin in the Sun.* 1959. Rpt. New York: Signet, 1966.

Harris, Trudier. *Martin Luther King Jr., Heroism, and African American Literature.* Tuscaloosa: University of Alabama Press, 2014.

———. *Saints, Sinners, Saviors: Strong Black Women in African American Literature.* New York: Palgrave, 2001.

Hartman, Saidiya V. *Scenes of Subjection: Terror, Slavery, and Self-Making in Nineteenth-Century America.* New York: Oxford University Press, 1997.

Hudson, Theodore R. "Ernest J. Gaines." In *The History of Southern Literature,* ed. Louis D. Rubin Jr. et al., 513–15. Baton Rouge: Louisiana State University Press, 1985.

Hurston, Zora Neale. *Their Eyes Were Watching God.* 1937. Rpt. New York: Harper and Row, 1990.

Jones, Suzanne. "New Narratives of Southern Manhood: Race, Masculinity, and Closure in Ernest Gaines's Fiction." In *The World Is Our Home: Society and Culture in Contemporary Southern Writing,* ed. Jeffrey Folks, 29–52. Lexington: University Press of Kentucky, 2000.

King, Gilbert. *The Execution of Willie Francis: Race, Murder, and the Search for Justice in the American South.* New York: Basic Civitas, 2008.

King, Martin Luther, Jr. "Letter from Birmingham Jail." 1963. Rpt. in *The Norton Anthology of African American Literature,* 3rd ed. Ed. Henry Louis Gates Jr. and Valerie A. Smith. Vol. 2: 594–607. New York: W. W. Norton, 2014.

Kreyling, Michael. *Inventing Southern Literature.* Jackson: University Press of Mississippi, 1998.

Kurtz, Michael L. "Reform and Race, 1950–1960." In *Louisiana: A History,* 6th ed. Ed. Bennet H. Wall and John C. Rodrigue, 351–75. Malden, MA: John Wiley and Sons, 2014.

Litwack, Leon F. *Trouble in Mind: Black Southerners in the Age of Jim Crow.* New York: Knopf, 1999.

Lowe, John. "Chronology." *Conversations with Ernest Gaines,* ed. Lowe, xvii–xix.

———, ed. *Conversations with Ernest Gaines.* Jackson: University Press of Mississippi, 1995.

Magill, David E. "'Make Him a Man': Black Masculinity and Communal

Identity in Ernest J. Gaines's *A Lesson before Dying.*" *Studies in the Literary Imagination* 49, no. 1 (2016): 61–76.

McPherson, James Alan. "A Region Not Home: The View from Exile." In *The Prevailing South,* ed. Dudley Clendinen, 196–209. Atlanta: Longstreet, 1993.

Morrison, Toni. "Rootedness: The Ancestor as Foundation." 1984. Rpt. in *The Norton Anthology of African American Literature,* 3rd ed. Ed. Henry Louis Gates Jr. and Valerie A. Smith. Vol. 2: 1067–71. New York: W. W. Norton, 2014.

Nash, William R. "'You Think a Man Can't Kneel and Stand?': Ernest J. Gaines's Reassessment of Religion as Positive Communal Influence in *A Lesson before Dying.*" *Callaloo* 24, no. 1 (2001): 346–62.

"Reverend Ike." www.britannica.com/biography/Reverend-Ike (accessed May 31, 2019).

Rothstein, Mervyn. "Round Five for a Theatrical Heavyweight." *New York Times,* April 15, 1990. www.nytimes.com/1990/04/15/theater/round-five-for-a-theatrical-heavyweight.html (accessed November 23, 2018).

Rowell, Charles H. "'This Louisiana Thing That Drives Me': An Interview with Ernest J. Gaines." *Callaloo* 3, no. 1 (1978): 39–51.

Shannon, Sandra G. *The Dramatic Vision of August Wilson.* Washington, DC: Howard University Press, 1995.

Shuler, Philip L. "Joanna." In *Harper's Bible Dictionary,* ed. Paul Achtemeier, 491. New York: HarperCollins, 1985.

"Sojourner Truth." www.nps.gov/articles/sojourner-truth.htm (accessed December 14, 2018).

Strain, Christopher B. "'We Walked Like Men': The Deacons for Defense and Justice." 1997. Rpt. in *The African American Experience in Louisiana,* ed. Charles Vincent. Vol. 11: 365–79. Lafayette: Center for Louisiana Studies, University of Louisiana, 2002.

Thompson, Carlyle V. "From Hog to a Black Man: Black Male Subjectivity and Ritualistic Lynching in Ernest J. Gaines *A Lesson before Dying.*" *CLA Journal* 45, no. 3 (2002): 279–310.

Tracy, Steven C. "The Blues Novel." In *The Cambridge Companion to the African American Novel,* ed. Maryemma Graham, 122–38. Cambridge, UK: Cambridge University Press, 2004.

"Tulsa Race Riot." history.com/topics/roaring-twenties/tulsa-race-riot (accessed December 17, 2018).

Walker, Alice. *In Search of Our Mothers' Gardens: Womanist Prose.* New York: Harcourt Brace Jovanovich, 1983.

——. *The Same River Twice: Honoring the Difficult.* New York: Scribner, 1996.

Ward, Jerry W., Jr. "Foreword." In *Black Southern Voices,* ed. Ward and John Oliver Killens, 5–9. New York: Meridian, 1992.

Washington, Booker T. *Up from Slavery.* 1901. Rpt. in *Three Negro Classics,* 23–205. New York: Avon, 1965.

"What Did Jesus Christ Mean When He Said 'In My Father's House Are Many Mansions?'" www.ucg.org/bible-study-tools (accessed August 15, 2018).

""What does Raoul mean?" Think Baby Names. www.thinkbabynames.com /meaning/1/Raoul (accessed October 26, 2017).

"Whitemouth." www.urbandictionary.com/define.php?term=whitemouth (accessed November 30, 2017).

Williamson, Joel. *A Rage for Order: Black-White Relations in the American South Since Emancipation.* New York: Oxford University Press, 1986.

Wilson, Charles E. "Black Manhood in Ernest J. Gaines's *A Lesson before Dying.*" *Journal of African American Men* 1, no. 1 (1995): 99–112.

Wright, Richard. *Native Son.* 1940. Rpt. New York: HarperPerennial, 1992.

Yon, Veronica Adams. "Gaines, Ernest J." In *The Greenwood Encyclopedia of African American Literature,* ed. Hans A. Ostrom and J. David Macey. Vol. 2: 599–604. Westport, CT: Greenwood, 2006.

Interviews and Conversations with Ernest J. Gaines

Brister, Rose Anne. "The Last Regionalist? An Interview with Ernest J. Gaines." *Callaloo* 26, no. 3 (2003): 549–64.

Brown, Anne Gray. "Scribe of River Lake Plantation: A Conversation with Ernest J. Gaines." *Southern Quarterly* 44, no. 1 (2006): 9–31.

Cash, Wiley. "'What Men Dream About Doing': A Conversation with Ernest J. Gaines." *Mississippi Quarterly* 60, no. 2 (2007): 289–304.

Ferris, William. "'I Heard the Voices . . . of My Louisiana People': A Conversation with Ernest Gaines." *Humanities* 19, no. 4 (July 1998): 4–7.

Gaines, Ernest J., Marcia Gaudet, and Darrell Bourque. "A Literary Salon: Oyster/Shrimp Po'boys, Chardonnay, and Conversation with Ernest J. Gaines." 2002. Rpt. in *Mozart and Leadbelly: Stories and Essays,* 131–59.

Gaudet, Marcia, ed. *Ernest J. Gaines: Conversations.* Jackson: University Press of Mississippi, 2019.

Gaudet, Marcia, and Carl Wooton. *Porch Talk with Ernest Gaines: Conver-*

sations on the Writer's Craft. Baton Rouge: Louisiana State University Press, 1990.

Gaudet, Marcia, and Darrell Bourque. "The Influence of Multi-Art Forms on the Fiction of Ernest J. Gaines: An Interview with Ernest Gaines." *Interdisciplinary Humanities* 20, no. 1 (2003): 76–92.

Lepschy, Wolfgang. "A *MELUS* Interview: Ernest J. Gaines." *MELUS* 24, no. 1 (1999): 197–208.

Levasseur, Jennifer, and Kevin Rabalais. "An Interview with Ernest J. Gaines." *Missouri Review* 22, no. 1 (1999): 95–111.

Lowe, John, ed. *Conversations with Ernest Gaines*. Jackson: University Press of Mississippi, 1995.

Films and Documentaries

The Autobiography of Miss Jane Pittman. Directed by John Korty. CBS Television, 1974.

A Gathering of Old Men. Directed by Volker Schlöndorff. CBS Television, 1987.

A Lesson before Dying. Directed by Joseph Sargent. HBO, 1999.

Louisiana Stories: Ernest J. Gaines. Produced by Rick Smith and Ruth Laney. Louisiana Public Broadcasting, 1992.

The Sky Is Gray. Directed by Stan Lathan. PBS, 1980.

FOR FURTHER READING

Babb, Valerie Melissa. *Ernest Gaines*. Boston: Twayne, 1991.

Bauer, Margaret D., and Charles Reagan Wilson. "Gaines, Ernest J. (b. 1933), Writer." In *The New Encyclopedia of Southern Culture*. Vol. 9: *Literature*, ed. M. Thomas Inge, 276–78. Chapel Hill: University of North Carolina Press, 2008.

Beavers, Herman. *Wrestling Angels into Song: The Fictions of Ernest J. Gaines and James Alan McPherson*. Philadelphia: University of Pennsylvania Press, 1995.

Bibler, Michael P. "Nation and Plantation between *Gone with the Wind* and Black Power: The Example of Ernest J. Gaines's *Of Love and Dust*." Chap. 1 in *Cotton's Queer Relations: Same-Sex Intimacy and the Literature of the Southern Plantation, 1936–1968*, 25–60. Charlottesville: University of Virginia Press, 2009.

Broeck, Sabine. "The Narrative Absence of Interiority in Black Writing: Suffering Female Bodies in *The Autobiography of Miss Jane Pittman*." *Palimpsest: A Journal of Women, Gender, and the Black International* 1, no. 1 (2012): 87–98.

Brown, Anne Gray. "Writing for Life: 'Jefferson's Diary' as Transformative Text in Ernest J. Gaines's *A Lesson before Dying*." *Southern Quarterly* 47, no. 1 (2009): 23–46.

Brown, Lillie Anne. "Introduction: New Criticisms on the Works of Ernest J. Gaines." *Studies in the Literary Imagination* 49, no. 1 (Summer 2016): v–xii.

———. "Onward Christian Soldier: Reverend Phillip Martin's Road to Redemption in Ernest J. Gaines's *In My Father's House*." *Studies in the Literary Imagination* 49, no. 1 (2016): 17–31.

Clark, Keith. "Que(e)rying the Prison-House of Black Male Desire: Homosociality in Ernest Gaines's 'Three Men.'" *African American Review* 40, no. 2 (Summer 2006): 239–55.

———. "Re-(W)righting Black Male Subjectivity: The Communal Poetics of Ernest Gaines's *A Gathering of Old Men*." *Callaloo* 22, no. 1 (Winter 1999): 195–207.

Costello, Brannon. "Class, Work, and Race in Ernest Gaines's *Of Love and Dust* and 'Bloodline.'" Chap. 4 of *Plantation Airs: Racial Paternalism and the Transformations of Class in Southern Fiction, 1945–1971,* 100–122. Baton Rouge: Louisiana State University Press, 2007.

Daley, Katherine, and Carolyn M. Jones. "Ernest J. Gaines's *A Lesson before Dying:* Freedom in Confined Spaces." In *From the Plantation to the Prison: African-American Confinement Literature,* ed. Tara T. Green, 83–117. Macon, GA: Mercer University Press, 2008.

Doyle, Mary Ellen. *Voices from the Quarters: The Fiction of Ernest J. Gaines.* Baton Rouge: Louisiana State University Press, 2002.

Egan, Alexis M. "'But I Was a Little Boy, and What Could I Do About It?': Contemplating Children as Narrators in the Short Fiction of Ernest J. Gaines." *Studies in the Literary Imagination* 49, no. 1 (2016): 49–60.

Estes, David C., ed. *Critical Reflections on the Fiction of Ernest J. Gaines.* Athens: University of Georgia Press, 1994.

Gibson, Scott Thomas. "Gift Exchange as Communal Resistance in Ernest Gaines's *A Lesson before Dying.*" *NANO,* no. 11 (July 2017), www.nanocrit .com/issues/issue11/Gift-Exchange-as-Communal-Resistance-in-Ernest-Gaines-Lesson-Before-Dying.

Gray, Dabney. "Ernest Gaines's *A Gathering of Old Men:* A Southern Perspective." *Journal of Intercultural Disciplines* 7 (Jan. 2007): 26–33.

Harris, Trudier. "Fear of Manhood in the Wake of Systemic Racism in Ernest J. Gaines's 'Three Men.'" Chap. 2 of *The Scary Mason-Dixon Line: African American Writers and the South,* 41–60. Baton Rouge: Louisiana State University Press, 2009.

Hebert-Leiter, Maria. "A Breed Between: Racial Meditation in the Fiction of Ernest Gaines." *MELUS* 31, no. 2 (2006): 95–117.

Hicks, Jack. *In the Singer's Temple: Prose Fictions of Barthelme, Gaines, Brautigan, Piercy, Kesey, and Kosinski.* Chapel Hill: University of North Carolina Press, 1981.

Hill, Michael D. "*A Lesson before Dying* as Style Guide." Chap. 3 of *The Ethics of Swagger: Prizewinning African American Novels, 1977–1993,* 70–92. Columbus: Ohio State University Press, 2013.

Lambert, Raphaël. "Race and the Tragic Mode in Ernest J. Gaines's *A Gathering of Old Men.*" *Southern Literary Journal* 42, no. 2 (2010): 106–25.

Manes, Claire. "Reading Ivan Turgenev with Ernest J. Gaines: Analyzing *Fathers and Sons* and *Catherine Carmier.*" *Studies in the Literary Imagination* 49, no. 1 (2016): 77–92.

Martin, Chante B. "'How a (Black) Man Should Live': Southern 'Places' of Memory, Instruction, and Transformation in Ernest J. Gaines's *A Lesson before Dying.*" *Journal of Men's Studies* 20, no. 3 (2012): 243–58.

Meyer, William E. H. "Ernest J. Gaines and the Black Child's Sensory Dilemma." *CLA Journal* 34, no. 4 (1991): 414–25.

Russo, Diane Chiriani. "'Whitemouth': A Bakhtinian Reading of Narrative Voice in Ernest J. Gaines's Transitional Novel *Of Love and Dust.*" *Studies in the Literary Imagination* 49, no. 1 (2016): 93–111.

Simpson, Anne K. *A Gathering of Gaines: The Man and the Writer.* Lafayette: Center for Louisiana Studies, University of Southwest Louisiana, 1991.

Spangler, Matthew. "Of Snow and Dust: The Presence of James Joyce in Ernest Gaines's *A Lesson before Dying.*" *South Atlantic Review* 67, no. 1 (2002): 104–28.

Stupp, Jason. "Living Death: Ernest Gaines's *A Lesson before Dying* and the Execution of Willie Francis." In *Demands of the Dead: Executions, Storytelling, and Activism in the United States,* ed. Katy Ryan, 45–58. Iowa City: University of Iowa Press, 2012.

Teutsch, Matthew. "'They Want Us to Be Creoles ... There Is No In-Between': Creole Representations in Ernest J. Gaines's *Catherine Carmier* and Lyle Saxon's *Children of Strangers.*" *Studies in the Literary Imagination* 49, no. 1 (2016): 113–27.

Thomières, Daniel. "Man's Way and Woman's Way in *The Autobiography of Miss Jane Pittman.*" *Mississippi Quarterly* 64, no. 1–2 (2011): 219–34.

Tucker, Terrence T. "(Re)Claiming Legacy in the Post–Civil Rights South in Richard Wright's 'Down by the Riverside' and Ernest Gaines's *A Gathering of Old Men.*" *Southern Literary Journal* 43, no. 2 (2011): 105–24.

Warfield, Adrienne Akins. "'In the South Pain Is Segregated': Waiting Rooms and Medical Ethics in Eudora Welty's 'A Worn Path' and Ernest Gaines's 'The Sky Is Gray.'" *Papers on Language and Literature* 53, no. 3 (2017): 211–36.

Williams, Dana A. "Lessons before Dying: The Contemporary Confined Character-in-Process." In *From the Plantation to the Prison: African-American Confinement Literature,* ed. Tara T. Green, 32–57. Macon, GA: Mercer University Press, 2008.

Young, Reggie Scott. "Ernest J. Gaines: A Portfolio." *Callaloo* 30, no. 3 (Summer 2007): 696–98, 702–13.

———. "Still Driven by That Louisiana Thing: On the Thirtieth Anniversary of *Callaloo*'s 1978 Special Edition on Ernest J. Gaines." *Callaloo* 30, no. 3 (Summer 2007): 699–701.

———. "Theoretical Influences and Experimental Resemblances: Ernest J. Gaines and Recent Critical Approaches to the Study of African American Fiction." *Contemporary African American Fiction: New Critical Essays,* ed. Dana A. Williams, 11–36. Columbus: Ohio State University Press, 2009.

Zeitler, Michael. "'Mr. Joe Louis, Help Me': Sports as Narrative and Community in Ernest J. Gaines's *A Lesson before Dying." Studies in the Literary Imagination* 49, no. 1 (2016): 129–40.

INDEX